BACKCOUNTRY SKIER

Jean Vives, PhD

Human Kinetics

Library of Congress Cataloging-in-Publication Data

Vives, Jean, 1949-
    Backcountry skier / Jean Vives.
        p. cm.
    Includes bibliographical references and index.
    ISBN 0-88011-650-1
    1. Cross-country skiing. 2. Skis and skiing. I. Title.
    GV855.3.V58   1998
        796.93'2--dc21   98-8130
                                                                                                CIP

ISBN: 0-88011-650-1
Copyright © 1999 by Jean Vives

Acquisitions Editor: Martin Barnard; **Developmental Editor:** Julie A. Marx; **Assistant Editor:** Laura Ward Majersky; **Copyeditor:** Jacqueline Eaton Blakley; **Proofreader:** Myla Smith; **Indexer:** Craig Brown; **Graphic Designer:** Robert Reuther; **Graphic Artist:** Tara Welsch; **Photo Editor:** Boyd LaFoon; **Cover Designer:** Jack Davis; **Cover Photographer:** David Stoecklein; **Interior Photographers:** Tom Roberts (pp. 52-53, 55-57); and unless otherwise noted, Jean Vives; **Illustrators**: Roberto Sabas and Joe Bellis; **Printer:** United Graphics

Human Kinetics books are available at special discounts for bulk purchase. Special editions or book excerpts can also be created to specification. For details, contact the Special Sales Manager at Human Kinetics.

Printed in the United States of America   10   9   8   7   6   5   4   3   2   1

Human Kinetics
Web site: http://www.humankinetics.com/

United States: Human Kinetics, P.O. Box 5076, Champaign, IL 61825-5076
1-800-747-4457
e-mail: humank@hkusa.com

Canada: Human Kinetics, 475 Devonshire Road Unit 100, Windsor, ON N8Y 2L5
1-800-465-7301 (in Canada only)
e-mail: humank@hkcanada.com

Europe: Human Kinetics, P.O. Box IW14, Leeds LS16 6TR, United Kingdom
(44) 1132 781708
e-mail: humank@hkeurope.com

Australia: Human Kinetics, 57A Price Avenue, Lower Mitcham, South Australia 5062
(088) 277 1555
e-mail: humank@hkaustralia.com

New Zealand: Human Kinetics, P.O. Box 105-231, Auckland 1
(09) 523 3462
e-mail: humank@hknewz.com

For Dad and Mom

Contents

Preface

My goal in writing this book was to provide a complete look at backcountry skiing while capturing the beauty of the backcountry. Therefore, *Backcountry Skier* is not just about skiing technique—it is also about living in the backcountry. It presents an objective and analytical look at the world of backcountry skiing through concise technique descriptions and over 140 illustrations. Whether you're a resort skier who is looking for something different or a cross-country skier who wants to extend your trips, you'll find this book packed with clear, usable information—including techniques borrowed from ski guides, mountaineers, ski patrollers, and snow rangers—that will make you an effective, knowledgeable wilderness skier.

Chapter 1 will bring you up to date on the most recent advances in cold weather clothing, while chapter 2 does the same for telemark and Alpine ski touring equipment, including skis, poles, boots, and bindings. Chapter 3 contains the most current information on conditioning for and staying healthy in the backcountry, with clear descriptions of weight training and flexibility exercises designed for backcountry skiers who must combine muscular strength and endurance to carry packs on ungroomed snow. The prevention of sport injuries related to skiing and high-altitude exposure is also covered.

Backcountry Skier combines the best of both telemark and parallel ski techniques into a unique, unified ski system in chapters 4 and 5, covering ascent and descent techniques, respectively. Telemark skiing is popular in the United States, but parallel skiing, most popularly Alpine touring (randonnée skiing) as it is practiced in Europe, is growing as skiers look for alternatives to telemarking.

Chapter 6 looks at mountain terrain hazards specific to skiing and includes a ski/snow compatibility table to help skiers learn how to match their techniques to the snow conditions. Chapter 7 provides readers with descriptions of how to use barometers as weather forecasting tools and includes a helpful sequence of photos showing the major stages of storm development, while chapter 8 covers the all-important skills needed to navigate safely in the backcountry, including altimeter use, global positioning devices, and latitude and longitude and UTM coordinate use. Terrain recognition skills are vital, and this chapter also contains a unique opportunity to cross-reference mountain terrain features to a photo and map of the same terrain. Chapter 9 describes how to recognize and then ski and climb around avalanche hazards and helps you determine what information about the route and snow conditions is important to obtain before leaving home. I also describe the use of safety and rescue equipment and techniques in case you're caught in an avalanche.

Chapter 10 gives you a new view of nutrition based on recent military and expeditionary food research and describes how to use new athletic food products to reduce pack weight, improve ski performance, and reduce fatigue during backcountry travel. Chapter 11 continues in this theme of backcountry touring by covering winter camping and expedition planning, explaining real-life tent camping techniques and hut and trail skiing etiquette. Finally, chapter 12 covers the critical components of surviving an emergency, focusing on the basic idea that if each individual is prepared to survive alone if necessary, the whole group becomes stronger. I advocate defensive skiing and equipment preparation, such as making your own survival jacket, and I've also included a complete survival pack list and encourage all skiers to learn winter bivouac camping techniques.

Backcountry skiing is exciting and fulfilling, but as with any sport some aspects can be potentially dangerous. I've used the techniques in this book for over 30 years in both mild and extreme weather conditions and found them to be safe and effective. If you're new to the backcountry, I recommend practicing all of these techniques in good weather conditions on easy terrain before moving into less forgiving situations.

I find backcountry skiing constantly beautiful, mentally challenging, and always fascinating. The mountains can change a person's life—they have mine. Have a great time out there!

Acknowledgments

Special thanks to:

- Peter Hackett, MD, Wilderness Medical Society
- Denny Hogan, Silverton Avalanche Center
- Rod Newcomb, American Avalanche Institute
- Dale Atkins, Colorado Avalanche Information Center
- MSgt. Jack Loudermilk, retired, U.S. Army
- Bill Clemens, MD, National Mountain Rescue medical director
- Larry Mclaughlin, photographer
- Paul and Kris Ramer, Alpine Research Incorporated
- Gary Neptune and the friendly staff at Neptune Mountaineering
- Catherine Jackson, PhD, professor of exercise physiology
- Laura E. Seitz, ACR Rescue Electronics
- Julie Ann Lickteig, MA, associate professor of nutrition

Thank you, Sandy, for all the help in the early days. To Sheila Lukins, a big thank you for supporting my wild ski projects. Finally, to my loving wife Chrystiane, for all your caring support; and to all my friends, especially Patrick—thank you for being there.

I need to thank my editors, Julie Marx and Laura Majersky, who did a super job in editing my book—they turned all the information it contains into a readable form. Special thanks goes to trade editor Martin Barnard, without whose help this book would not have been possible.

1
chapter

Staying Warm and Dry

Advances in cold-weather clothing have been nothing short of spectacular. Although everyone needs good clothing for winter sport fun, beginners as well as younger and older skiers especially benefit. Good clothing is a great investment in your enjoyment of backcountry skiing and all outdoor sports. Experienced mountaineers know that good winter clothing makes winter outings all the more pleasurable.

Buying Clothing

Clothing is most cost-effective when it can be used for several sports. Storm jackets and pants can be used for rainwear in the summer. Because good clothing is expensive (see table 1.1), consider building up your clothing selection over a few ski seasons while you are improving your skills and increasing the scope of your ski activities. Insuring your ski gear under a homeowner or renter insurance plan is an absolute must. Having your equipment stolen is a terrible experience and can set your skiing back a whole winter.

Table 1.1

Clothing Costs

There are many sources available for finding winter clothing. Top-end clothing is usually stronger, lasts longer, and is more stylish; however, lower-priced functional gear that can perform just as well as more expensive counterparts can be found. Today, there are chain stores throughout the country that sell used sports clothing and equipment. Ski swaps, on-line discount stores, and bulletin boards at ski shops often list good buys. You can also check local newspapers for people who might be selling gear at discount prices.

TYPICAL CLOTHING COSTS

	High	Low
Synthetic medium-weight underwear top	$40	$20
Synthetic medium-weight underwear bottom	$35	$20
Synthetic expedition-weight underwear top	$45	$20
Synthetic expedition-weight underwear bottom	$45	$20
Drylite T-shirt	$20	$10
Ski hat	$30	$10
Balaclava	$20	$5
Heavy gloves/mittens (Gore-Tex if possible)	$80	$35
Lightweight cross-country gloves	$25	$10
Heavy ski socks	$18	$9
Ski sock liners	$6	$3
Gore-Tex storm suit top	$350	$175
Gore-Tex storm suit bottom	$350	$145
Down or Polarguard vest	$95	$55
Polar pile jacket (optional)	$170	$60
Camp booties	$35	$10
Gaiters	$50	$15

How Clothing Works

The climate in the mountains is one of extreme cold and heat. Garments must serve two seemingly contrary purposes: to repel external moisture while still allowing sweat to evaporate from the garment, especially during hard work. Therefore, breathability, wicking, and venting are three very important factors to consider when purchasing clothing. Choosing the proper clothing for the conditions can make the difference between an enjoyable ski tour and a damp or freezing experience.

Interacting With the Environment

As you ski, heat and sweat in the form of vapor exert an outward pressure against the inside of the garment. Whether this vapor can escape depends on the garment and the weather conditions. Heat and moisture flow from areas of high temperature or humidity to areas of lower temperature or humidity. When the air inside the garment is warm and moist and the outside air is cold and dry, heat will escape more quickly. When the temperature outside the garment is higher than the temperature inside, as during spring skiing or when snow is mixed with rain, the hot air inside the garment escapes more slowly, making it more difficult to maintain a comfortable temperature inside the garment. If it is raining outside (100 percent humidity), will sweat still escape? Yes, but not as well as when the outside weather is dry.

Heat can be pulled or taken away from the body by the wind in a process called *convection.* It can also be drained from the body when it comes into contact with something cold such as snow, rock, ice, or moist air in a process called *conduction.* Cold, humid air is able to wick heat away from the body better than cold, dry air. This is why the damp maritime climates of coastal ranges such as the Sierras and Cascades feel colder than continental interior ranges.

Radiation can also be a problem, especially when it comes to controlling the amount of heat inside a garment. A dark-colored garment will always absorb more heat than a light-colored one, which explains the popularity of black garments among skiers. Even though the air temperature may be quite cool, the heat of the sun on a clear day can be absorbed by the garment. This is why it can be 90 degrees Fahrenheit (32 degrees Celsius) on the surface of a red ski jacket while the air temperature is 40 degrees Fahrenheit (4 degrees Celsius). In staying warm, though, skiers who wear dark-colored garments risk not being able to stay cool on warmer days. Dark garments absorb radiation, keeping the skier warmer with less clothing (which saves weight), while light-colored garments reflect radiation, minimizing heat buildup.

Thermal Density and Loft

Thermal density describes the amount of heat that clothing captures within its filaments, fibers, or feathers. When air is captured in a still area of clothing, its temperature can be raised by body heat. This warm air is conserved about the body and maintains body heat if it remains protected from convection or conduction forces from the outside. This is the concept behind the idea of dressing in layers (see pages 4-11).

The thickness of the insulation space in a garment or a sleeping bag is called *loft* and is especially important when goose or duck down are the insulating materials. Unfortunately, when down gets wet the loft collapses, losing all its insulation properties. When a typical garment is wet, the microspaces between the fibers cannot hold warm air because they are full of water. Fantastic new hydrophobic (water-hating) fibers that have been developed, such as synthetic fleece (Polartec, etc.), do not absorb any water at all from the inside (sweat) or the outside (snow) and are fast-drying as a result.

Shape

The shape and fit of a garment determine its ability to hold heated air around the body. Microconvection air currents can enter a garment, wicking heat off the body. The closer the garment is to the body, the fewer convection currents exist. (That's the reason for getting close-fitting underwear.) Be sure that all underwear and shirts are long enough to fit snugly below your belt line to keep heat in.

Dressing for the Backcountry

As already stated, you need to capture and keep air in your clothing so it can be heated by your body, which in turn will keep you warm. Dressing in layers of clothing is an efficient way to capture air and heat it. Each layer has a purpose. In the following sections we will see how each layer of clothing works.

Layer One: Dryness

Underwear keeps you dry and warm. Polypropylene, Capilene, and Hollofil materials, when directly against the skin, delay the conden-sation of sweat vapor so that it can evaporate. Underwear usually comes in light, medium, and expedition weights. A lightweight layer can be used under an expedition-weight layer during colder conditions and then used separately during warmer conditions. Newer wool blends (Devold, Smart Wool) are getting more attention from skiers who normally prefer traditional materials.

The underwear layer is usually made up of two separate pieces, top and bottom (see figure 1.1). One-piece underwear (longjohns) might seem like a good idea at first. Most have a drop seat for toilet use, and the one-piece design prevents bunching. The top part can't be used by itself, though, making it less versatile in changeable conditions.

Besides being long enough to tuck in, the top should have a turtleneck with a zipper for maximum temperature adjustability. Cuffs at the wrists keep your wrists warm and prevent heat escape. The bottom garment should have cuffs at the ankles, and for men, a fly in front. For maximum comfort when snow camping or hut skiing, you can rotate two sets of expedition- or medium-weight underwear,

Figure 1.1   Layer one—dryness.

changing into a second set at night for pajamas and leaving it on to become the first layer of your ski clothes the next day. In winter, your underwear becomes an integral part of your sleeping insulation system. A short-sleeved, quick-drying, nylon jogging T-shirt (made of a dacron polyester blend) worn right on the skin keeps you even dryer than a long-sleeved undershirt by itself. It also works great during spring touring when you just want something on your skin to protect you from the sun.

Layer Two: Insulation

The insulation layer (see figure 1.2) usually consists of a sweater or heavy expedition-weight thermal underwear, and a vest (which can be fiberfill, pile, or goose down), or any combination thereof. The vest helps to maintain core temperature, and it can be used without the sweater during warmer conditions. A full jacket (fleece, down, or Polarguard) is used less often because of the heat generated in ski

Figure 1.2   Layer two—insulation.

touring. However, a jacket can be used if it is cold enough. A pile vest with an outer nylon shell works best since it is snowproof and windproof when used by itself. Pile pants (also shown) teamed with a storm pant can be used in very cold conditions, while stretch Lycra, biking tights, or stretch pile can be used during warmer conditions.

A jacket, sweater, or shirt should always be long enough that it won't pull out of your pants during exercise. A good test when buying these items is to reach for the sky with each arm to see if the bottom of the garment comes over your belt or if sleeves pull away from your wrists. If either of these things happen, buy the next size up. Be sure your clothing has high collars for protection from wind. Don't buy anything with loose threads, and be sure the garment was made properly. Always keep your receipts and don't be afraid to take an item back if it doesn't feel right.

Many different types of insulating materials have been used over the ages. Fur was the first insulator, and in many regions of the world it is still the material of choice. Let's review some the contemporary materials used for insulation.

• **Wool**—The wool industry hasn't been resting during the synthetic revolution. Today's wool underwear feels luxurious and doesn't shrink (or stink!) like it used to. Some experts say wool is more comfortable over wider temperature ranges, and on long expeditions it stays warmer longer than synthetics. Wool is not hydrophobic, though, and can absorb up to 30 percent of its weight in water. Powder snow sticks to wooly knickers like glue and should always be worn with a nylon shell for increased water resistance.

• **Goose down**—Goose down is a great insulator and has a high thermal density, but only when dry. When it gets wet, it loses all insulation, and it is very difficult to dry, even over a raging campfire. It works best when paired with a Gore-Tex garment or a DryLoft-covered sleeping bag. DryLoft is a type of Gore-Tex that keeps the down dry and allows the feathers to get air to maintain dry insulating loft. Goose down comes in different grades or power of fill: 500, 600, even 800 loft is sold. (Higher grades are loftier and more expensive.)

• **Pile fleece garments**—Pile fleece (Polartec among others) is actually made of a fine polyester plastic. It comes in several grades of thickness from lightweight to expedition weight, with corresponding 200, 300, and 400 weights. The plastic is spun into a wool-type material that has a very high thermal density. It is hydrophobic, which makes it a good insulator even when wet. The newer versions seem to get more luxurious with each passing season. You can even get stretchable windproof fleece garments for added warmth.

- **Polyester fills**—The best polyester fill comes in the forms of Polarguard HV and 3D, which consist of a long continuous filament that resists shifting during use, therefore allowing the garment to stay warmer longer. Polarguard is used in place of down as stuffing for vests, jackets, and sleeping bags. Dacron materials are less expensive and easier to maintain than down, and unlike down insulate even if wet. Their only drawback is that they don't compress as easily as down, so they take up more room in your pack. A compression sack can help remedy this.

- **Cotton**—Cotton fails completely as a cold-weather insulator because it absorbs water and sweat and conducts heat away from the body. Jeans or cotton T-shirts (not to be confused with nylon jogging T-shirts) shouldn't be worn skiing. Jeans can get very wet after a few falls in the snow and won't dry. Many ski patrollers have had to cut and peel wet or frozen jeans off skiers who had broken their legs while skiing—a painful process to say the least.

Layer Three: Wind Protection

The insulation layer helps to trap air around the body and keep you warm. The outermost layer, the storm suit (see figure 1.3), will further help maintain body temperature. This layer consists of pants and a jacket, and is vital because it protects all the other layers from the environment. It should be waterproof, breathable, and easily ventable (the terms *waterproof* and *water resistant* are used interchangeably for simplicity).

The outer layer must breathe. Sweat vapor must be allowed to escape if your clothing is to remain dry. Don't ever believe that you'll be able to dry your clothing off with body heat. Who can guarantee that you'll have any to spare? You will need it for yourself to stay warm. You also can't assume that the weather will be warm enough to dry clothes, or that you will be able to find enough wood for a fire. Your cold clothes will be wicking heat away from your body while you are looking for firewood!

You should envision yourself in the worst weather conditions possible when choosing your outer-layer garments. With proper care, outer-layer garments should last you for at least five years with moderate weekend use. Most manufacturers make both lightweight and expedition-weight garments. Although expedition-weight gear is nice, it is also heavier. Unless you are a beginner who falls a lot, you will be able to get away with the lightweight version. Check to see whether lightweight jackets and pants have reinforced knees, elbows, and seats, which are necessary for handling abuse.

Materials

The shift in backcountry clothing has been to breathable, waterproof materials, and it is often more important to look for what garments are made of than what company made them. The two most effective materials for this outer layer are coated nylon and Gore-Tex.

• **Coated nylon**—Coated nylon skiwear is far less expensive and lighter than Gore-Tex, and it works well if vented properly. Wearing coated nylon can be similar to wearing a plastic bag—your sweat can't escape, so it makes your clothing wet. This sweat vapor that is trying

Figure 1.3   Layer three—wind protection.

to escape is blocked, so it backs up through your layers of clothing until it reaches your body, making you cold. Goose down under coated nylon is really a problem. Adding zippers at the underarms helps eliminate moisture. It is better to use synthetic or wool insulation under coated nylon since goose down fails when wet.

• **Gore-Tex**—Gore-Tex gear is probably the biggest breakthrough in outdoor clothing today. This material allows sweat vapor to escape from the garment and keeps moisture out. Evaporation of sweat keeps the body drier—a critical factor in staying warm. Gore-Tex is Teflon that is electrostatically laminated to the inner shell of the garment. Don't be fooled by all the new Gore-Tex clone fabrics (such as Omnitech, H2NO Storm, HellyTech)—studies by independent testing labs have shown that Gore-Tex brand materials are superior to any other material in terms of breathability and water resistance. Gore-Tex can remain waterproof after 500 hours of continuous water exposure while maintaining a low resistance to vapor transfer. Gore-Tex comes in three-ply and two-ply versions, which are used on separate parts of garments—three-ply is more abrasion proof and is usually used on the shoulders and elbows, while two-ply is often used on the body of the jacket.

Storm Jacket

A Gore-Tex jacket is best, but a jacket of coated material can be used if it is well-vented. The jacket should have zippers under the armpits for ventilation and large pockets for warming hands or storing a camera. It should also have a large hood with an elastic cord, big enough to fit over a ski hat and able to be adjusted snugly around the face. The wrist closures should be Velcro or elastic and must be expandable enough to fit over gloves. Elbows should be reinforced. There must be a Velcro wind flap over the main zipper that can close the jacket in case of zipper failure.

Storm Pants

The pants should have full-length zippers so that the pants can be put on while leaving skis and boots on. They should also be reinforced at the knees and buttocks. The pants should have snaps and elastic closures at the waist, making for easier toilet use, and at the ankles to act as gaiters (see page 11). Always buy the type with built-in suspenders so you can drop the seat without taking off your clothes— a real plus in terrible weather! Get suspenders if you can't find pants with built-in ones, since pants always slide down during touring. The ankles should be reinforced on the inside to prevent cutting of the pant material by ski edges.

One-Piece Ski Suits

One-piece ski suits can be insulated or noninsulated. One-piece racing suits are very lightweight and are used for track skiing, but they are difficult to use when nature calls. They are usually made of Lycra and are not very warm, so they can only be used during very good weather. One-piece downhill ski suits or Alpine climbing suits are insulated, making them too warm for all but the very coldest ski tours. The traditional two-piece jacket and pant system seems to be the best for all-around use. Bib knickers are great if they have a seat zipper for toilet use. Without a zipper, you need to take off all your clothes to relieve yourself—a real hassle.

Clothing Color

The color of the clothing used in wilderness skiing is very important. Clothing must dry quickly, so black is a popular color for outerwear because it dries so well. Unfortunately, in warm weather it can be very hot and uncomfortable. From a rescue standpoint, storm suits should be brightly-colored (yellow, red, or blue) for maximum air-to-ground visibility. Tests have shown that contrasting colors such as black and yellow or black and red are more visible than single colors.

Accessory Clothing

Don't neglect the details! In the following sections, I'll discuss some of the accessories you'll want to add to your basic outerwear to get the most out of backcountry skiing: gaiters, gloves and glove liners, socks and sock liners, and hats. Each of these items will add to the comfort and safety of your trip. For example, your hat and gloves cover areas of the body where your blood comes closest to the cold (wrists and head). If they are not protected, you'll still be cold! An extra hat or pair of gloves weighs very little but can add greatly to your enjoyment of the sport.

Gaiters

High-top gaiters (16 inches [41 centimeters] high) are mandatory for skiing off the track, especially when using knickers. Gaiters keep your legs and feet warm by keeping snow out of your boots. They can also protect the ankle of your expensive pants from getting cut by skis or rocks (see figure 1.4).

Coated nylon gaiters are not ideal—they accumulate body moisture on the inside of the gaiter, which in turn gets your clothing wet. But if that's all you have, just unzip your gaiters occasionally at rest stops to vent the moisture out. Naturally, Gore-Tex gaiters are best because they vent moisture and are warmer as a result. Gaiters with Velcro closures are preferred over those with zippers, which can break. If you do have gaiters with zippers, installing zipper pulls (see page 18) will also make it easier to open and close your gaiters with cold fingers. Newer gaiters have replaced the usual nylon cord in the instep with a strap-and-buckle arrangement, saving everyone a lot of frustration with broken cords. You can buy and install that upgrade on your old gaiters if they don't have them.

Overgaiters and Overboots

An overgaiter is just a bigger version of a gaiter that covers the whole boot. It is especially good when using leather boots. Newer, warmer,

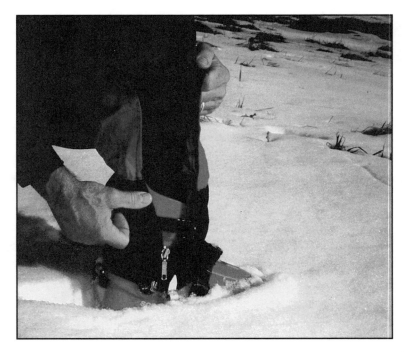

Figure 1.4 Make sure your gaiter zippers allow access to boot buckles or laces for easy adjustment.

plastic boots have eliminated the use of these coverings. Overboots are different only in that they cover the bottom of the boot as well. They are great for skiing in very cold conditions or for those whose feet tend to get cold. They keep your boots drier, and as a result warmer. Overgaiters and overboots also protect your boot from sharp rocks and skis. Those made with Gore-Tex are preferred, as they keep the boot drier. They usually seal around the welt of the boot using an elastic rubber cuff (which must be replaced occasionally, depending on use—replacements will be more frequent when one walks on pavement or rocks).

Gaiters for Alpine Ski Touring Boots

Most gaiters open on the front and back, but rarely on the side where your ski buckles are. Alpine ski touring gaiters that have an extra-long strap to go under the plastic boot have remedied this. Some people use this gaiter for their high-performance telemark boots as well.

Gloves and Mittens

Many people prefer the warmth of a mitten over a glove, but people with warmer hands prefer to have the dexterity of the glove. Some newer designs using removable pile liners offer the warmth of a mitten with the convenience of a glove. People with extra-cold hands (or feet) shouldn't be afraid to get electric hand and boot warmers that use rechargeable batteries for day touring. Chemical heat packs are great to have along on longer tours. Spraying antiperspirant on the hands (and feet) adds warmth by keeping them dry. I discuss gloves, mittens, and glove liners below.

 • **Ski touring track gloves**—Leather cross-country track gloves have a tendency to get wet from sweat and snow. Better gloves are now made completely of synthetic materials and are more water resistant. Some have a convenient terrycloth top surface for wiping sweat from the face.

 • **Downhill ski gloves**—If you are a downhill skier already and own some of the newer downhill gloves, they will be warm enough for occasional off-trail skiing. Look for gloves with Dacron (Thinsulate, Hollofil) insulation and a Gore-Tex shell.

 • **Mountaineering gloves**—These gloves are fitted with a long sleeve and rubberized material and are used with a removable inner pile liner. These gloves usually have articulated fingers that are premolded in a grip position so that it takes less effort to flex them. They are very tough and warm, and last forever. Skiers should buy them a size larger than their normal size so a liner can fit inside.

- **Mittens and mitten shells**—Wool mittens absorb snow and turn into a wet mess very quickly, causing freezing hands—so they should never be used without a nylon shell. The shell should be reinforced in the palm area to minimize wear to the material, and should have an elastic or Velcro closure. A shell made for mountaineering is the most durable.

- **Glove liners**—Glove liners are a must in very cold weather. They keep the hands warm when you take your gloves off to work on clothing or take a photo. They also protect the gloves' insulation material from getting wet with sweat, which would lessen their insulation effectiveness. They are usually made of polypropylene or Capilene. Look for liners that have a cottonlike finish, are not slippery, and allow for increased finger dexterity.

Ski Socks and Liners

Many people wear rag wool socks out of tradition; however, today we have many varieties of socks made out of superior materials. Nylon-Dacron and polypropylene-wool blends are always more durable than wool by itself. Modern ski boot socks retain dead air space even when compressed. Polypropylene helps keep the sock dry because it is a solid fiber and doesn't absorb moisture. The new synthetic fleece socks are excellent. Gore-Tex socks are also getting rave reviews. Neoprene socks used for water sports should never be used for cold-weather sports at high altitude. Neoprene rubber has cells inside that fill with water or sweat. This water is warmed, which keeps the feet warm. However, at high altitude, the air spaces in the neoprene swell with decreasing air pressure. The rubber swells and comes up against the boot shells. When it cannot swell any further, it swells inward and squeezes the foot, cutting off circulation and possibly resulting in frostbite.

Liner socks help keep the ski sock cleaner, drier, and therefore warmer. A dirty sock is a cold sock because the dirt takes up air space that heat could occupy. Liner socks wick away moisture so sweat can't build up on the skin. Dry skin is warm skin, and is less prone to get blisters because the skin-sock interface develops less friction. Beware

© Carl Skoog

Skiing the powder at Crystal Mountain, Cascade Range, Washington.

of slippery liner sock materials that allow the foot to slide around inside the boot during use. This makes for less precise footing and causes blisters from the friction created. Those having a rough finish are best.

Snow Hats

We have often heard that 40 percent of our body heat is lost through the head. But that is from a dry head! When the head and hat are wet, that figure can rise to 75 percent, not including the wind factor! Hats should be warm, windproof, and water resistant. Your hat should fit comfortably under your storm jacket hood. Choose a knitted hat with a smooth finish that sheds snow since those with a rag or fleece finish can collect snow and get soaked during heavy snowfalls. A wool/synthetic blend ski hat is a good choice for both resort and backcountry skiing. It's wise to spray hats with a waterproofing material like Scotchgard to maintain water resistance. It's hard to beat a waterproof Gore-Tex nylon-shelled, pile-insulated hat in bad weather. Face masks and balaclavas are also very useful in windy, cold conditions. Windproof fleece is softer on the face than neoprene, which can hold moisture. Always bring an extra hat—it's light insurance!

Sun Hats

Your body needs protection from sun as much as from cold. Sun is a potent force in the mountains. Skin cancer concerns give just cause to wear some type of hat to keep the sun off your face and neck on warmer days when ski hats aren't worn. The old-fashioned cotton baseball cap works great. What is even better than a baseball cap is the desert-style hat with cloth that covers the neck. This is one instance where cotton works well because its absorbs sweat, gets wet, and keeps the head and neck cool.

Caring for Clothing

Remember that you aren't just washing or repairing regular clothes—you are maintaining expensive gear, so take special care. Always follow the manufacturer's instructions on garment care. If in doubt, ask the shop where you bought the garment for cleaning advice before leaving the store.

Cleaning and Waterproofing

Clothing and sleeping bags insulate better when they are clean. When clothing fibers hold dirt instead of air, there is less dead air space and loft, resulting in a reduced ability to insulate and keep you warm.

Clothing should be clean, dry, and at room temperature before applying a spray or liquid waterproofing to protect garments against grime. Many new high-tech cleaning-waterproofing products use water-repellent polymers to help remove dirt and body oil and give down jackets and sleeping bags an increased degree of water resistance.

Don't forget to take proper care of your boots—wet feet are cold feet. Mink oil, Biwell, and Sno-Seal all work well when used in moderation, but too much of any one nullifies the waterproofing effect. Oil destroys tread and makes leather soft. Too much wax can build up into a conductor of cold or clog leather pores, causing wet feet. Always apply wax or oil in thin coats. Boots should be prewarmed in front of a fireplace or in front of an open oven door.

Sealing Seams

The seams on many garments and tents today are presealed electro-statically at the factory. Seams appear mostly on storm jackets and pants, and on tent floors and roofs. They also appear around the welts of boots. If the seams on your garments have not been presealed, purchase the appropriate seam sealer and apply to dry, warmed surfaces only in a heated, well-ventilated room. Apply one coat and let it dry for a few hours, then apply the next coat.

Zippers

Zippers seem to have a mind of their own and can break at the worst possible moment. Lubricants such as silicon or Teflon help maintain easy-pulling zippers, and suntan lotion even works in a pinch. Be sure you can work all of the zippers on your clothing and other gear quickly by adding pull loops (see page 18). Every time you have to take off your gloves to use a zipper, you lose body heat and your hands get colder. In the meantime, your friends are waiting! In the field, carry some safety pins in your repair kit just in case a zipper breaks. Dental floss can be used as emergency mending, so place a sewing needle in your floss box.

Conclusion

Clothing can make a difference between enjoying backcountry skiing and hating it. Investing in good clothing is the first smart thing you can do to ensure your enjoyment of the sport and your safety in bad

MAKING ZIPPER PULLS

Most zippers are too small to use with large gloves or mittens in the middle of a blizzard, so each zipper should have a pull loop. Go down to your local mountain shop and buy about 20 feet (6 meters) of round 4 mm Perlon accessory cord, which is easier to grip than flat webbing. Twelve-inch (30-centimeter) pieces of cord work best for clothing. Use 14-inch (36-centimeter) cord on sleeping bags, backpacks, and tent zippers. Burn the ends of each piece with a butane lighter after cutting or have the shop cut them electronically. Tie the ends with a square knot, stick one end through the loop and loop through the knot, and you've created a zipper pull. You'll be happy you had them!

weather conditions. In the ultimate sense, your clothing *is* your first shelter, and good winter clothing provides the foundation for all your outdoor exploits. You can spend more time skiing and less time heading indoors to warm up, and you'll have more patience and endurance, which will help you make good decisions in bad weather. Mountain rescuers have often found survivors with only their clothing to keep them warm. It's something to think about.

chapter

Gearing Up for the Backcountry

While ski clothing will keep you warm and dry, good ski equipment will help you ski faster and farther with less energy. In fact, good ski equipment can lift your skiing ability to a whole new level of performance. The applications of space age materials and construction technologies are providing skiers with a whole new range of ski equipment that is more effective and fun in backcountry conditions.

Types of Equipment

Over the years, ski equipment has evolved into specialized versions for different types of skiing. *Track and skate skiing* takes place on a machine-groomed track with a ski that is 55 mm wide. *Cross-country (XC)*, or *Nordic, touring* uses slightly wider skis on established trails or open rolling terrain (not on a groomed track). *Classic telemark* equipment uses three-pin bindings, telemark boots, and a metal-edged "skinny ski" (55 mm) in the mountains, forest, and tundra.

Latest Trends

Today's telemark skiers at the resort or in the mountains (sometimes called ski mountaineers) are using a heavy-duty Nordic touring system employing a high-top (over ankle height) boot with a three-pin binding and a wide (over 70 mm) ski. Parallel skiers may prefer an *Alpine touring (AT)* system (called *ski randonnée* in Europe) that uses a plate binding that can lift up during touring and lock down during downhill runs. At advanced levels on steep terrain, both disciplines use plastic boots and Alpine-width (70 mm) skis. You can parallel ski or telemark (see chapter 6) with either setup, but obviously both are specialized. Both types of equipment have been used on multiday ski expeditions.

Merging of Equipment

It is getting harder to see the differences in upper-end telemark and AT equipment. High-top telemark boots are increasingly being used with adjustable-release bindings, a feature once unique to AT bindings. Today, only one characteristic separates advanced telemark and AT equipment: the pivot point. AT bindings incorporate a plate and a machined metal pivot for heel lift during locomotion, while telemark bindings use the boot's own flex for heel lift. Telemark purists dislike the rigidity of the AT plate and thus stick with the three-pin model. Which is more efficient in uphill climbing? My research has shown that the two modes are identical in energy expenditure, even though AT gear is heavier, which shows how efficient a machined pivot is compared to the bending of a boot. Some newer AT gear is even lighter than newer telemark equipment. Even the prices are similar for these two forms of equipment (see table 2.1).

Table 2.1

Approximate Equipment Costs

Mfg.	Model	Weight/pair	Cost
TELEMARK BINDINGS (NONRELEASABLE)			
Black Diamond	XCD	14 oz.	$65.00
Cabletrack	NNNBC	1 lb. 8 oz.	62.00
Rainey	Superloop	1 lb. 6 oz.	95.00
Riva	Riva II	1 lb. 7 oz.	85.00

Mfg.	Model	Weight/pair	Cost
TELEMARK BINDINGS (RELEASABLE)			
Rottefella	TRP-100	2 lb. 8 oz.	$275.00
Voile	CRB	3 lb. 0 oz.	98.00
RANDONNÉE/AT BINDINGS			
Diamir	Fritschi	3 lb. 12 oz.	$350.00
Dynafit	Tech	1 lb. 10 oz.	295.00
Silvretta	SL	2 lb. 5 oz.	339.00
TELEMARK BOOTS			
Andrew Leather	Rifugio	4 lb. 6 oz.	$189.00
Andrew Leather	Solitude	6 lb. 0 oz.	335.00
Asolo Leather	Snowfield	4 lb. 10 oz.	290.00
Asolo Plastic	Telebreeze	6 lb. 10 oz.	280.00
Scarpa Plastic	Terminator	8 lb. 14 oz.	515.00
Trak (Merrell) Plastic	Supercomp	9 lb. 2 oz.	510.00
RANDONNÉE/AT BOOTS			
Dynafit	Tourlite Tech	6 lb. 14 oz.	$379.00
Nordica	TR9	8 lb. 8 oz.	420.00
Scarpa	Denali	8 lb. 12 oz.	450.00

Mfg.	Model	Profile	Weight/pair	Cost
TELEMARK SKIS				
Black Diamond	Desolation	91-69-80	6 lb. 6 oz.	$400.00
Black Diamond	Resolution	99-66-92	7 lb. 8 oz.	576.00
Black Diamond	Syncro-X	72-54-63	5 lb. 6 oz.	320.00
TUA	Mega	88-64-78	6 lb. 0 oz.	485.00
AT SKIS/WIDE TELEMARK				
Dynastar	Big Powder	115-90-110	6 lb. 0 oz.	$550.00
Kneissal	Tourstar	90-70-80	6 lb. 7 oz.	469.00
Volkl	Snow Ranger	103-80-97	7 lb. 4 oz.	550.00
SKI POLES				
Black Diamond	Flicklock Adj.	2 section	22 oz.	$90.00
Leki	Lawisound	2 section	22 oz.	94.00
Life-Link	Extreme	2 section	19 oz.	80.00

All boot weights are for a men's size 9 including weights for Alpine touring boots.

Telemark or Alpine Touring?

As a general rule, telemarking equipment is best suited for gentle slopes and light packs, while AT gear is perfect for steep slopes and heavy packs. If you like trail skiing but do an occasional hut tour, choose wider metal-edged Nordic skis that will give you better control on icy trails and offer the ability to telemark on untracked snow. Longtime parallel skiers who want to stick with parallel techniques with some occasional telemarking in the backcountry will like AT equipment. It's not necessary to learn a whole new technique for the backcountry when you already know one.

Renting equipment is the best way to determine which gear is most comfortable for you. While AT gear is becoming more popular in mountainous areas, most shops will rent only telemark gear. Each winter, outdoor magazines have backcountry ski equipment test reviews that rate different skis in varying snow conditions. Studying the latest equipment reviews can help you stay current on new ski models. Beginners shouldn't be afraid of so-called performance equipment; it will help them ski better with less effort. Finally, a ski doesn't have to say "backcountry" on it to be used there—many people ski the backcountry with "resort" skis. Whatever you choose, use the same equipment for both resort and backcountry use—this builds up strength and technique overall.

Skis for the Backcountry

Skiing can be twice as hard with equipment that is not suited to your strength or the snow conditions, so it is imperative that you choose the ski that works best for you. With that in mind, consider the following characteristics when looking for skis (see figure 2.1).

- **Width**—Today's backcountry skiers use wider skis than in the past (see figure 2.2). Narrow skis were designed for machine-made tracks, not natural snow conditions; it is impractical to sideslip or turn in thick, mucky snow or wear a heavy pack if you are using narrow skis. For skiers used to AT gear, anything over 70 mm is considered a wide ski. But to a telemarker, anything over 55 mm is wide. Both AT and telemark proponents would agree that a wider ski has distinct advantages. It offers more flotation than a narrow ski on powder, crud, slush, and sun crust—especially when wearing a pack—because of its increased skiing surface area. A shorter, wider ski has as many cubic

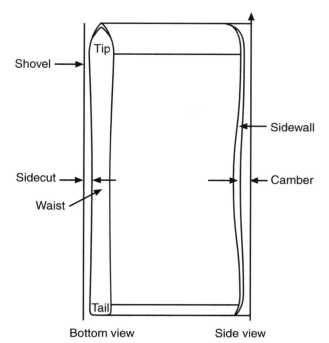

Figure 2.1 Parts of the ski. Adapted, by permission, from J. Yacenda, 1998, *High-Performance Skiing,* 2ed. (Champaign: Human Kinetics), 27.

Figure 2.2 Backcountry skis are becoming wider and more efficient. From top: Dynastar Big Powder and Volkl Snow Ranger (telemark/AT); and Black Diamond Resolution, Desolation, and Syncro-X (telemark).

centimeters touching the snow as a very long, narrow ski, but spreads body weight sideways as well as forward and backward, which reduces sinking into deep snow. Because wide skis are easier to turn, beginners will fall less and learn faster.

- **Length**—The old method of standing in your boots and touching your palm to the tip of the ski still applies to narrow skis (55 mm) when choosing the proper length. Now, however, with wider skis there are so many ski models out that you must trust your ski shop to pick the right length for you. A ski must be matched to the ability level, aggressiveness, and weight of the skier. Generally, skiers of higher ability and aggressiveness tend to have longer skis.

Skis are measured in two different ways: cord length and running length. Cord length is measured by running a tape measure along the ski's top surface from the heel of the ski to the tip of the ski. The running length is a measure of the surface of the ski that actually touches the snow. On a 195-cm ski, this may amount to 177 cm. While shorter skis are lighter—which translates into increased endurance, reduced travel time, and easier packing—keep in mind that longer skis put more edge on the snow. More edge on the snow increases security on ice, which is especially important for the steep terrain specialist.

- **Weight**—Heavier skis tend to carve through heavy snows better. But that's not a good enough reason to use them; long-haul backcountry skiing involves hours of touring and climbing between relatively short moments of downhill skiing. Always get the lightest ski available.

- **Ski core**—*Ski core* describes the materials that make up the ski. Skis are generally built from sandwiched combinations of three materials: foam, wood, and metal. Foam and fiberglass are used for flexibility. Wood adds stiffness and dampening. Metal adds torsional stiffness, and durability. Wood and metal skis will probably hold binding screws better than a pure foam core. Most skis have a reinforced midsection called a *binding plate* that gives binding screws solid anchorage into the ski (see discussion on ski bindings, page 30). Modern skis are built very strong and they rarely break.

- **Torsional stiffness**—This is the amount of flex or twist the ski has along its long axis. The ski should be stiff enough to hold on ice and hard snow. Performance on ice is important, because a fall on ice can cause more injury than a fall on fluffy powder. There are many types of skis that work well in all conditions, but all-metal skis work the best on ice due to their superior torsional stiffness. Cap skis, also made of the foam-wood-metal combination, use a top cap of fiberglass which is heat molded to a torsion box construction making it torsionally stiffer. These have become popular due to their increased edging power for both telemark and AT skiers.

• **Vibration dampening**—When a ski vibrates, that means it is spending time in the air and not on the snow, holding an edge. To maintain control on hard snow and ice, the ski must be able to dampen vibration. To test this, hold the ski vertically with your fingertips. Lightly drop the ski down from an inch above the ground. Does the ski vibrate? The less it vibrates, the better it will be on hard pack and ice.

• **Flex**—Generally, the ski should have a predictable, even flex, tip to tail, for skiing powder and crud. However, the tip of the ski may flex a little more than the rest of the ski, allowing the ski to deflect off crud or rocks to minimize the effect on the ski's tracking. An aftbody, or rear of the ski, that is stiffer than the front of the ski is good for edging on ice and finishing turns in all conditions.

• **Side cut**—Side cut is the amount in millimeters that the waist of the ski differs from the tip or tail of the ski. This measurement determines the ease with which the ski can be turned. Maneuverability in tight spaces among trees and rocks is important in the backcountry. So-called shaped skis with 30 mm of side cut (*parabolic* or *hourglass* skis) do speed turning response. However, the downside is that a waist that is too narrow allows the ski to collapse in the middle when skiing powder or crud. So-called fat skis with 20 mm of side cut are better suited for backcountry conditions, since these combine increased flotation and turning ease. When purchasing skis, sidecut information is listed by the manufacturer on the ski packaging, and it can also be obtained from magazine ski tests and knowledgeable ski shop personnel.

• **Sidewalls**—The side of the ski is prone to damage from rock and ice, so it must have a proven record of durability. Some newer skis have beveled sidewalls that theoretically minimize resistance to turning in heavy snow. This design feature may help in some conditions, but probably not to any great extent in most conditions. A good way to evaluate sidewall is to pay attention to the edges. Metal edges are mandatory for backcountry skis. Steel offset edges not only provide holding power, but protect the ski's sidewall from injury.

- **Camber**—Camber is the amount of spring or life that a ski has, which allows the ski to spring back after being compressed on the snow. Traditionally, Nordic skis had a double camber, allowing the ski to be unweighted slightly and thus enabling forward sliding, which was convenient when using wax or skins (see chapter 4, page 70). Today, most modern telemark and Alpine skis do not have a double camber, as downhill performance has been given a higher priority than trail performance.

When buying skis be sure that they don't have too much camber—your body weight should be able to compress the skis fully. To test the camber, lay the skis down on a flat, hard floor, and slip a piece of paper under each ski. Then, step on top of both skis together, making sure your weight is equally distributed on both skis. Have a friend pull the pieces of paper out from under the skis simultaneously. If he can pull the paper out from under the skis, those skis are not the right length—go to the next longer length. If he cannot pull both pieces of paper out, then those skis are the correct length for your weight. The idea is to be able to make contact with the snow as well as float on top of it. This is very important for climbing and for skiing on hard snow and ice.

- **Bases**—There are two methods of base processing for ski bottoms. A sintered base is made from melted plastic chunks, while extruded plastic bases are made from preformed sheets of P-tex. Sintered bases are porous, so they hold wax better. Bases come in different levels of hardness. A level 2,000 P-tex base is very hard, so it won't get hurt by rocks. The flip side is that it is really hard to tune the skis yourself since the base material is so hard to file.

- **Color**—A dark-colored ski bottom won't melt snow any faster or slide better than a light-colored ski! But bright-colored skis are easier to find if they get away from you. Base color may be significant in ground-to-air signaling, according to French tests in which yellow fluorescent bases were visible by helicopter from three miles (5 kilometers) away.

Ski Tuning

Backcountry skis get beat up because they are used on ungroomed slopes, but they still need to be maintained at a high level. Sharp edges and good bases are essential for good turning. Should you tune your own skis? With harder base materials and metal edges, you'll find that it takes too much time. There are some good books on ski tuning if you want to do it yourself (see the bibliography), but certified technicians with professional tools do a great job and many of them are backcountry skiers themselves. Besides, the $30 you spend to tune your skis is a small price to maintain a $400 investment! Tune them just before the ski season starts, when many ski shops have tuning specials. Always get your skis tuned right before spring skiing so they will be sharp on morning ice. In the field you can take out nicks in the edges of your skis with a small sharpening stone, but leave the heavy files at home—overzealous attempts at tuning can ruin your new skis.

Ski Boots for the Backcountry

Boots are the most important piece of equipment you will buy since they make the vital connection between ski and body. Good-fitting boots mean increased strength, endurance, and comfort, and can reduce falling by transmitting turning forces quickly and forcefully to your skis. This is vital on ungroomed backcountry snows. Poor-fitting boots mean cold feet, blisters, pain, and reduced endurance. In addition to getting a good fit, be sure to match the boot to the ski. Generally, the wider the ski, the heavier the boot that should be used. Do not, for instance, put a low-cut telemark boot on a heavy, wide downhill ski.

Don't expect to just walk into the first shop you visit and buy a pair of boots. Talk with the shop's boot-fitting expert and try on several pairs. Fit boots using the socks you normally wear while skiing: probably a polypropylene liner sock and a medium-weight ski sock. Wear the boots around the house for a few hours after you make your purchase to check the fit. If they don't fit, return them. There are a lot of good boots out there, so it's the fit that counts, not the brand. If $50 to $100 separates you from the boot you need, consider putting it on layaway. Remember that a pair of boots can last several years, making for a minimal yearly investment over the long term—a one-time purchase price of $300 to $400 for boots that last 10 years (or more) means only $30 to $40 per year.

Telemark Boots

Ski boots must also be snow boots. Treadless Nordic shoes have caused countless people to slip and injure themselves on icy parking lots even before they got their skis on! High-top telemark boots are warmer because most are double insulated and are safer during walking because they have rubber mountaineering soles. A square toe allows for fitting in a three-pin Nordic binding, and many have buckles for increased stiffness and ease of use with cold hands (see figure 2.3). All are hinged at the ankle for forward and backward flex. For those boots that have laces, round laces come untied frequently—they should be replaced with flat laces for convenience.

Plastic telemark boots are permanently waterproof and are far safer in survival situations than leather boots, which can get wet or break down with use. Plastic provides more control over the ski and transmits release forces to releasable bindings more effectively than a leather boot, thereby avoiding release malfunction. Leather boots do have a nice feel to them and will be around as long as there is a market, but they just don't hold up as well as plastic telemark boots. Keep leather boots in a cool, dry place during the off-season. A boot tree will keep your leather boots looking new; in addition, shoe polish will not only help keep your boots looking new, but also will help them stay water resistant.

Figure 2.3 Telemark boots have evolved from light touring boots into specialized downhill skiing machines. From left: Andrew Rifugio and Solitude, Trak Supercomp (formerly Merrell), and Scarpa Terminator.

Most plastic telemark boots are double boots. This eliminates using too many socks, which can cause the foot to swim around inside the boot and thereby reduce the turning force transmitted to the ski. An inner boot is a stiffer structure, providing a more accurate fit. Double boots are substantially warmer than single boots, making hut skiing and snow camping much easier. Inner boots can be removed and dried inside a sleeping bag, hung above a hut fireplace to dry, or worn around the hut. The better inner boots have heavy-duty bottoms for wear around the hut. Worn-down inner boots can be replaced with factory-made Gore-Tex inner boots or a custom heat-molded inner boot (Raichle Thermoflex, etc.). Both work well but the advantage goes to the heat-molded inner boot because it saves weight and eliminates lacing completely.

Alpine Touring Boots

All AT boots have been plastic for some time and prefaced the development of the plastic telemark boot. These boots also have a removable inner boot for warmth while skiing. The ski boot itself has a Vibram climbing sole, so it can't be used with regular downhill bindings (see figure 2.4). AT boots lack a flexible footbed, making the boot uncomfortable for extended walking or downclimbing. Bring running or trail shoes if extended walking on pavement (over 2 miles [3 kilometers]) is required. For skiing and touring, forward and rear flex is arrested by a ratchet lock on the rear of the boot that can be manipulated easily.

Downhill Boots

Some skiers have put Vibram soles on their downhill ski boots or try to use their "comp" (competitive) telemark boots for touring. Unfortunately, these boots keep the skier in a constantly forward-flexed position, making flat skiing or walking miserable. (This is not a recommended practice.) This can be remedied somewhat by unbuckling the top two buckles of a front-buckle ski boot. For a peak ascent, it's easier to pack your ski boots and hike up in trail boots.

Fitting Problems

If you are bowlegged or knock-kneed, you will have a harder time turning your skis. A ski boot specialist can fit you with an orthotic or custom-molded footbed that will hold the foot in a neutral position that

Figure 2.4 AT boots. From left: Dynafit, Dachstein, and Scarpa.

spreads body weight over the whole boot bottom evenly, making weight changes and edging easier and more precise. If you are constantly getting blisters, check this out. Avoid hard plastic orthotics, which do not conform to the foot. Skiers who have narrow ankles and those with cold feet can remedy both with a custom heat-fitted inner boot.

Ski Bindings for the Backcountry

Simply stated, bindings should hold the boot to the ski when desired and release the boot when desired. The three-pin telemark binding is basically a clamp. The telemark boot flex acts as a hinge, allowing the skier to walk and glide. Generally, an AT binding uses a plate on which the boot fits. This plate is attached to a metal hinge that can be adjusted for release. All AT bindings have a release function. While more telemark skiers are seeking bindings with a release function, most are not because releasable bindings are not fashionable for the telemarker. Overall, plastic telemark boots can fit into AT bindings, but AT boots will not work with telemark bindings.

Telemark Bindings

Telemark bindings are typically three-pin bindings that rely on the engagement of the bindings' three pins into the three pinholes on the bottom of the ski boot (see figure 2.5). These bindings are often used along with a cable attachment. By itself this type of binding isn't releasable, but by luck, sometimes these boots tear out of these bindings during a violent fall when enough force is generated. Today, telemark boots are getting so big that in a bad fall they can tear the binding out of the ski. This can cause the ski to break in half (a good way to get stranded in the backcountry). Many ski industry people are now advocating the use of releasable telemark bindings to save skis in addition to preventing knee injuries, which can be both physically and financially devastating.

Releasable three-pin bindings work best with plastic telemark boots, since plastic boots transmit release and turning forces to the binding more accurately. The front two screws of the binding are typically placed directly at the ski's center as marked by the manufacturer. This allows more weight to be placed on the rear of the ski for better completion of turns. You must calibrate some bindings yourself during skiing, while other bindings with more accurate DIN (Deutsch Industrial Normale—an internationally accepted standard of engineering and testing) standards must be adjusted by a technician.

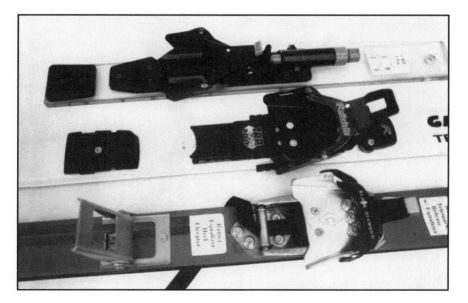

Figure 2.5 Telemark bindings can be mounted on a releasable plate that also has a release function. From top: Voile, Rottefella, and Ramer.

Cable Bindings

Cable bindings are popular because they save the boot from damage that occurs at the three pinholes with hard use (see figure 2.6). Some cable bindings have a screw mechanism that can be tightened when a cable gets stretched. Others attach to the toe piece itself with two hooks. A cable system helps to keep the boot centered on the ski during turns. The Voile CRB binding uses both three pins and a cable, which allows the skier to take off the cable during long, flat stretches, increasing heel lift and comfort. Cables by their nature will stretch over time, so spare cables should be carried on longer ski tours. By themselves, cable bindings do not release, but they can be mounted on a releasable plate if desired.

NNBS Nordic System

Although it is considered a telemark binding from a marketing standpoint, from an engineering standpoint the NNBS binding system is more similar to an AT binding than a telemark binding because it uses a metal pivot point for locomotion. A metal bar (built into the bottom of the toe) snaps into a special binding clip—it's basically a step-in binding, and you use your ski pole to release the boot from the binding by pressing a small lever (see figure 2.7). The only drawback is that the clip gets jammed with ice at times. Heavier telemarking

Figure 2.6   A basic telemark cable system: Black Diamond Riva II binding, Asolo boots, and Kazama skis.

boots are now being adapted to this system so they can be used with an adjustable-release binding.

Heel and Toe Plates

A good metal heel plate prevents your boot from sliding off the ski during turning but not during a fall. Plastic heel plates are worthless because they allow ice to build up under the heel, thus allowing it to slide off the ski during turns, with a simultaneous loss in turning force. With releasable bindings, use only the heel plate that comes with the binding. Some heel plates have a built-in heel elevation device that can be used to reduce heel drop and fatigue during climbing. Toe plates minimize the buildup of ice under the foot just behind the three-pin binding. This prevents snow buildup under the toe area, which can cause the boot to bend tightly over the toes and lead to toe pain, bruising, and cold toes. Old-fashioned heel location devices used a shoe-mounted post that dropped into a ski-mounted V-slot, preventing the boot from leaving ski center during turning. During a twisting fall, the skier's leg was locked into the ski, which usually resulted in injury. As for telemark plate bindings, I can personally testify to the dangers of using a plate binding without a release system.

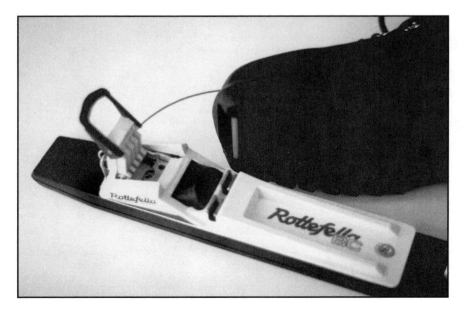

Figure 2.7 NNBS ski binding system.

Stacking

Stacking increases the distance between the telemark boot and ski with plastic spacers (available at ski shops). By increasing this distance, the more aggressive telemark skier is able to increase the mechanical advantage of the leg over the ski, increasing the *crank* (the power the leg can apply to the turn). It also keeps the boot from hitting the snow during radical turns.

Alpine Touring Bindings

Adjustable-release AT plate bindings (see figure 2.8) have been in constant use in Europe for over 50 years. They allow the foot to be locked down or "free-heeled." This allows the skier to switch between telemark and parallel techniques during the same run, if desired. Most have standardized DIN release settings.

Before plastic telemark boots, AT bindings were the only design that accepted a plastic ski boot. All have some type of heel elevation system for climbing efficiency. Some AT plate bindings

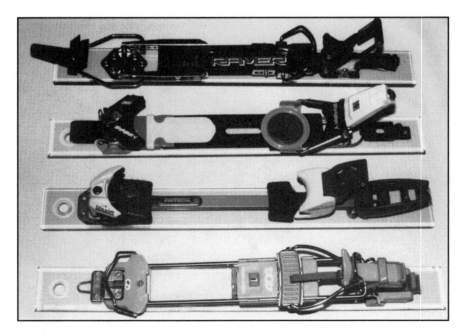

Figure 2.8 AT bindings. From top: Ramer (no longer made, but in widespread use), Emery, Diamir-Fritschi, and Silvretta.

also accept climbing boots, allowing them to be used to reach winter climbs. The Fritschi Diamir is the only true step-in binding in backcountry skiing and can speed mode changes due to its fast step-in features.

AT bindings are becoming more sophisticated in design each year. For example, the Dynafit binding consists only of a heel and toe piece, using the boot itself for the plate function. This saves weight, making them as light as some telemark bindings. While they lack the higher heel elevation of some bindings like the Fritschi, you can't ignore the pleasure of skiing on air!

Good AT bindings share the following characteristics:

• **Lockdown mechanism**—The binding can shift easily between touring and climbing modes. Some bindings require that you get out of the binding to change modes. This can be inconvenient, since during an ascent the skier may want to lock the binding in the down position for a fast downhill escape or for a long stretch of side-stepping.

• **Return spring**—Some bindings have a return spring that boosts the return of the ski to the boot during kick turns and flat striding. The spring plays a more important part in kick turns, where it gives the skier greater control of the rear of the ski.

• **Heel elevators**—Heel elevators lift the heel during climbing, reducing calf and thigh fatigue (see figure 2.9). They are so effective that they are now available on telemark bindings. They should not be used on flat terrain, where they become very uncomfortable. Most AT bindings have multiple elevation settings, making them adaptable to different slope angles.

Touring Adapters

There are several AT binding adapters that fit into the bindings of downhill skis. This eliminates the need to purchase new equipment, which would be a compromise for the person who just wants to backcountry ski occasionally. While problems don't arise with the adapters themselves, don't forget that some downhill gear is very heavy. Remember also that downhill boots with their permanent forward lean are painful even on short tours.

Release Considerations

Most AT bindings and some releasable telemark bindings are DIN calibrated and can be adjusted by using tables that compare your body

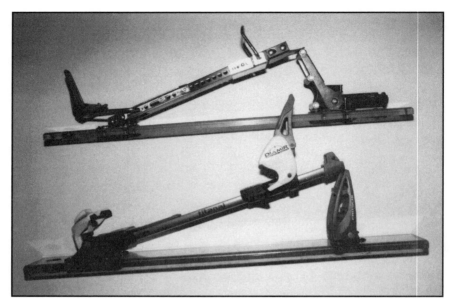

Figure 2.9   Heel elevators save energy during climbing. From top: Ramer, Diamir.

weight and ski ability. Have your binding adjusted by a certified technician according to manufacturer specifications, or ask to be shown how to do it yourself. The following conditions can illustrate how your bindings might respond to different ski and snow conditions.

• **Difficult terrain and snow**—The binding should be elastic enough so it doesn't pop off with every little vibration or with additional pack weight. Experience with your own binding will guide you on whether to increase or reduce its setting depending on the snow you are skiing. On extreme ski descents, where a premature release can be dangerous, experts often eliminate the binding release altogether.

• **Prior history of leg injury**—Children, older adults, and people with previous history of leg injury should use a lower setting. The skier should make the shop aware of past injury or history of knee weakness.

• **Snow conditions**—Heavy spring snow requires a lower setting on some bindings due to the increased incidence of slow, twisting falls. Ask the ski shop about any needed adjustments under these conditions. It's a good habit to have the shop check your bindings at the same time you get your skis sharpened.

Binding Noise

AT bindings are notorious for making a clacking noise during touring. Even telemark bindings squeak due to friction between binding and boots. This can be remedied by spraying silicon on the boot edges where they meet the binding. AT clack can be softened by covering heel elevators or ski surfaces with rubber electrical tape. Plastic boot noise can also be helped with silicon spray at the cuff and hinge parts.

BETTER BINDING MOUNTING FOR WOMEN

Recently, more ski shops have been mounting bindings farther forward in order to improve ski performance for women. Research has shown that women ski better when bindings are mounted slightly forward of center, because women have a tendency to sit back on their skis. This is due to the fact that women's body mass is concentrated in the hips and thighs, while men hold their mass in the upper body. Further support for this binding placement procedure can be found in *Womenski* by Claudia Carbone.

Runaway Straps

Runaway straps prevent losing a ski in terrain where walking out may be impossible, which may force a bivouac. The wire clip used on many telemark bindings that is clipped to the skier's bootlaces is a ski retention device meant for resort use only—they are difficult to use with gloves. String or cord is not a substitute because knots can freeze up, preventing release. Many resort skiers avoid runaway straps because they can cause the ski to "windmill" during high-speed crashes and cause head injuries; however, backcountry ski speeds rarely approach resort speeds. The most effective solution is to use runaway straps that are attached to the binding. Runaway straps are best constructed of nylon webbing with a Velcro closure that can be released or attached quickly (cost: $25). Any attachment should be released *before* crossing a suspected avalanche zone.

Ski Crampons

Sometimes snow is too hard for skins to adhere (see chapter 4, page 71). It could be a patchy situation where adhesion comes and goes. On very hard snow or ice, *ski crampons*—metal teeth that can be pushed into the snow—can be helpful for climbing while ascending low-angled traverses. They come in two styles, with advocates for each: one attaches to the binding (see figure 2.10), while another model attaches to the ski. The binding type allows the ski edges to remain in contact with the snow while you advance the ski to the next crampon placement, but if this type of crampon is used with heel elevators while climbing, the elevators will prevent the teeth from reaching the snow—not a problem for the ski-mounted type. But, ski-mounted types can make you feel like you are on stilts if they don't penetrate the snow, making you feel very unbalanced.

Ski Poles for the Backcountry

The ski pole is to the skier what an ice axe is to the mountaineer. It can be used to maintain balance, initiate turns, and prevent falls. During

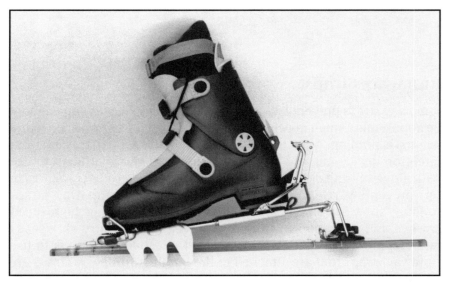

Figure 2.10   Ski crampons make climbing on crusty spring snow much easier (Silvretta binding and crampon shown).

bushwhacking it can be used to beat down a trail, and at night you can use it to anchor your tent. You can use it to probe for crevasses on glaciers or to determine the strength of ice on ponds and rivers. When crossing that stream or log, you can use it for support, and on the approach hike you can use it as a walking stick. It can also be used to probe for weak layers when digging avalanche pits. The ski pole has many uses—so buy some good ones! Some qualities to look for:

- **Strength**—The use of Nordic bamboo or fiberglass track ski poles for backcountry skiing is a mistake. The track pole was designed to have a certain flex and propulsion effect on the skier during track skiing, but in the backcountry, strength has priority over flex. Spend the extra money and buy adjustable-length metal ski poles that can act as avalanche probes. They are double walled, thereby twice as strong as a single pole, and you can adjust your ski pole length at will for uphill, downhill, or level skiing.

- **Length**—A track pole is longer because it is used for longer strides. However, during backcountry skiing this longer pole will put the skier in a perpetually unweighted posture, reducing skin/wax grip and balance, and increasing fatigue. Shorter poles help you plant the pole closer to the body instead of off to the side, where much energy is wasted. To measure your pole, stand tall on your skis. With the pole upside-down and touching the ground, grip it under the basket. With the proper length, the forearm should be 15 degrees above parallel to the ground. An adjustable pole makes these measurements unnecessary since you can adjust the pole at any time to any length that is comfortable.

- **Tips**—A straight ski pole tip is more effective for self-arrest than a ski pole tip that is curved for faster withdrawal during track skiing. The self-arrest capability must be the first priority in choosing ski poles. Tips should be kept sharp and replaced if damaged. Dull ski pole tips can cause you to miss pole plants and self-arrests! Ask your ski shop about the best method of sharpening your ski pole tips.

- **Baskets**—Large traditional Nordic ski baskets cause several problems: snow loads on the baskets during trail breaking in deep powder, greatly increasing fatigue and arm strain; they snag tree limbs, causing falls during downhill skiing; they also prevent fast self-arrests because the basket gets between the pole tip and the snow. A standard-diameter Alpine ski pole basket of four inches is sufficient.

- **Handles**—In the past, old leather ski pole handles used to soak the leather gloves of skiers' freezing hands, causing frostbite. Today, leather has been replaced with durable plastic and rubber composites. Standard Alpine ski handles are best for backcountry skiing because they offer a definite platform for the hand during skiing and help to dissipate shock, reducing fatigue to the arm and the shoulder joint. Other handles have a self-arrest blade built in so you can self-arrest on steeper slopes.

- **Straps**—The strap is an important part of the propulsion system because you push back on it during the latter part of the stride. Straps should be adjustable in length and wide enough to disperse stress over a wider area of the hand for better comfort. Quick-release straps tear out of their handles when the pole is caught by a tree. They should be standard on more backcountry ski poles to reduce unwanted falls and hand, arm, and shoulder injury.

Improving Your Grip

A ski pole is no good if you can't hold onto it. Wool gloves or mittens ball up with snow, allowing your hand to slide off the pole. Rubber electrical tape wrapped around the ski pole shaft can increase your grip during icy conditions. You can also rub ski touring wax along the length of the shaft. Your emergency duct tape supply can be wrapped around the ski pole 12 inches below the handle for use as a lower grip during long traverses or downhill skiing.

Maintenance

At the beginning of the ski season and before especially cold ski tours, lubricate all sliding parts of the ski pole with silicon spray so they don't freeze together. A rifle cleaning kit with a ramrod is very effective in cleaning the inside of the ski pole tubes. There are several systems used to adjust ski pole length, and some use a nylon bushing inside the pole. When the bottom part is twisted, a screw within the pole shaft expands the bushing within the pole, allowing adjustment of the pole length. These nylon bushings have a tendency to break with wear and tear at low temperatures, so always keep spare bushings in your repair kit. The biggest mistake is to overtighten the mechanism. Once it engages, twist the pole only once more to make it tight.

Ski Repair Kit

You must know how to fix your equipment out in the field, since problems always seem to happen when it's cold and you're exhausted. Find out from your ski shop what spare parts you should carry to repair your ski bindings and poles. A suggested list of items for a repair kit appears in the equipment list on page 264.

EQUIPMENT EMERGENCIES

- **Binding tears out of ski**—Duct tape won't keep a wet binding on a wet ski. Even if the ski is warm, the tape will be cut by the metal edges within a few miles. With a multipurpose knife, you can drill new holes with the leather punch. Now insert drywall expansion sleeves that are used with larger screws. You will find that this is so strong you might not even need to fix it once you get home.

- **Jammed ski pole sleeves**—If the two halves of an avalanche ski pole get jammed together and refuse to come apart, warm the poles in a hut or over a camp stove so they are just warm, not hot. Find a sturdy tree branch or hut roof beam. Tie Prussik knots around each part with shoelaces. In the Prussik knot, shoelaces are wound around the ski pole and threaded through themselves twice. The Prussik knot is prevented from sliding up or down the ski pole by duct tape holding it in place. Tie the upper Prussik knot around a tree branch, then stick your foot through the lower knot and put your body weight on it slowly until the poles come apart.

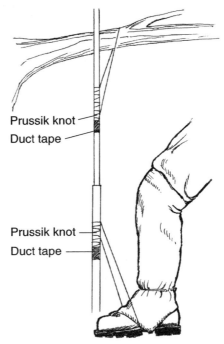

Prussik knot
Duct tape

Prussik knot
Duct tape

- **Broken ski pole shafts**—Find a stick just big enough to fit *inside* the two halves of your broken shaft, and trim it down with your knife (don't use old wood, it could break). Once you have joined the two shaft pieces, wrap the whole thing with duct tape. Use additional wood pieces if one is not enough.

- **Broken baskets**—A ski pole shaft without a basket is especially dangerous to those around you, and you won't be able to push off the snow without a basket anyway. Make a temporary basket with duct tape and small sticks—be creative.

- **Broken skis**—Old wooden skis *can* break in half. The best fix is to mount the binding on the tip half of the ski, so the ski will stay on top of the snow.

- **Broken ski tip**—Don't throw the broken tip away. Duct tape it back onto the ski. Always carry a spare ski tip when using wooden skis.

Conclusion

The purchase of effective ski equipment can greatly help you learn how to ski backcountry snow conditions. It can also increase your travel speed in variable snow and weather conditions. Durable, worry-free equipment doesn't stay durable and worry-free all by itself—skis, bindings, boots and poles must all be maintained professionally for best results and maximum performance. In addition, skiers must be prepared for equipment breakdowns—both with their own as well as the equipment of others.

3
chapter

Backcountry Conditioning

We often marvel at the ski pros. How do they ski so well? How do they stay in shape? You would ski great, too, if you lived at a ski resort and skied every day! However, the majority of us don't live at a ski resort. We usually have to get in shape in a gym in an urban area. Not as romantic as being in the mountains, is it?

Everyone has an opinion when it comes to training—and most people don't even like the concept. The outdoor athlete is usually, well, outdoors! Staying in shape comes naturally to the experienced, but not to beginners. Specific strength training can increase power, strength, and endurance, as well as speed learning, prevent injury, and basically allow for lots more fun. Indoor training can pay off big on the slopes! Although knowledge of ski technique is vital, the development of sport-specific strength cannot be ignored.

How to Train for the Backcountry

Backcountry skiing is a physically demanding sport, and conditioning away from the slopes can help prepare your body for those demands. You are most injury prone during the first hours or days of a ski tour. Ski touring has its own training effect that is more sport-specific than any exercise you could do in the gym. Conditioning before a trip prepares you for the initial exercise stress of the trip, preventing muscle breakdown. Losing excess body weight and doing cardiovascular training improves power and endurance—we can out-ski nightfall and bad weather when we can climb faster and ski longer.

Aerobic Versus Anaerobic Conditioning

Most of our day-to-day existence utilizes *aerobic* metabolism (meaning "with air"), whether we are sitting around or engaging in low-level exercise. But anaerobic (meaning "without air") metabolism uses more available biochemical fuel instead of oxygen when your body cannot take air in quickly enough during short bursts of exercise. During steady exercise, anaerobic and aerobic states are in constant flux. The worse shape we are in, the more anaerobic metabolism we use, and thus we "feel the burn" more. As we get into better shape we use aerobic metabolism more often, because we are adapting to a higher level of exertion. Well-trained skiers use aerobic metabolism more often and use stored fat, saving energy reserves for the spurts of harder exercise ahead.

Training for backcountry skiing is not like training for cross-country skiing. Strict aerobic training like long-distance running is not enough! Not only do we travel long distances, which requires aerobic training, but we also must carry heavy packs and climb hills, which require anaerobic training.

Cross-Training

Cross-training has been loosely defined as a means of adding variety to your workout by playing several different sports. It became popular with triathlon training, an endurance event in which participants must swim, bike, and run. Using these three sports was acceptable because they all involve similar blends of *aerobic* and *anaerobic* metabolism. But neither metabolism was really conditioned to its fullest because muscles consistently go from one metabolism to another. The person who is seeking to achieve maximal muscle growth should separate the two metabolisms, which can actually work against each other if they are combined on the same day. Weightlifting enhances distance running performance, but running reduces the gains from lifting. Additionally, cross-training detracts from consistent sport-specific training that targets particular muscles.

This is especially important for those who feel they have strength deficiencies. You should perform aerobic training (distance running, biking, skiing) and anaerobic training (weightlifting, wind sprints) on alternate days.

Training for Altitude

As we ascend in altitude the maximum volume of oxygen ($\dot{V}O_2$max) that we can utilize decreases along with our potential for exercise. An altitude of 7,000 to 8,000 feet (2,133 to 2,438 meters) seems to be the threshold altitude at which the body starts to make physiological adaptations. If you live at sea level and cannot train at altitude, your best preparation is to train the metabolic pathways that are most involved in physical work at altitude: train *an*aerobically. At altitude the body prefers anaerobic pathways for metabolizing energy since there is less available oxygen at altitude. By preconditioning those pathways, they are primed for maximum strength gains once you are at altitude. Wind sprints (50- to 100-yard running sprints or one-lap swimming sprints) and weight training are all variations of anaerobic training. When we train anaerobically, we feel a burning sensation in our muscles. This is caused by the accumulation of lactic acid—a muscle metabolite that results from hard exercise. This is different from the pain of a muscle injury that is accompanied by the total failure of the muscle to continue working. Sport breathing (discussed in more detail in chapter 4) will also maximize efforts at altitude, which is why it is so encouraged throughout this text. To maximize physical performance on a ski tour follow the long-accepted advice: climb and ski high but sleep low, for best recuperation at night. Be sure also to follow a high-carbohydrate diet—a good example is presented in the nutrition chapter.

Periodization

Ski training can fit into a yearlong fitness schedule. *Periodization* is the practice of timing conditioning so that you are at your physical peak at the optimal time. In the past, elite skiers would design their training so that they would be in peak condition just before a major competition. You can adapt this idea to be in the best shape possible when the ski season begins or just before a major ski trip (see table 3.1).

Summer is a great time for aerobic training, which forms an aerobic base that prepares the body for harder training. Studies have shown

Table 3.1

Weekly Off- and During-Season Conditioning Program

	Mon.	Tues.	Wed.	Thurs.	Fri.	Weekend
Off-season	Weights	Bike/run	Weights	Bike/run	Weights	Trip/rest
During-season	Bike/run	Weights	Bike/run	Weights	Rest	Skiing

that without an aerobic base, strength and muscle mass gains are reduced and more difficult to achieve. Most skiers like mountain biking, mountaineering, swimming, and backpacking, and these are great training modes year-round. Running up hills and stadium steps (within the parameters of knee health) will help form your aerobic base. In the fall, focus conditioning to include more ski-specific training. This means weightlifting three times a week until December, when you enter a maintenance phase during the ski season. During the season, if skiing on weekends, you may lift two days per week. This continues until April, when you may wish to train for summer sports again such as mountaineering or mountain biking.

Getting Started

Backcountry skiing can give you a good reason to get into shape, but it can be more than just that. It's easier to stay in good shape if you make a habit out of it, so developing good exercise and eating habits is very important. Good health should be the goal of any conditioning program. The older skier may walk every day, while the younger skier may maintain an aggressive weight training schedule. Whatever your age or gender, backcountry skiing is not the domain of the super-athlete—it is the type of physical activity everyone can participate in over an entire lifetime. This is conditioning that's not only good for skiing—it's good for life!

Get a Physical

Prior to training, one should have a complete physical exam. Particular emphasis should be given to the hip, knee, and ankle joints since

Hiking is a great way to get into shape. Snowmass Peak,
near Aspen, Colorado.

they are so important in skiing. Older skiers may require a graded exercise stress test, if so determined by the physician.

Get Back to Good Habits

If you smoke, you should quit or at least cut back as much as possible—nothing will make breathing harder! Drink plenty of water and reduce alcohol consumption. Reduce the fat in your diet and keep junk food to a minimum. Take a simple daily multivitamin—few of us have a balanced diet.

Get a Positive Attitude

A good attitude is really important to stay motivated. Get psyched! Watch some ski movies to remind yourself why you're doing this. Don't get into any guilt trips if you miss a workout—just pick it up the next day. Do what you can. If you are too tired to run a mile, walk! Doing a little each day can help you develop a new habit of physical fitness that will improve your health and skiing. Having a friend or loved one train with and support you in your goals is a big plus.

Train Outdoors and Indoors

When the weather is good, you can train outside. But during the winter, a good athletic club can help you maintain and increase your fitness level. Although home gyms are becoming more popular, many people find working out with others at a health club or recreation center to be more fun, not to mention that the company of others helps them keep up their workout routines. Utilize facilities where there are helpful weight room personnel. Not all clubs are conducive to training, so it pays to ask around as you search for a good workout spot.

You can easily get in shape for backcountry skiing without getting bored. Any opportunity to walk and climb stairs should be seen as just that—an opportunity, not drudgery. More specifically, mountain biking or road cycling combining long rides with sprints will give you a great workout. Indoor biking on stationary cycles, especially using sprinting (try the new "spinning" classes), can really build anaerobic power. In addition to cycling, trail running or backpacking with ski poles is very sport-specific, as is in-line skating.

MONITOR YOUR HEART RATE FOR MAXIMUM TRAINING RETURN

Knowing your heart rate really helps you get the training results you want. Professional cyclists and football and basketball teams have long used heart rate monitors to maximize their workouts. There is a direct relationship between heart rate and maximal oxygen consumption ($\dot{V}O_2$max). Most ski touring occurs within a range of 65 to 85 percent of one's maximum age-adjusted heart rate. Altitude generally increases resting heart rate by 10 percent upon arrival, but the rate will drop down to normal with acclimatization (about five days). Athletes have long used the following equation for target heart rate range to monitor their level of fitness.

Maximal heart rate (men) = 220 – age
Maximal heart rate (women) = 226 – age

	TARGET HEART RATE (FOR 47-YEAR-OLD MALE)	
	Lower Limit (65%)	**Upper limit (85%)**
Maximal heart rate	173	173
Conditioning intensity	173 × .65 = 112 beats/minute	173 × .85 = 147 beats/minute

You can still use these training principles without a monitor. After 30 minutes of skiing, find your pulse by putting two fingers just in front of your watchband, or put two fingertips on the edge of your throat and press lightly. Don't press too hard or you may not feel anything. In either method you have to take off a glove. Count the number of beats in 10 seconds and multiply by 6 to get the number of beats per minute. Compare that on-snow pulse rate to the pulse rate you achieved while working out. Try to get your training rate as close as possible to your actual skiing rate. You should try to slightly overtrain and get above your skiing heart rate as often as possible. When biking or hiking, you should be at your cruising rate of 65 percent of your maximal heart rate (HRmax) for 70 percent of the time and at your upper limit of 85 percent HRmax for 30 percent of the time. That's what pace is all about. If you try to max out all day, you won't go all day!

Planning a Workout

The workout can be broken into four areas:

1. Warm-up and stretch
2. Aerobic training
3. Weight training
4. Flexibility training

Warm-Up and Stretch

Each session should start with a warm-up that consists of 15 minutes of stationary cycling or brisk treadmill walking. You should keep warming up until you feel warm. If you don't warm up, lifting will be unproductive and difficult, and the potential for injury is higher. Stretch only after you have warmed up! Cold muscles don't stretch well—they tear better.

Aerobic Training

Aerobic training prepares the body for the reduced oxygen absorption at altitude by increasing the number and size of mitochondria. Mitochondria are responsible for the utilization of oxygen at the cellular level. The more mitochondria, the better we are able to utilize what oxygen there is at altitude. Long, slow distance training stimulates mitochondria growth by stressing muscle cells with increased blood flow and oxygen extraction demands at submaximal exertion levels. Most backcountry skiing occurs within 65 to 85 percent of your maximum heart rate—so your training heart rate should match this range. While many world-class bicyclists do five-hour training rides, the following training regimes are sufficient to build aerobic endurance for backcountry skiing: a one-hour bike ride (stationary or road), one- to five-mile (1.6 to 8 kilometer) hikes, one-mile swims, and so on. These should be done on aerobic training days, which should occur two to three times per week off-season, and one to two times per week during the ski season.

High-intensity bicycle training, such as spinning classes that utilize stationary bikes, can really increase endurance and power. When used correctly, stair-stepping machines also provide a good workout because they duplicate climbing motions so well. Be sure not to rest your arms on the support rails, as this defeats the weight-bearing purpose of the machine. You can set the stepper to a manual setting and do longer periods, up to 40 minutes for long, slow distance training that is good for weight reduction and building an aerobic base. Or you can preset the machine so it takes you into Fartlek training (meaning "speed play"), which is great for building cardiovascular and anaerobic conditioning. The main thing is to break a sweat and get physical. Remember, it's going to be a lot easier to get in shape here than out there!

Weight Training

The weightlifting methods illustrated in this chapter are meant to be done three days a week during the off-season and two days a week during the season. You can use the weight training descriptions on pages 51-57 as a guide to create your own workout. Always breathe during all resistance exercises. The standard breathing for most exercises is to inhale as the muscles lengthen and to exhale as the muscles contract. During the season you can go to Tuesday and Thursday workouts for the week prior to your ski weekend. On Friday, resting and carbo loading (see chapter 10) will be more important than lifting.

Weight training is important for several reasons. Weight training has been used by professional and amateur sports teams for years to build toughness and strength. The U.S. Ski Team found that strength gains from training improved their skiing skills. Weightlifting also can keep you stronger and leaner as you age. Even in active individuals, the body decreases its metabolic rate by 3 percent per year because it loses a half pound of lean muscle mass per year after age 30. Metabolically active muscle mass burns inactive fat tissue off even when you are sleeping. While fat insulates the body, it doesn't generate warmth at night, but muscle does by shivering.

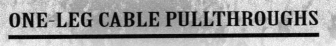

ONE-LEG CABLE PULLTHROUGHS

Hip flexors for trail-breaking power

Stand with your back to the cable machine and hook your toes behind a pull strap attached to the lower cable. Pull your knee up until your thigh is parallel with the floor—hold onto adjoining equipment for balance, if necessary. Pretend you're breaking trail! For best results, perform 3 sets of 12 on one leg and then switch to the other leg.

LEG EXTENSIONS

Quadriceps for knee strength and injury protection

Sit in the seat with your safety belt tightened. Hook the top of your feet under the roll pad of the machine arm, and extend your legs up as high as possible while holding both sides of your seat. Hold the weight for two counts at the top of the lift for a deeper contraction. Lower the weight slowly until the heels are behind the knees. Perform 3 sets of 12, using a full range of motion so the legs stretch out completely.

LUNGES

Quadriceps for telemark strength

Hold a barbell across your neck; you can place a towel under the bar for comfort (or you can hold a dumbbell in each hand). Stand upright with your feet together, head up, and chest out. Take a big step forward as if going into the telemark position, lowering yourself so that both knees bend to form 90 degree angles with the floor. Don't allow the front knee to extend past the ball of that foot. For best results, perform 3 sets of 12 with one leg, then switch to the other leg.

LEG CURLS

Hamstrings for knee strength and injury protection

Lie face down on the leg curl machine bench and hook your heels under the padded roll bar. Your knees should be at the rear edge of the bench. Bring your heels up as high as possible, hold for two counts at the top of the lift, and lower the weight slowly. Perform 3 sets of 12.

HEEL RAISES

Calves for climbing power

Hold a barbell across your neck; you can place a towel under the bar for comfort (or you can hold a dumbbell in each hand or use the calf raise station on a universal machine). Stand upright with your toes on a two-inch (five-centimeter) thick block of wood with your feet together, head up, and chest out. Raise your body so that you are standing on your toes and hold briefly, then lower your body slowly to the starting position. Keep your legs straight and knees firm (but not hyperextended). Try varying your foot positions (toes pointed in, toes pointed out) to work all areas of the calf. Perform 3 sets of 12.

SIT-UPS

Abdominals for back strength, backpack carrying,
and injury prevention

Lie on your back with your knees bent, heels close to your body, and feet flat on the floor; or rest your legs on top of a low bench. Place your hands behind your head (or cross them on your chest). Keeping your elbows behind your head and your chin pointed to the ceiling, tighten your abdominals and lift your shoulders and upper back off the ground. Remember not to pull on your neck to lift your body—your hands are there only to support your neck. Slowly lower the shoulders back to the ground. Feel the crunch in your abdominals and hold the last few repetitions of each set. Perform 3 sets of 25 daily.

BARBELL WRIST CURLS

Forearms for hand strength

Sit at the end of a bench with your legs about shoulder-width apart and place your forearms, palms up, on your thighs with the backs of your wrists slightly beyond your knees. Use light weights for this exercise. Grip the bar with your palms up, open the hands, and extend the wrists slowly, allowing the bar to roll down to the ends of your fingers. Curl the fingers and wrists to return the bar to the starting position. Don't let your forearms leave your thighs. Perform 3 sets of 12.

CABLE SIDE RAISES

Triceps and shoulders for extreme poling movements

For the left arm, stand sideways to a cable machine with a low pulley and reach down and across the front of your body with your left hand to grasp the handle. Pull the weight up and out until the arm is extended straight out in front of the body, then lower the weight slowly to the starting position. Be sure to keep the elbow slightly bent and the wrist rigid. Perform 3 sets of 12 with one arm, then switch to the other arm.

BENCH PRESS

Triceps, chest, and shoulders for pole movements, backpack
carrying, and overall strength

Lie on the bench with both feet flat on the floor and grasp the barbell
with your hands a little farther than shoulder-width apart, your palms
facing forward, and your elbows slightly bent (you can also perform
this exercise with dumbbells or on a bench press machine). Lift the
weight off the rack, hold the bar straight above your chest, and slowly
lower it to your chest as you breathe in and then press the weight back
up as you breathe out. Don't bounce the bar off your chest and don't
arch your back! Always have a training partner spot you when doing
bench presses with free weights. Perform 3 sets of 12.

TRICEPS PUSHDOWNS

Triceps for poling strength

Face an overhead pulley and stand with your knees slightly bent, your back straight, and your feet shoulder-width apart. Grasp the bar palms down and push the bar down by straightening your elbows until your arms are fully extended, keeping your upper arms firmly against your body. To complete the movement, slowly bend your elbows until your forearms are parallel with the floor. Perform 3 sets of 12.

STANDING BARBELL CURLS

Biceps for ski pole withdrawal

Stand with your feet shoulder-width apart and grasp the barbell palms up, resting it against your upper thighs (you can also perform this exercise with dumbbells or a universal machine). Curl the bar up until your forearms just touch your biceps, keeping your upper arms close to your sides. Hold the weight at the top for two counts, then lower it following the same path. Perform 3 sets of 12.

DUMBBELL FLYS

Chest expansion for improved sport breathing

Lie on the bench face up with a dumbbell in each hand and your feet flat on the floor. Start out with light weights (5 to 10 pounds); eventually you can work your way up to heavier weights. Keep your arms slightly bent while extending them out to the sides and inhale as you lower the weights, then exhale as you return the dumbbells to the starting position. At the lowest point in the movement your arms will be parallel with the floor. Make sure your upper arms never go beyond this point. Perform 3 sets of 12.

Repetitions, Sets, and Frequency of Training

All movements during weightlifting should be done smoothly at a steady speed, involving the entire range of motion. Jerking weights instead of lifting them smoothly can cause injury to the muscle you are training and to the rest of your body, especially the back.

The most widely used protocol for lifting to produce strength *and* endurance is to perform 3 sets of 12 repetitions with a one-minute rest between sets. That is, do 3 sets of as many repetitions as you can do, but no more than 12 per set. Lifting until failure stimulates your muscles to work to develop size and strength. If you do 8 reps and have to stop, fine. If you can only do 5 reps, reduce the weight by 5 pounds; if you still can't do 8 reps, reduce it by 5 pounds again. It's better to start off slow and build up to more reps using good form and proper technique than to jerk and cheat to get the weight up. You're not looking for an injury that could keep you off the slopes!

A high-quality workout of one hour is sufficient. If you have never lifted, start the first week by doing only 2 sets of 8 reps. Then do 3 sets of 8 during the second week. Weight training should take place every other day (usually Monday, Wednesday, and Friday) in the off-season, but no more than three one-hour, high-quality workouts per week are needed for good results. Two workouts per week can maintain your level of training, especially if you are skiing on weekends or doing additional outdoor exercise.

Order of Exercises

You should emphasize the importance of your leg muscles to skiing by training them first, since you have more energy at the beginning of the workout than at the end, then finish the workout by training your arms and hands. Begin weight training only after a good warm-up of at least 15 minutes of walking or cycling at low intensity.

Flexibility Training

Stretching increases intramuscular circulation and range of motion by reducing muscle tightness, which increases speed and immediately reduces minor soreness. Always warm up *then* stretch properly before skiing or doing any other physical activity. Leg flexibility is vital for the prevention of ski injuries, but neck flexibility is greatly overlooked. Hikers and ski tourers have a bad habit of looking at the ground instead of keeping their heads up. Neck rotations and side-to-side stretches should be done routinely. Use the stretches on pages 59-61 to start your program, and ask a trainer at your fitness club for stretching advice if you are having a hard time figuring out a proper stretching routine. The stretches on the following pages, with a few modifications, can be done outside right before starting your day or in the gym to maintain flexibility. Breathe deeply as you stretch, and hold each stretch for 10 counts.

TRUNK ROTATIONS

Stand with your feet parallel and legs shoulder-width apart. Your skis may be on or off in this exercise. Hold your ski poles across your shoulders behind your head, and rotate to the left and right at the waist.

HAMSTRING STRETCH

Stand with your feet parallel and legs shoulder-width apart, with your skis on. Lift one ski so that the tail sticks in the snow with the tip up, using your ski poles for balance. Repeat with the opposite ski. You can perform this stretch indoors by lifting your heel and resting it on a chair seat or tabletop.

FOREARM STRETCHES

Extend one arm out in front of your body, bending at the wrist so your fingers point up. Keep the arm straight while you grasp the fingertips with your other hand and gently pull them back to stretch the lower side of the arm. Next, bend your wrist the other way so your fingers point down and gently push the fingers toward your body to stretch the top of your forearm. Repeat on the opposite side.

NECK ROTATIONS

Rotate your head slowly in one direction and then the other. While rotating, try to touch your ear to your shoulder and tuck your chin to your chest.

QUADRICEPS STRETCH

Stand with your feet parallel and legs shoulder-width apart, with your skis off. Flex one knee to lift your heel backward to your buttocks, and grab your raised foot with the same side arm. You can hold onto a wall, tree, or fence for balance. Inhale and slowly pull your foot upward toward your buttocks to stretch the front of your thigh. Repeat on the opposite side.

© Chris Brown

CALF STRETCH

Lean forward toward a wall, fence, tree, or other vertical object with one leg forward and the other leg straight back. Your skis may be on or off in this exercise. Keep your rear foot flat on the floor and both feet pointing straight forward. Bend your arms as you lean toward the wall, keeping your back straight. Repeat on the opposite side.

© Chris Brown

SHOULDERS AND TRICEPS STRETCH

Reach one hand up and back over your shoulder with the elbow pointing straight up, as if you were scratching the center of your back. Reach the other hand up to hold the pointed elbow and gently pull the elbow behind your head to stretch the arm. Switch arms and repeat.

© Chris Brown

Overtraining

With any form of physical activity, pain is your body's way of telling you to stop. You should feel the burn, not the hurt. Some muscle strain is good, but pain can signal that an injury is coming. Listen to your inner voice. Stop yourself! Remember that you could put yourself out for the winter. Tomorrow is another day, and rest is as important as training. You shouldn't train when you are overly tired and can't exercise properly.

Staying Healthy in the Backcountry

Most accidents that happen in the mountains are not serious. However, an accident can still injure you and negatively affect your athletic future. This section provides an overview of first aid for sport injuries due to skiing, as well as injuries due to cold, heat, travel, and altitude.

First Aid Training

A little red bag with a white cross might help you fix small cuts and bruises, but it won't help you fix a broken leg. Some will be disappointed by my medical kit, which stresses minor stomach and blister medications (see the equipment list on pages 264-265), but keep in mind that almost everything you carry can be used in a first aid response. Handkerchiefs make fine bandages, and duct tape is a good skin tape. Knowledge and a cool head are important in backcountry emergencies. All skiers should take a first aid course dealing with mountain emergencies. Several excellent mountain medicine texts are listed in the bibliography. This book cannot be a complete treatise on first aid, but it will emphasize some areas needing attention. If you have a chronic condition, don't forget to take along the medicines that you need (such as insulin or asthmatic inhalers).

Skiing Injuries

Always use the appropriate protective devices during skiing. Kneepad protectors should always be used by telemarkers, especially during tree skiing or wherever tree stumps exist in the snow pack. Those with a history of knee injury should also wear orthopedic knee braces to protect the joint. Lower-back braces can be used by those with a history of back injury. Massage is good therapy for most general aches and pains.

With any twisting injury (whether to the knee or the ankle), one might experience severe pain and swelling. Fracture pain differs from other pains—it is more severe and persistent and will not allow weight bearing. Pain from a twist may subside somewhat with continued skiing, but it should not be ignored. The faster you care for the injury, the sooner it will heal. Use the RICE formula—*R*est, *I*ce, *C*ompression, and *E*levation. In camp, elevate the whole leg and use a large freezer bag full of snow held in place with an elastic wrap for an icepack. Cold has tremendous healing power. Apply the icepack for 15 minutes every 2 hours for the first 72 hours. An anti-inflammatory drug such as ibuprofen, aspirin, or naproxen should also be taken (with food or milk, if these drugs upset your stomach).

Blisters and Foot Care

Blisters are always a problem in outdoor sports. Slippery sock liners don't prevent blisters; they actually cause them by increasing sliding and friction inside the boot. Always use dry, clean polypropylene sock liners. Pretape nuisance spots with white medical tape or duct tape *before* skiing. Treat blisters promptly, before they get too big. Deflate blisters at their edge with a sharp pin that has been sterilized with a flame. Carry a "blister kit" that contains second skin, moleskin, and medical tape or duct tape. Apply in the following order:

1. Second skin—gelatin padding that reduces pain
2. Moleskin—tougher outer padding
3. Tape—keeps other layers on

Also, before skiing don't forget to clip your nails and spray your feet with antiperspirant to reduce wetness. In camp, take your socks off and allow your feet to dry. Foot massages are always good for general pains and can eliminate cold sensations within a few minutes.

Hypothermia and Frostbite

Severe hypothermia occurs when the body temperature falls below 90 degrees Fahrenheit (32 degrees Celsius). With severe hypothermia, shivering stops; the person usually cannot ski; and the person may be unconscious. Mild hypothermia involves shivering, apathy, and loss of coordination. A body temperature just at 90 degrees Fahrenheit causes mild confusion to occur (a dangerous time to be making navigational decisions). Because there is a danger of hypothermia and

EVACUATION BY SLED

Evacuation by sled can be used to help skiers suffering from fatigue, altitude sickness, hypothermia, or frostbite. However, moving a critically injured person is different from moving one who is tired or suffering from frostbite or hypothermia. Order air or ground evacuation (that is, helicopter or snowmobiles) if you suspect neck or back injury. Those not showing signs of neck or back injury such as numbness or tingling in the feet, legs, or back can be moved short distances (1 to 2 miles [1.6 to 3 kilometers]), but the route should be as smooth as possible; you should scout it out thoroughly before attempting transport because rough handling can cause the victim to go more deeply into shock.

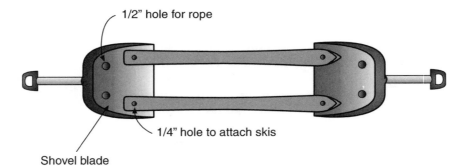

1/2" hole for rope

1/4" hole to attach skis

Shovel blade

It is better to make camp at the injury site if the site is safe from dangers such as avalanche or rockfall. Keep the victim warm and comfortable, and in this case, let professional rescuers do the moving. If, however, the injured person must be moved before professional help arrives, you can construct an emergency sled.

Emergency sleds built from skis are not as solid as a rescuer's fiberglass toboggan, but if the victim's chances of survival are slim if he isn't moved out of a dangerous avalanche zone or to a place of shelter, an emergency sled can be considered. If you are prepared with a few minimal supplies, you can build one. Four aluminum bolts with wing nuts and washers can be used to hold two skis together on two large avalanche shovels. Drill quarter-inch holes at the tails and tips of each ski, and also through two snow shovels, if holes do not exist in those places already (many snow shovels are made with holes in their shovel blades). Attach ropes for guiding the sled to the shovel handles or thread them through half-inch holes drilled in the shovel blades.

frostbite when air temperature is below –20 degrees Fahrenheit (29 degrees Celsius), exercise should be limited. Many mountain emergencies evolve due to the loss of judgment and ability to reason that occurs with this condition.

Hypothermia is often accompanied by frostbite. Frostbite was once thought to be caused by the freezing of intercellular water resulting in cell rupture and tissue death, but it is currently thought to be caused by the obstruction of blood vessels in the affected area. Frostbite begins as the freezing of the skin—something that can occur even on a sunny day, when cold and wind exist together. The skin appears patchy white (especially on the nose and ears) due to a constriction of blood vessels. After the blood returns, the skin becomes red and swollen. In severe frostbite, the skin becomes purple and then black *after* rewarming. Always rewarm affected areas after returning to shelter where rechilling cannot occur. Immersion in warm (not hot) water should be done gently, and the affected area should not be massaged. Seek medical advice if severe frostbite is suspected.

The best defense against hypothermia and frostbite is smart skiing—avoid fatigue and bad weather, use the proper clothing, and stay hydrated. Since metal conducts cold, avoid wearing earrings during periods of extreme cold as this will promote frostbite. It's not uncommon for a whole group to be hypothermic without even knowing it. You can usually ascertain a group's comfort level by the amount of talking in the group; on the trail, quiet people are frequently cold people. Strike up conversations to keep people talking and to keep their minds off the cold. Some skiers might never admit being cold in front of a group, so periodically ask individuals how they are feeling and make sure everyone is eating high-energy food and drinking plenty of water (dehydration leads to hypothermia in cold conditions). Thermos containers filled with hot Gatorade are also good to take on colder day tours, and chemical heat packs last four to six hours and are fantastic for heating up cold hands and bodies while providing a great psychological lift. In stormy conditions, keep everyone moving. If a map stop is necessary, find a spot in a dense grove of trees where wind protection is available. In severe cases of hypothermia or frostbite, those affected should be hospitalized upon reaching the trailhead.

Travel Contamination

Giardia, a parasitic protozoan, is responsible for most waterborne illnesses. Resistant to cold temperatures, giardia can be found in snow (if animal waste is nearby, but not in freshly fallen snow), in flowing streams, and in open water holes in frozen streams and lakes. Always avoid discolored snow (especially red) when collecting snow for water, as it can contain harmful microorganisms. Also, all water should be treated, pumped, or boiled.

Contamination with bacteria such as giardia can cause gastrointestinal cramping and illness. You can decrease your chances of contamination by boiling any water you use. According to research done by the Wilderness Medical Society (1992), boiling water for two to three minutes is sufficient to kill bacteria. Also, iodine or other water purification tablets are lightweight and very effective, if you can handle the aftertaste; they also save stove fuel. Larger groups may want to use a water filter. Prevent contamination by always washing your hands or using alcohol wipes after toilet duties. If gastrointestinal illness from contamination occurs, a stomach kit (see equipment list) will come in handy.

Acute Mountain Sickness

Altitude illness doesn't occur just in the Himalayas. People occasionally get ill at ski resorts that lie between 8,000 and 12,000 feet (2,438 to 3,657 meters) above sea level. The effect of altitude depends on the degree and rate of the change in altitude. Illness can occur when there is a change in altitude of 6,000 feet or more, where the normal healthy body can take up to two weeks to acclimatize.

Acute mountain sickness is not a specific disease, but describes several symptoms caused by high altitude. Symptoms may include extreme fatigue, headache, dizziness, breathlessness, and hyperventilation. Tourists usually feel these symptoms above 8,000 feet (2,438 meters), while high-altitude inhabitants most often feel them above 14,000 feet (4,267 meters). Conditioning won't prevent the onset of mountain sickness, but it may increase the ability to deal with the debilitating symptoms. A past history of altitude problems may mandate a slow ascent to altitude and a stay of a few days close to the trailhead before a major ski tour. For example, many people stay a few days in Denver (5,260 feet [1,603 meters]) before ascending to the ski resorts at higher altitudes. Alcohol consumption usually makes the symptoms worse. Symptoms tend to worsen at night with reduced physical activity and usually decrease in 24 hours. If they don't, the victim should descend to the lowest possible altitude immediately. Always be sure the person is hydrated and resting.

Those with heart conditions should always get a physical before going to high altitude.

Heat Exhaustion

You can get hot while mountain skiing, especially in the spring. Sunstroke and heat exhaustion, basic overloads of the body's cooling system, are marked by very high body temperature; red, hot, dry skin; abnormal breathing; and mental confusion. Both should be treated with rest out of the sun, cooling, and *lightly* salted liquids. From an athletic standpoint, for every 10 degrees that the air temperature rises, the body must double its effort to produce the same amount of work. Reduce clothing *before* you get too hot. Don't cover your calves in hot weather, because they release a lot of body heat (you can wear shorts or knickers, or unzip your ski pants for ventilation—see figure 3.1).

Figure 3.1   Unzip pants to provide cooling in warm weather.

Wear lightweight gloves to allow heat release at the wrists. While visors allow heat to escape from the head, keeping the skier cooler, caps will protect the head from sunburn. In very warm conditions, wearing a polypropylene or Dry-Lite running shirt will keep you cooler and drier than a cotton T-shirt. Be sure to rest more often and drink more liquids in hot weather—this will also help keep you cool.

Sport Vision

Sunglasses and goggles are safety equipment for your eyes—if you can't see, you can't ski. Solar radiation (UVA and UVB rays) increases by 10 percent every 5,000 feet (1,524 meters). High-altitude radiation can damage the eyes as easily as tree branch collisions and other accidental impacts. Plastic lenses work best—they are more scratch resistant than polycarbonate, and they cannot break. Mountain sunglasses should provide 100 percent protection from UVA, UVB, and IR (infrared) rays, and they should also be impact resistant. A brown-yellow tint is best for bright light, whereas yellow lenses should only be used for cloudy days where flat light, or no shadows or depth perception, exists. Yellow driving or shooting glasses are excellent for those who sweat profusely and have problems with their glasses fogging. Side panels can protect the eyes from incidental radiation that causes subconscious irritation that can greatly increase both fatigue and your temper! A sunglass-retaining strap can prevent accidental loss and breakage. Use an anti-fog cloth for cleaning, or apply a commercial anti-fog product to the inside of lenses to minimize fogging. Anti-infammatory eyedrops are an excellent remedy for eye irritation.

Skin Protection

At high altitude, it doesn't have to be hot for you to get a sunburn. Most wilderness medicine specialists advocate the use of sunblock with SPF 30 to 45, but an SPF 15 can be effective *if* you apply it evenly and often. Also, use a product that will not sting your eyes when you sweat. Second-degree burns are common among those whose skin is not sun conditioned. Sunburned arms and shoulders are not fun when you are carrying a 50-pound pack! Calves are also important to protect during spring ski tours. For dry, cracked skin from the sun and the dry mountain air, backcountry skiers have long used veterinarian-bag balm creams.

© Thomas A. Lepisto

Mountain biking on Hermosa Creek Trail in the San Juan National Forest, Colorado Rockies.

Conclusion

Preparing your body for backcountry skiing is as important as preparing your equipment. A well-conditioned body can handle the exertion of skiing and the effects of altitude more efficiently than a nonconditioned body; as a result, you can learn faster, fall less with fewer ski injuries, and have more fun skiing. In the field, the use of proper precautions related to environmental hazards such as altitude, sun, and cold is just plain common sense. Tare care of your body out there—it's your most important piece of equipment.

4
chapter

Climbing Techniques

Climbing is an integral part of backcountry skiing. Instead of dreading the next hill, anticipate what you're going to see once you reach the top! While skiing on the flats is not as exciting as going downhill, skiing over the "great white desert" can be a pleasant experience if you learn to relax your mind and go with it. If you're expedition skiing, you'll need to cover a lot of ground between those downhill sections. Skiing or climbing up the slope you intend to ski down is a good practice and lets you inspect snow conditions (see chapter 7 for more tips). In this chapter I'll discuss the pros and cons of climbing skins and wax, then describe the basic climbing techniques you'll need for the backcountry.

Climbing Skins Versus Wax

Climbing skins and Nordic wax provide the basic snow locomotive force in skiing: the ability to grip and glide over the snow. Traditionally, wax has been used instead of climbing skins for long-distance ski tours on rolling or low-angle terrain. More skiers are now using skins for flat skiing and climbing because the glide available with wax is negated when you carry a heavy pack or trail break in deep snow.

Nordic ski wax has the unique property of allowing glide and grip at the same time due to its unique molecular structure. The steeper the climb, the more wax you should apply. A wide-spectrum two-wax system such as Swix Gold and Silver is easy to learn and use. A binder wax such as Blue Klister may be applied early in the season so the wax stays on longer.

Wax provides more glide than skins, which in turn saves energy and increases mileage. For tours on rolling terrain and settled snow of consistent temperature, wax is fine. The problem is that snow usually doesn't stay at the same temperature or consistency for long, and snow can stick to the wrong wax. Suddenly, instead of gliding your skis are sticking to the snow, making every stride difficult; you then have to stop and scrape the old wax off and apply a different wax for the conditions. After many years of playing with wax in the Sierras, I decided to use skins exclusively even though they are slightly slower, and I haven't changed back in 15 years.

Climbing Skins

Climbing skins—strips of material that are fastened to the bottom of the skis with adhesive or buckles—enable the ski to grip snow while allowing for glide (see figure 4.1). Skins were originally made out of real sealskin because fur has a nap (that is, the fur is slanted, so these skins allow you to slide skis forward but not backward because the skin bristles up, gripping the snow). Most modern climbing skins are mohair, nylon, or plastic. Nylon skins are preferable because they absorb less water, ice up less, and have better glide than mohair or plastic skins.

Most climbing skins use an adhesive that can be reapplied after it has worn off. Older skins had several buckles that allowed snow to accumulate between the skin and ski, causing the ski to come off. But on hard-pack or icy traverses, buckles can prevent the ski from being edged completely, thus causing slips.

Compared to skins, wax is impractical due to its lower adhesion qualities on steeper climbs of varying snow conditions. The idea is to save energy. Climbing skins allow you to climb steeper snow on icy or very hard snow that wax doesn't handle well. Skins make steeper climbing safer in places where a fall or slip can cause a twisting backward fall on dangerous ground. You are more surefooted on climbing skins because of their powerful adhesive capacity. They can be left on for skiing downhill to reduce speed when the skier is fatigued or is carrying a heavy pack.

Figure 4.1   Applying climbing skins.

You should learn to change skins quickly—some people can take off their skins without taking off their skis! For speed in bad weather, you and your skiing partners should take off each others' skins so you won't have to remove skis. This saves a lot of time and energy.

Skin Adhesives

As I mentioned earlier, most skins are attached to the ski with an adhesive that needs to be reapplied as it wears off. Some adhesives don't work well at temperatures below 0 degrees Fahrenheit (–18 degrees Celsius) or when the skins get really wet. Some hot-melt adhesives stay sticky at much lower temperatures, but must be reglued at the factory after they wear out, which may not appeal to some. Ask your ski shop which glue seems to work best. Reapply your adhesive before starting a long ski tour. It is also smart to take along some backups in case your skins just won't stick, such as violet or silver cross-country wax, duct tape, or an old pair of Nordic-width skins.

Skin Sizes

There are several brands of climbing skins that come in several different widths, from 50 to 80 mm, for use with wide skis. If properly measured, the skin will cover almost the entire bottom of the ski, allowing about a half inch on either side of the skin so that complete edging of the ski can occur. Alpine or full-width skins can be used for peak ascents or touring, but on tours with lots of rolling terrain and few steep climbs, full-width skins lose some of their efficiency. The solution is to put narrower Nordic skins on your wide telemark or Alpine skis. This system allows for grip and a great glide that equals that of wax in some conditions. However, it won't work well on steep climbing traverses because the narrower skins can't reach the snow to provide grip.

Using Skins During Skiing

Skins glide best when they are clean. Any old adhesive stuck to the snow side of the skin can hold snow and ice, diminishing the skin's effectiveness. Skin waxes or special anti-stick sprays can be effective in helping skins glide more smoothly, especially in wet spring snows. Glue touch-ups may be required if the skins get dirty or wet or are used in very cold conditions. Keep the skins warm and sticky between runs by putting them inside your jacket. When skiing downhill, place the skins in a waterproof nylon bag larger than the one they came in. This makes the skins easier to access and will keep your clothes drier. Be sure your skins have rubber tail clips and tighteners. These will keep the skin on securely even if the adhesive is not working. If you have new wider skins, be sure the skin's tip hardware fits over the tip of your ski. You can add a thumb loop to the metal tip part for easier grasping in cold weather if desired. When drying skins, always fold them with the sticky sides together to preserve the glue.

Kickers or Half-Skins

Like Nordic skins, kicker skins are well adapted for use on low-angle rolling terrain where steep ascents are not encountered. *Kickers* or *half-skins* attach under the middle third of the ski (often called the kicker zone or wax pocket). The middle third of the ski receives most of the skier's weight, and therefore can deliver the most traction. However, the leading edge of some half-skins causes much resistance to sliding. Plus, the body weight of the skier is not always in the center of the ski during climbing. As the body weight moves forward and backward, so do the center of gravity and traction.

Wax

If you prefer wax, you should reapply cross-country wax in an even, moderately thick coat from tip to tail before attempting longer climbs

Alpine ski tourers during an early morning peak climb in the
Austrian Alps.

over 500 vertical feet (152 meters). You'll need the tip-to-tail coverage
because as you climb, you transfer weight to different areas of the
ski—and every inch of ski that is in contact with snow is utilized for
climbing adhesion. *Don't* smooth out your wax with a cork; a rough
wax actually provides better grip than a smooth layer.

Waxless Skis

There is no ski-base system that can really do what skins can. The
greatest barrier to the waxless ski idea is the inability of a ski-base
system to climb up ice and very hard snow. Waxless skis, although
suitable for moderate slopes, do not approach skins in sheer climbing
power. Use your waxless skis on rolling terrain—but take some
climbing skins for steeper climbs.

Climbing Basics

If you don't like climbing, you are missing out on 50 percent of the enjoyment of backcountry skiing. It doesn't have to hurt! By using the proper equipment and techniques you can learn to enjoy climbing and even get good at it! Technique is an important part of the art of climbing on skis.

Every climbing challenge has a solution, and trying to use muscle instead of brains is a sure way to burn out fast while climbing. Climbing traverses, while technically longer, can save you energy for the long haul. Sometimes going slower at higher altitudes allows you to complete a longer climb without stopping at all. You'll be skiing past the sprinters who will be stopping to rest as you head for the summit.

Safety

Before you start a longer climb (anything over 500 vertical feet [152 meters]), consider the following safety measures. They will make your climbing more efficient and safer because you'll last longer and climb faster.

- Be sure this is a climb that everyone in your group can do in a reasonable amount of time. Give more pack weight to stronger climbers to reduce climbing time.
- Be sure your avalanche transceiver is on (see chapter 9).
- Plan your route for maximum avalanche protection (see chapter 9).
- Plan to make turns or rest stops under natural protection such as rock outcroppings or heavy trees to protect yourself from falling snow or rocks.
- Be sure your climbing skins are on securely so they don't fall off on the way up. If you are using wax, be sure it has been applied properly so you don't have to rewax.
- On steeper, harder climbs, be sure to eat and drink before climbing. You'll need the energy, and this way you don't have to stop your climb to eat.
- Reduce or adjust clothing before climbing to minimize stopping during climbing. Loose shoelaces are fine for uphill climbing, but should be tightened for downhill skiing.

Sport Breathing

Correct breathing is the most overlooked technique in skiing, which is unfortunate because it can make your ski touring a lot easier. Climbing pace is set by your breathing pace, not the other way around. On low-angle slopes, for example, bring your right ski forward and breathe air deeply into your lungs. Feel your lungs expand. Now transfer weight onto that foot and press down and breathe out (sometimes called pressure breathing). As the slope steepens, take smaller steps and breathe in and out on alternating strides. On very steep sections you may inhale and exhale each time you move a leg forward. At rest stops, bend your body down between your ski poles with your upper body parallel to the ground so that gravity helps you increase your chest expansion. Practice this conscious breathing when you are weightlifting or hiking with a heavy pack.

Climbing Posture

The most common mistake ski tourers make during climbing is to lean too far forward while climbing steep slopes. This reduces weight on the middle of the ski, where the skins or wax are doing most of their work, increasing the chances of a slip.

Don't bend over at the waist to weight your skis; bend at the knees and keep your back straight. This reduces stress on your back, especially if you are carrying a pack. Pack weight also improves the traction of your skins or wax and can actually help you climb—but only if you keep your back straight! Strength *and* good technique are both important during climbing.

Stopping While Climbing

Stop only at secure positions on the slope. Put your skis across the slope and stomp out a good platform to rest on—stopping with your skis facing up the mountain might cause you to slip backward! Don't stop on ice or where it is very windy. In addition, stay off steeper, angled slopes if a rest stop is needed. If you are fatigued on a very steep, exposed slope, slow down and get to the top no matter what. Never take your pack off on a very steep slope. It may fall down the slope, plus you'll waste much energy taking it off and on and could lose your balance.

The Mental Game

Maintain a positive attitude—climbing can be tough. Clear your mind, go at your own pace, and enjoy the day. You won't be any good to yourself or your friends if you get into a bad mood, which robs you of energy. Don't try to keep up with everyone else. Find a speed and rhythm *you* enjoy and stick with it. Take a deep breath and relax every muscle you are *not* using. Try counting your steps, and add a few extra steps between rests. You'll be surprised at how a game can take your mind off the task. Pace yourself and keep a reserve of strength for emergencies—that's real safety.

Backcountry Climbing Techniques

Different techniques can be used for more efficient climbing on different terrain. This section covers how to perform these techniques and which ones work best in various situations and conditions you may encounter while climbing. The shading you'll see in many diagrams represents which arm or leg bears the weight at different points in the technique.

Diagonal Stride

The diagonal stride is the key to effective backcountry skiing (see figure 4.2). The motion is very similar to ice skating or roller skating. During the leg thrust, transfer your weight from the pushing leg to the leg that is already forward. Imagine gripping the snow with your toes. Follow with a pushoff that begins at the heel and finally rolls off the inner edge of the big toe as your leg passes to the rear. Think of rollerblading with a pack on. Always rely on your legs, not your arms, for climbing or touring to maximize your energy.

In cross-country racing, ski poling is fluid and aerobic. In backcountry skiing, it is slower and more dynamic. Plant the poles straight down at the ski's side, ahead of the bindings, not out sideways. This pushes the upper body forward. As you shift the weight to the forward ski, begin pole planting with the opposite arm. AT skiers may increase their speed on inclined "flats" by releasing their heels and utilizing the diagonal stride without using climbing skins.

Figure 4.2   The diagonal stride is used to climb on low-angle terrain.

Depending on your energy level, you can often climb straight up low- to moderate-angle slopes using the diagonal stride. Although a straight line is always the shortest route, it may not be the easiest. As you climb, keep your skis on the snow—lift only your heel off the ski, *not* your ski off the snow. If the ski party's track is too slick to climb or descend safely, put one ski or both skis in the untracked snow next to it and go up that way. Your skis will grip better on the ascent and you will come down slower on the descent.

Occasionally, on very short, steep, straight-up pitches you may lean forward and use a choked grip (see page 81) when on skis or on foot. Advance your ski poles in short distances, and resist reaching your hands over the height of your shoulders when climbing straight up with ski poles—this will put you off-balance. Don't unweight one ski completely until you are in a position to weight your new forward ski. Aggressively transfer your body weight from the rear ski to the forward ski. Stomp down on the front ski if necessary so that the wax or climbing skin will grip the snow. This is often a problem in wet snows or on ice, where both skins and wax have a hard time gripping. Use your body weight to push your arms back assertively! Plant your ski poles close to your body so you can push straight down and back with them instead of having them push sideways.

Herringbone

The herringbone technique allows you to make easy turns on lower angled slopes. The ski's tips are spread wider than shoulder-width apart while the tails are just touching. For straight up climbing, pick up each ski off the snow, placing it higher than the last. Then edge the inside edges of both skis by bending the knees to the inside (remember, you can't edge your skis with straight legs). Plant the poles close to your body, between the bindings and the rear of the ski (see figure 4.3), and push them down and backward using a walking cane grip.

Herringbone turns don't work well on steep slopes where kick turns would be easier. For the herringbone turn, start in the traversing position (see chapter 5) and stem the uphill ski first, then immediately stem the other ski. When climbing and turning uphill, weight the inside edges of both skis. Don't stop in the middle of the turn—keep turning your skis until you are in the new desired position. Use small steps to maintain balance, especially on ice. Keep your poles moving, planting them just ahead of your bindings. While climbing, the poles can be held normally until the apex and steepest part of this climbing turn, when you can shift your ski pole grip into a walking cane position allowing you to push down and back to complete the turn (see figure 4.4).

The normal manner of gripping your ski pole handle is to push your hand up through the handle strap and then back down so you are gripping the strap and handle within the hand (see figure 4.5). This allows you to apply arm pressure down on the strap, providing you with more climbing and touring force.

When overcoming terrain obstacles, utilize the entire shaft of your ski pole by using a choked grip (see figure 4.6). In this technique you grip the ski pole down the shaft from the handle. On steeper traverses or climbs this keeps the body from leaning downhill, therefore maintaining balance and reducing energy use. Wrap duct tape or electrical rubber tape at one foot intervals on the shaft of the ski pole to provide for a better grip over the whole shaft of the ski pole.

Sidestep Climbing

Sidestepping involves climbing up the slope sideways with both skis parallel across the fall line and edging both skis into the hill at the same time. You should be able to sidestep up slopes both forward and backward to avoid obstacles and unnecessary kick turns. Climb up in

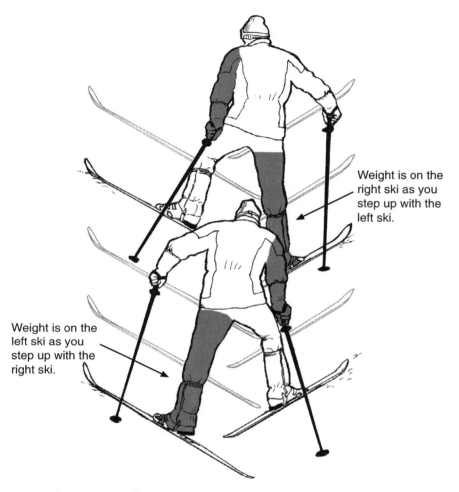

Weight is on the right ski as you step up with the left ski.

Weight is on the left ski as you step up with the right ski.

Figure 4.3   The herringbone allows for uphill climbing on low-angled slopes.

short steps while using a choked grip on the uphill hand and get as close to the slope as possible. Step up with one ski and plant it firmly on the snow above the obstacle, then shift your weight over the uphill ski to be sure it won't slide out from underneath you. While supporting yourself with both ski poles do a leg press up to your new stance, using the walking cane grip to push on the downhill pole during the sidestep up. While climbing, always keep three points of contact with the snow in case you slip: two poles and one ski or two skis and one pole. Reduce superfluous pole movements. The more

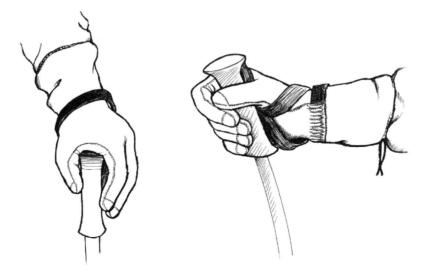

Figure 4.4 Walking cane grip.

Figure 4.5 Normal grip.

Figure 4.6 Choked grip.

time you have your pole tips in the air, the less time they are in the snow supporting you. Keep your back straight and your head up for balance. ATers can lock down their heels when sidestepping for extended periods or in awkward situations for easier and more precise climbing.

Traverse Climbing With Kick Turns

The kick turn is an essential technique for beginners and experts alike during ascending or descending. Kick turns can be done facing outward during descending (downhill kick turn) or facing the slope during climbing (uphill kick turn). The uphill kick turn has the advantage since you can readily get into a self-arrest position if you slip on steep terrain, whereas a slip from the downhill kick turn position can throw you into an uncontrolled fall. Both turns are very similar except for the pole positions.

For the downhill kick turn, first kick a flat platform in the snow. Now, plant your poles securely into the slope behind you for support in case you slip. Your upper body is facing down the slope. The skis must be parallel to each other and strictly across the fall line or else they will slip out from under you. Next, pick up your downhill ski by bending the knee and lifting at the thigh (see figure 4.7a). Don't be lazy and rotate the tail of the outside ski in the snow. It will jam into the snow, causing a fall. Pivot the ski around in the air while keeping your poles where they are, and plant the ski back in the same place, but facing the opposite direction now. Once the ski is firmly planted, pick up the other ski and bring it parallel to the first, bringing the other ski pole with it.

The uphill kick turn is similar but with the following exceptions— you do a kick turn going uphill, above the same-sided ski pole, and in the direction of the turn. The left pole is planted behind you, a few inches above your uphill ski, between the binding and the end of the ski. Then the uphill ski is pivoted so it lies above the ski pole (see figure 4.7b). The more parallel the skis, the easier the uphill kick turn will be. Transfer weight onto the uphill ski and bring the remaining ski and ski pole around together into the new direction. Beginners will do themselves a big favor by becoming experts in both turns, as both turns are invaluable in the backcountry. Practice on low-angled slopes, increasing the steepness with experience.

The platform is the key to this turn. It must be perfectly level, especially on steep, exposed slopes. To increase the speed and safety

a

b

Figure 4.7 *(a)* Downhill and *(b)* uphill kick turns allow you to go up or down any slope.

of the whole group, advanced skiers should stomp out kick turn platforms for less experienced skiers. Use low-angle climbing traverses (see chapter 5 for basic traverse description) between kick turns to conserve energy. Tip your knees outward slightly to keep your skis and skins flat in relationship to the slope for better traction when traversing.

Climbing With Ski Crampons

Ski crampons (see chapter 2, page 38) can give you extra footing on hard snow or ice. Both models of ski crampons add security while you are climbing or traversing icy slopes. Like climbing skins, you should anticipate their use *before* you start up an icy slope. On hard snow or ice, use small upward steps going from one crampon placement to the next. If you're using binding plate-mounted ski crampons, avoid using heel elevators since they prevent the crampons from reaching the snow.

Climbing Using Heel Elevators

Heel elevators artificially reduce the angle of climb by providing a higher resting position. This reduces calf and thigh fatigue and helps you conserve energy. The best heel elevators are offered on AT gear because more lift positions are available. As with ski crampons, you should anticipate the need for heel elevators before they are needed. Heel elevators are available for both AT and telemark skis (see figure 4.8). Heel elevators are best used during straight-up climbing or steep traverses. They should not be used on long, low-angle traverses where they can keep you unbalanced and cause a fall.

Courtesy of Peter Bridge

Figure 4.8 These telemark skiers demonstrate that heel elevators aren't used only by Alpine ski tourers anymore.

Climbing on Foot

Sometimes it is more efficient to walk or climb on foot than on skis. Those conditions could be:

- when climbing a face, ridge, or shoulder devoid of snow;
- when climbing ice or snow that is too steep to climb effectively on skis and where crampons or boots may be more efficient;
- where thin snow prevents safe continuous skiing, as during early winter or late spring; and
- during high winds where a skier can be blown off-balance, causing a fall. In this case, the snow may not be soft enough to hold an edge to prevent side winds from blowing one sideways.

On low-angle snow slopes, climb straight up like a duck (en canard) with toes out to rest your calves. As the angle steepens, try walking sideways up the slope like a crab—this is fun and works great! You should use your ski poles for support and safety at all times (see figure 4.9).

Figure 4.9   Hiking over snow or rock may be necessary when high winds shred snow off the slopes. Note how the skis are carried.

Kicking steps with telemark or AT plastic ski boots is much easier than using leather boots. You don't need to slam your boot into the snow for it to stick; this just wastes energy. Use the boot's weight and swing it from the knee in a relaxed fashion. Kick your steps straight into the snow horizontally to prevent the boot from slipping out of the snow. Keep your heels down while climbing to avoid stressing your calf muscles.

Carrying Skis

Most modern packs have side compression straps that are excellent for carrying skis if used correctly. Some packs may require ski-carrying patches where straps can be attached. If your pack doesn't have these, they can be easily installed. Bicycle toe straps work great for attaching skis. Skis should be packed securely. If skis are carried too low, they can hit your heels or the terrain, especially when descending on foot. If placed too high, they can hit your head or snag on tree branches. Carrying skis crossways on top of the pack is the worst situation. This last method is unsafe because the skis can throw the skier off balance—especially dangerous on icy terrain or steep traverses (see figure 4.10).

Boot Crampons and Ice Axes

Boot crampons and an ice axe may be necessary on more serious ski tours where steep slopes or glacier travel may be encountered. Boot

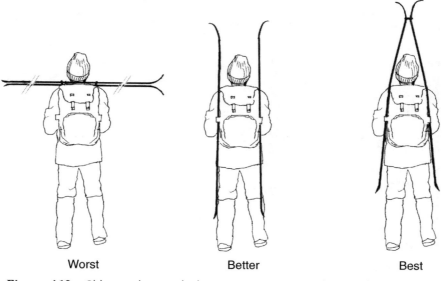

Worst	Better	Best

Figure 4.10 Skis can be carried many ways—some better than others.

ROCKCLIMBING AND ROPE HANDLING

It's likely that you'll encounter rockclimbing only on high-mountain tours. If you encounter any rock formations during your ski tour, remember that stiff ski boots hold well on *big* footholds, but they are not rockclimbing shoes. Plan your route carefully to avoid rockclimbing, which cannot be navigated using basic ski climbing techniques.

A good knowledge of rockclimbing and rope handling techniques can be valuable to the backcountry skier heading to higher mountains. This is not to say that you will always carry climbing gear on ski tours, but knowing basic rockcraft can give you an added sense of security, especially when you have to climb a short section of rock while carrying your skis to get from one slope to another or climb up a peak. It is also a valuable tool in emergencies.

The need for a rope in backcountry skiing is unusual—at least in the United States, where glacier travel typically doesn't occur in the contiguous 48 states. But rope use is not restricted to glacier travel. For larger groups, carrying a rope may be a good idea. It can be used for rescue purposes, such as pulling someone out of a creek with high banks, or making and hauling a sled. A typical rope approved for glacier travel by the UIAA (Union Internationale des Associations d'Alpisme) would be a 165-foot (50-meter), 8.5 mm Perlon rope (special touring ropes are 8.0 mm). A rope "throw bag" similar to the one used on whitewater rafts that contains 100 feet (30 meters) of 7 mm Perlon rope is an alternative that could be quickly dispatched. Always remember—never throw a rope to someone unless *you* are anchored.

crampons can help you climb steeper slopes surely and quickly. However, keep in mind that if your crampons won't penetrate the ice or snow you're trying to climb, you should think twice about skiing the same terrain. Adjustable 12-point crampons with step-in bindings are much easier to use than strap attachments. Rigid plate crampons are fine for steep climbing but are harder to walk with on lower-angled slopes, so adjustable crampons are preferred.

Always put on crampons *before* conditions become difficult enough for you to need them. Learn how to put on and remove crampons quickly, and practice doing this at home with the gloves or mittens you expect to be using. Be sure your crampons fit your ski boots *before* your trip, and keep your crampons sharp—dull crampons can cause a fall. Don't overtighten crampon straps when wearing leather boots; this can cut off circulation and cause cold feet. Finally, learn to pick

Colorado Haute Route near Berthoud Pass, Colorado.

up your feet when you climb so that the points of one crampon won't snag your opposite gaiter and cause a fall.

A good basic mountaineering ice axe made of lightweight aluminum is the most versatile. A medium-length axe (about 70 to 75 centimeters) can be used on steeper terrain and also as an anchor in softer snow. *Climbing Ice* by Yvon Chouinard and *Mountaineering: The Freedom of the Hills* by The Mountaineers are both good titles for learning how to use crampons and ice axes.

Conclusion

Those who haven't learned how to properly use climbing tools will experience more difficulty in the backcountry, and probably won't enjoy skiing the backcountry as much as they could. Skins are far superior to wax for sheer climbing power. The ski pole is a very important tool when we are climbing the mountain—it is an extension of our senses as we learn to probe for snow strength, depth and skiing potential. Learning sport breathing is the most overlooked aspect of backcountry skiing, as it is with most sports. Increasing our efficiency and our climbing ability increases our pleasure of the backcountry experience. There is a psychological game in climbing: those who are able to relax their minds and the muscles that aren't being used will have the greatest endurance at the end of the day.

5
chapter

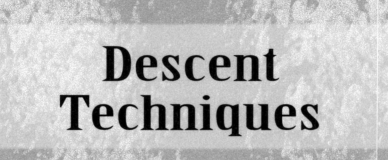

Descent Techniques

Telemarking has been heralded as *the* ski technique for backcountry for years. However, a lot of good telemarkers use parallel techniques as well! (In fact, more than a million Europeans ski the backcountry without using any telemark techniques at all!) The two techniques complement each other when teamed together. If you are a resort skier with good basic skills, you are at the doorway to new adventures in the backcountry.

Backcountry Descent Techniques

Notice that the word "descent" is used instead of "ski." That's because sometimes we have to walk or climb down a slope instead of simply skiing it. In the backcountry we have to be adaptable to conditions and use the right technique for the terrain at hand. Whether you prefer parallel or telemark techniques, the following information will prove useful.

General Descent Safety

Consider the following points before descending an unknown slope.

- Make sure avalanche transceivers are on.
- Skiers with shovels should ski last (if shovels are limited).
- Wear gloves to protect hands from cuts from ice and snow abrasions. Wear kneepads for protection from trees and other obstacles when needed.
- Scrape off excess wax for speed and ease of turning. Timid skiers should leave wax and climbing skins on to reduce speed.
- Beginners and fatigued skiers should review the pole drag technique (see page 101).
- Give each other plenty of room, especially in poor snow or reduced visibility.
- Never turn above a skier. You could miss your turn and cause a crash.
- Ski in control: this is the essence of backcountry skiing. Stop before you get too tired or are unable to ski safely.

Downclimbing on Foot

Skiing is not the whole story in winter backcountry travel. Sometimes you just have to walk down, such as when you encounter slopes stripped of snow (see figure 5.1). If you're walking down a snow-packed slope, always downclimb by driving your heel into the snow before taking your next step. If downclimbing in excess of 200 feet (61 meters), skis can be more safely carried on the pack and not in your hands (see chapter 4, page 86). Use your ski poles for support.

Sidestepping and Sideslipping

At times you may have to sidestep down, as shown in figure 5.2. If you do not have the energy or inclination to ski a short slope, sideslip or sidestep down it. On steeper slopes, sideslipping allows you to get a better idea of snow conditions before committing a turn.

Sideslipping will control your descent on steep, hard-pack snow or ice. During sideslipping, the upper body should face downhill (anticipation) with skis across the fall line. If necessary, plant the upper pole using a lower choked grip to keep the body in balance. Downhill pole plants should occur in a vertical line below the bindings. Knees are angulated into the hill. Feet are weighted flat on the skis so that body weight is equally distributed over the whole ski fore and aft—don't overedge on ice or you might lose your grip. Unweight the edges by simply rolling your ankles and knees outward. Regain your edges by

Figure 5.1 Skiers downclimbing unskiable terrain on the Sierra Haute Route, California.

Figure 5.2 Sidestepping will take you down tight situations. Notice the choked grip on the uphill pole.

FALL LINE

Looking for a line is jargon meaning looking for a line of descent. It could be down a trail, down a face, or through some trees. Your line should follow the same rules that a climbing route does: safety from avalanche and rockfall, consistent snow conditions, lack of obstacles, and so on. How deep is the snow and how does it compare with your past experiences? How long is the run? Can you handle it? If you fall, where will the fall take you? Many of the answers will depend upon where the fall line is. To determine the fall line, imagine the route a drop of water would take down the mountain. The route it travels is the true line of gravity—the fall line. Always think in terms of your fall line. Instead of fighting gravity, learn to use it. Put your skis across the line and you stop; point them down the line and you go. Sideslipping is a good exercise in experiencing the fall line. A double fall line is more difficult to navigate.

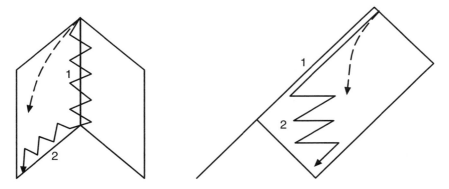

Number 1 is the primary fall line, while number 2 is the secondary fall line. Picture an open book. If you tilt the book, it looks like the illustration above. It will be easier to ski number 1 than trying to ski the resolution of the two fall lines together (dotted line). Avalanches will also follow this vector resolution. Taking one fall line at a time is easier and more fun.

cranking them into the slope, but don't plant your downhill pole too close or too deep—you could ski onto it, causing a fall.

Falling Leaf

This maneuver, which involves sideslipping forward and backward, is used very often—though most people are not aware that it is an actual technique! The falling leaf is great for navigating tight spaces between trees or boulders and descending icy trails and steep chutes. It's also good for controlled descent on steep slopes with unknown obstacles, or when hands are being used to push back tree branches or hold a sled. When sideslipping forward you should feel the front of your ankles against the top of your boots as you bend at the knees to weight the front half of your skis (see figure 5.3). Feel the sides of your feet edging into the hill. When sideslipping backward, feel your weight on your heels and the tails of your skis. Feel the back of the calves hit against the top of the back of the boot. Keep your knees bent! Your upper body should face downhill. When looking at terrain above or sideways, turn your head only by itself without rotating your body, because you could fall. Falling leaf is an excellent exercise for any skier who wants to learn how pressure and stance affect skiing.

Traversing

Traversing allows you to ski across a slope from one side to another. While easy on good, soft snow, it can be difficult when carrying a heavy pack or when the slope is icy or exposed.

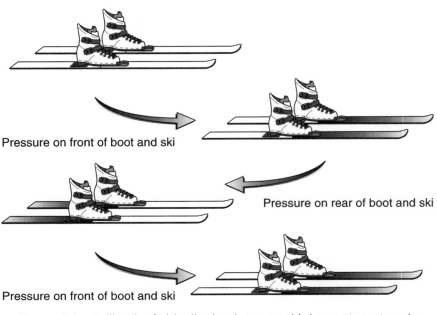

Pressure on front of boot and ski

Pressure on rear of boot and ski

Pressure on front of boot and ski

Figure 5.3 Falling leaf sideslipping lets you ski down steep terrain while positioning yourself for your next turn.

Your skis should be across the fall line, shoulder-width apart. Knees are bent, with the ski's edges angled toward the hill. A shallow low-angle traverse allows you to cross the slope slowly; a steeper angle increases your speed. Your uphill ski should always be a half-foot *ahead* of your downhill ski for balance (most of your weight is on the downhill ski) and to prevent crossing of the skis. Your shoulders can be slightly dipped to the outside to weight the downhill ski. Keep your hands above your waist. On steeper slopes, your uphill hand can grip the ski pole lower on the shaft (choked grip) to keep your shoulders square to the slope and your body balanced. Fear may cause you to overedge on steep slopes; avoid overedging as it will cause your skis to slip out from under you (see figure 5.4).

On very low-angle slopes you will be able to relax and let your skis run straight down, parallel to each other. This is a good time to work on posture, even while wearing a pack. Feel your feet and your skis encounter minute obstacles in the snow. Practice bending your knees and keeping your body weight centered. Keep both skis equally weighted and your head up, not looking down at the snow.

Skate or Step Turn

The skate or step turn is useful in accelerating on low-angle slopes or dodging obstacles. As if you were ice skating, simply push off one ski to the other ski, which is pointing in the direction you want to go (see figure 5.5). Transfer your weight aggressively while gliding on the first ski. Bend your knees a little before the transfer—this will give you more spring into the new ski. Double pole at this time to give extra

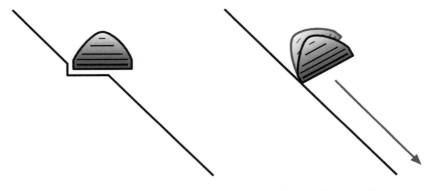

Figure 5.4   Don't overedge during traversing, especially on ice—you might lose your grip and fall.

Figure 5.5 Skate or step turns are excellent for direction changes on the flats.

forward momentum and maintain balance. Remember to pick up your skis at the thigh instead of just picking up your heels, which allows the ski tails to drag.

Snowplow

The basic snowplow technique is used by skiers and even ski patrols because it allows them to go slow while inspecting the snow ahead for obstacles. The snowplow technique can also be used to control your speed, turn, or stop completely.

- **Straight-running snowplow**—This is very good for speed control on any snow except thick crud, where a telemark stop or pole drag is useful. Practice the straight-running snowplow on a low-angle, hard pack slope where you can point the skis straight downhill without actually sliding. You should be able to hold yourself in a racer's starting position with the ski poles planted at shoulder width at a point between the bindings and the tips. Hands are in the walking cane position. Push your heels outward while keeping the tips of the skis together. The wider apart the tails are, the more you can bend your knees to the inside, edging your skis to slow you down. Beginners should practice this position until they can hold their body weight using just the skis. Knees are bent and the inside edges are equally weighted. When you are ready, pull your poles out of the snow and rotate your ankles outward, releasing the edges. Stay in the snowplow position while skiing straight down the hill.

• **Half snowplow**—The half snowplow is good for speed control on steep, narrow trails while carrying a pack. Keep one ski pointed straight down the trail's edge while pushing (stemming) the other ski across the trail, edging it. If the trail is tilted (has a double fall line), stem and brake with the lower ski.

• **Snowplow turn**—Experiment with turning your skis on a well-packed, low-angle slope. From a straight-running snowplow position, apply weight to the opposite (outside) ski of the desired turn direction (to turn left weight the right ski; see figure 5.6a). Ski poles should point straight back with hands at waist level. The harder or thicker the snow is, the more pressure you need to exert to control your speed or turning direction. Snowplow turns are very good on fragile snows such as sun crust or windslab.

• **Snowplow stop**—The snowplow stop is a very stable method for slowing down or stopping on ice, windslab, or powder while inspecting snow ahead. It is less disruptive to fragile snow, resulting in fewer falls. While in the straight-running snowplow position, simply apply equal pressure to both inside edges and push out at the tails of the skis (see figure 5.6b). The more you edge the skis, the slower you will go until you stop at maximum edge set.

Stem Christi

The word "stem" is orginally from the German word describing the pushing sideways of the skis at the tails so a "pie wedge" shape is formed with the skis. The stem christi starts off as a snowplow turn

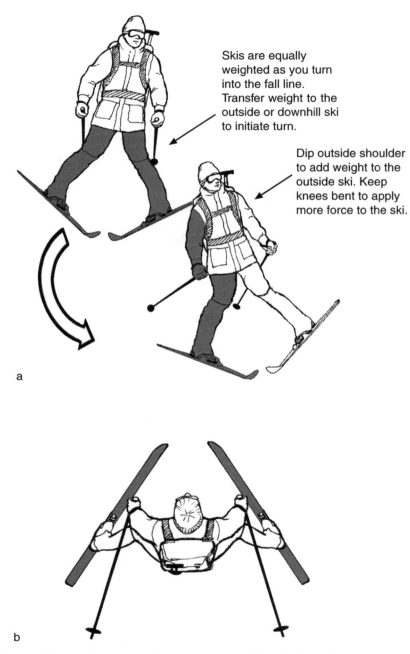

Skis are equally weighted as you turn into the fall line. Transfer weight to the outside or downhill ski to initiate turn.

Dip outside shoulder to add weight to the outside ski. Keep knees bent to apply more force to the ski.

a

b

Figure 5.6 *(a)* The snowplow turn is a solid technique for speed control. *(b)* The snowplow stop works in all conditions.

but ends up as a wide-stance parallel turn (see figure 5.7). Begin in the traverse position and go into a snowplow turn weighting the outside ski as you normally would. But this time make it a smaller snow-plow—more of a pie wedge. As centrifugal force turns you, slide the inside unweighted ski alongside or parallel to the outside ski, keeping it flat. Accompany this with a pole plant for balance and turn initiation. Equally weight both skis to complete the turn. This turn is very good on a hard windslab that supports your weight. The stem christi can be linked together with short or long traverses.

Wide-Stance Parallel Skiing

The stem christi leads naturally into wide-stance parallel skiing (see figure 5.8). While pole planting, pivot both skis across the fall line. Immediately bend your knees into the hill, edging the skis. Hopping

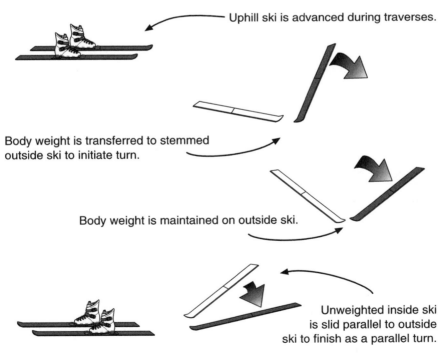

Uphill ski is advanced during traverses.

Body weight is transferred to stemmed outside ski to initiate turn.

Body weight is maintained on outside ski.

Unweighted inside ski is slid parallel to outside ski to finish as a parallel turn.

Figure 5.7 The stem christi is an excellent technique on crud, even on steeper slopes. The uphill ski is always in front during the traverse.

Figure 5.8   Wide-stance parallel skiing.

up slightly while pole planting will unweight your skis, allowing them to release their edges and turn. The tails will swing out due to centrifugal force. Have the inside ski follow the outside ski while applying more body weight to the outside ski. In powder, keep both skis together and weight both skis equally as if you were surfing. Keep the knees into the hill during turns. Parallel turns can be linked together with no traverses to become Wedeln or linked short-radius parallel turns on steeper terrain. (Wedeln is an Austrian term for linked short-radius turns; small short-radius turns can be linked together for control on steeper slopes.) The upper body must face downhill in anticipation of the next turn.

Hockey Stop

The hockey stop is just a parallel turn back up the hill coupled with an edge set hard enough to stop you (see figure 5.9). A strong pole plant helps you to pivot the skis across the fall line into a hard edge set of both skis across the fall line. This is an excellent technique for stopping on icy trails. Practice edge setting into hard hockey stops while skiing at a ski area to get the feel of it.

Courtesy of Chrystiane DeMers

Figure 5.9 Hockey stops are good edge-setting practice.

Pole Drag

The pole drag is an excellent beginner's technique that allows you to control speed in crud and powder in narrow situations. It gives beginners the ability to slow down on hut trails and lets experts get down tree runs when they are fatigued. From a snowplow position, simply put both ski poles between your legs and push them into the snow (see figure 5.10). Kids and small adults may be able to actually sit on their poles (be sure they are metal poles). Be sure the poles are pushing down on the snow and not on your ski tails. Pull up at the handles (straps off) with one hand and push down at the rear with a straight arm for more stopping power. The pole drag doesn't work on ice, so you may have to walk down.

Two Telemark Progressions

No two skiers are alike. Some have more parallel skiing experience, while others have more ski touring experience. Telemark can be reached from either discipline. The following steps can be used in learning telemark.

Figure 5.10 Both beginners and experts can control their speed with the pole drag.

Both progressions have been used successfully with many students. Try to practice these skills in the order in which they are presented.

Progression One: Telemark for Ski Tourers

1. Diagonal stride into telemark over bumps
2. Diagonal stride into telemark through dips
3. Diagonal stride into telemark during creek crossings
4. Diagonal stride into graduated telemark turns on gentle slopes
5. Diagonal stride into telemark turns on gentle slopes

The first progression approaches telemarking from the standpoint of the ski tourer, who navigates small obstacles constantly and in turn has learned to absorb small dips while holding the telemark position during trail skiing.

EXTREME SKIING

It's a big jump from basic parallel to extreme skiing, which was once defined as skiing where a fall would result in death. Slopes don't have to be very steep to cause a dangerous fall, though. Skiing steeper slopes depends on solid parallel or telemark turns made with clean and decisive pole plants. On steeper terrain you can use longer poles to reach farther downhill and support the upper body during unweighting. Skiing steeper terrain and controlling speed work together. You often get the feeling of going from one hockey stop to another. Consistency helps control speed; make each turn the same size. Use equally hard edge sets. Only advanced skiers should attempt steep skiing—even with their expertise, they should always practice steep skiing on slopes that provide smooth slopes below in case of a fall. Self-arrest techniques must be practiced as well.

© Carl Skoog

Extreme skiing down the Mowich Face of Mt. Rainier, Mt. Rainier National Park, Cascade Range, Washington.

Diagonal Stride Into Telemark

The telemark position often looks as if one is genuflecting (see figure 5.11). By placing one ski forward, the telemarker is able to absorb big dips over two ski lengths instead of one, preventing falls. To cross a small dip or stream, use the telemark position; by having one ski at a time enter the dip you can balance your body forward and backward (see figure 5.12). You can take smaller dips head on, but larger dips (like a frozen stream bed) may require you to enter at an angle to lessen the shock of the transition into the depression. Lean the body back in anticipation of the sudden stop you may encounter at the bottom of the dip. When you do stop, the backward lean and the sudden deceleration will equal out so you don't fall forward onto your ski tips. Use the sudden deceleration to spring off the bottomed-out ski and jump onto your new leading ski, which you should plant aggressively on the bank in front of you. Get your body weight onto this forward ski as quickly as possible to ski through the dip without missing a stride. Plant your ski pole on the opposite bank for support.

Diagonal Stride Into Graduated Turns

As described in the previous section, most ski tourers use the telemark position when traversing small dips on the trail. It is the same position

Figure 5.11 Basic telemark position.

Keep your head mostly up and the rear ski weighted.

Ski poles shift from rear position to forward position to prevent you from falling forward.

Figure 5.12 Telemark position while crossing a creek or dip.

you will use for skiing downhill. For practice, use a low-angle slope that is evenly packed or has light powder. A groomed beginner slope at a local ski area is ideal. While in a telemark position, do several traverses across the hill, increasing the steepness with each run. Think of the telemark position as a flattened-out diagonal stride frozen in midstride. Try several variations—see how low you can get or how high you can telemark while still in balance. Keep your hands low to keep your body downweighted. If you stay square to the leading knee, you will have positive pressure on your forward ski during straight running and bigger turns. Picture a T with your foot, forward knee, and head forming the vertical line and your shoulders as the top of the T. With your arms out to your side in a low and wide position, you've got a powerful position to make a strong turn. Try it! As you get more confident, try steeper traverses with more speed. Perhaps by mistake you will exaggerate a turn so much that you are facing uphill when you stop—congratulations, you just did a telemark stop!

Progression Two: Telemark for Parallel Skiers

1. Snowplow turn
2. Stem christi turn
3. Linked stem christi turns
4. Stem christi into telemark
5. Traverse into stem christi and telemark

The second progression approaches telemarking from the parallel skier's standpoint. Most resort skiers are familiar with parallel skiing, snowplow turns, and stem christi turns.

Stem Christi Into Telemark

On a low-angle beginner slope, you can initiate a telemark turn from a stem christi turn. As you stem your uphill ski laterally to the outside, apply your weight to it (see figure 5.13). Now let the rear ski tip slip behind the forward ski as if you were making a mistake in doing a stem christi. As the skis come around, bend at the knees and transfer your body weight to the outside-forward ski. The rear ski's tip should just meet the forward ski between the forward ski's tip and binding. Push the outside-forward knee toward the center of the turn and edge its inside edge. Your body weight is mostly on the forward or outside ski while 30 percent of your weight is on the rear ski, which serves to maintain balance. The stem of the rear ski gradually decreases until the traverse position is regained. Keep your hands and arms low and

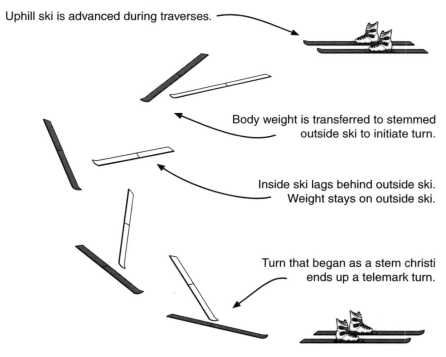

Uphill ski is advanced during traverses.

Body weight is transferred to stemmed outside ski to initiate turn.

Inside ski lags behind outside ski. Weight stays on outside ski.

Turn that began as a stem christi ends up a telemark turn.

Figure 5.13   The stem christi easily shifts into the telemark position by pushing the outside ski forward.

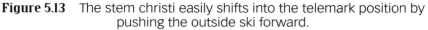

out to the side—don't let them drop behind your body. Keep your upper body facing in the direction of the turn.

Fine-Tuning Telemark

Now that you have the idea of telemark, focus in on some of the details that will make telemark even easier to use in the backcountry. Returning to such turning basics as good pole plants, bent knees, and proper upper body position will pay off when skiing ever-changing backcountry snow conditions. Breathing during downhill skiing is just as important as it was when climbing up—you can put much more strength into your turn if you're not holding your breath!

Pole Planting

Pole plants increase balance, power, and speed control during turns. Combining telemark with pole plants helps to angulate the upper body and increase upper-body stability, resulting in fewer falls. On hard-pack snow, pole plants are vital to speed control and they help to define the radius of turns. Hold your ski pole snugly and stab the snow—forceful pole plants make your turns more definite (see figure 5.14). You sometimes see people with hands very high over the head while telemarking; unfortunately, this unweights the skis and nullifies the turning effort. Keep your hands down!

Telemark Stop

If you want to come to a complete stop in crud, use a telemark stop. This is done by exaggerating the telemark turn as if you were trying to telemark going uphill. As you make your turn, apply all your weight to your downhill ski and edge it aggressively. The upper body faces downhill. Hands are at waist height aiming downhill. Your eyes should be looking downhill throughout the turn. Do several telemark stops in a row to develop speed control, harder edging, and a good upper-body position for doing small-radius turns.

Weighting Your Skis

It's important to weight the rear ski while telemarking, especially during long-radius (large) turns, but it is also useful in short-radius (small) turns. Try to balance your weight between the rear and front

© Laurant Mclaughlin

Figure 5.14 Downweighting and solid pole plants define turn shape and control speed.

skis. With practice you will start to feel your rear ski almost as much as your front ski. Get used to feeling the pressure on the ball and toe of the rear foot. You will feel as if you are snowboarding or surfing on your ski. This is a great sensation, especially in powder. Now that you are telemarking with both skis, you will be doing long-radius turns with one long metal edge!

Another trick is to try to preweight your uphill ski before twisting your ankle into the direction of the turn. By preweighting you will help the ski "track" into the turn more smoothly—a definite plus in heavy snows. Also, as you rotate and edge the ski, it will respond more quickly to the turning force applied through your boots.

Turn Size and Terrain

Telemarkers can use short-radius turns for better control on steeper terrain. Your upper body faces downhill at all times. As soon as your skis decelerate and come to a complete edge set, you can use that sudden deceleration and the snow that bunches up underneath your skis as a platform for the next turn. Jump or hop your trailing ski over the lead ski into the next edge set. When you hop over your lead ski, be very aggressive and decisive. Your pole plants will be important as they will help you maintain balance, especially in heavy snow. Stay in the fall line and keep your hands low. Pole plants should be made directly downhill in line with your ski boots. Larger, long-radius turns should be used on lower-angled, wide-open slopes where hard edge sets can collapse the snow.

Teaming Telemark and Parallel

Powder and ice often occur together in patches on windblown slopes. Telemark to the edge of the ice and keep your weight forward to

TIPS FOR BEGINNERS

It's difficult to be a beginner! You're always falling, and then everyone gets mad at you for holding them up. Don't despair! Take a deep breath and remember that three techniques can help you get down almost any hill:

1. Kick turn and linked traverse
2. Pole drag
3. Sideslip

Avoid These Mistakes

1. Don't ski "cold." Warm up your body with some easy flat skiing and stretch your muscles.
2. Always maintain good posture—stand up straight and bend at the knees, not at the waist.
3. Don't stare at your ski tips. Keep your head up!
4. Use just the muscles you need to use and relax everything else.
5. *Don't forget to breathe!* Without knowing it, you might hold your breath because you are nervous. Breathe fear out and breathe power in! Visualize doing beautiful turns, turn by turn by turn.
6. Attitude is everything! Try to laugh at your falls and don't take them personally. Believe it or not, learning how to ski is an exciting time!

counteract the acceleration due to the ice, then go into a stem christi or wide-stance parallel and/or hockey stop on the ice. Telemarking on ice with a pack usually causes the rear ski to slide out unless you have great technique and are very strong. Parallel or stem christi on the ice and then drop back into a telemark position when you hit the powder again. The heavy snow will cause you to decelerate suddenly, making you fall forward over your ski tips—this is where telemark is very helpful, so be ready. Keep your weight back just before hitting the heavy stuff. When telemarkers are learning to parallel, they often have problems unlearning single leg action and relying on stemming to initiate turning. After telemarking for 15 years I had to unlearn some of those habits myself!

Falling Correctly

Most of the fear of skiing is the fear of falling. Falling in powder is fun. But falling on hard-pack snow, especially with a pack, can hurt. You might land not only on snow but on the rocks underneath. Before heading down, judge the angle of the slope, the type of snow, the length of the run, and the possibilities of falling (see figure 5.15). Once you decrease the fear of falling and its stigma of failure, you can progress faster in learning to ski. You can learn how to fall and minimize injury by using some of the following techniques.

Preventing Injury

You can prevent injuries during falls by following these guidelines.

- Be honest with yourself. Ask yourself two questions: "Can I ski it?" and "If I fall, where will I end up?" Maximize your fall survival potential. Don't pick a ski line that crashes you into a boulder or takes you off a cliff if you miss a turn! Ski defensively. On more exposed terrain, pick descent lines that provide for a long runout/space to fall just in case.

- Practice correct falling techniques. For example, the first reaction in a fall is to extend the arm straight out with the palm down. But by putting your body weight on a locked arm, tremendous pressure is applied to the shoulder joint, which can dislocate the shoulder. Stop falls with a *bent* elbow, which absorbs the fall much better without applying injurious forces to the shoulder and thumb joints.

Figure 5.15 Falls like this can be avoided by skiing defensively and anticipating fragile snow conditions.

- Keep your ski pole straps off during the descent.
- Wear abrasive ski clothing. Lycra ski pants are fashionable but can add lethal speed to your slide.
- Climb up the slope that you intend to ski, and inspect it for hollow snow and icy patches. Plan your descent! If your boots can't penetrate the snow, it will be difficult to do a self-arrest later on. Pick another route with softer snow.

Preventing Runaway Skis

Beginners have a tendency to sit down on the tails of the skis when they actually mean to sit in the snow. When you sit on the tails of the skis, the skis accelerate, which can be especially hazardous on steep, icy trails. Always fall to one side of the skis into the snow.

Headfirst Falls

"Headers" are a common fall in skiing. Usually short falls, they can turn into long, sliding falls on steep, hard slopes. When falling headfirst, you instinctively extend your hands out in front of you to keep your face off the snow and ice where it could get cut; however, spring slopes have many small, icy ridges that are sharp enough to cut your hands (so always wear gloves during spring skiing). A rollover stop can help you stop more quickly on steeper slopes (see figure 5.16). This stop was first attributed to ski instructor and guide Bill Briggs of Jackson Hole, Wyoming, who was famous for his extreme ski descents. The rollover can be done forward or sideways. It is best done on steep slopes with soft snow, but can be done on hard snow as well. As you go into a headfirst fall, keep on falling, bringing your skis all the way over your head and pointing back downhill, all in one move. Get your skis across the hill to protect your body from impact with unseen obstacles such as trees or rocks.

Ski Pole Self-Arrest

The self-arrest is an important survival technique in backcountry skiing. Always get on your stomach after a fall and arrest immediately. Get your skis spread out downhill from you across the hill to protect your body from impact with unseen objects. Grab both ski poles just above the baskets and jab both ski pole tips into the snow (see figure 5.17). *Do not extend your arms!* Keep your body weight over your ski pole tips instead of relying on strength alone. If at first you can't get the tips in, wait a second, then try again when you reach softer snow. Arrest early before you start picking up speed. Even if your speed is increasing, don't abandon this technique; keep trying repeatedly while keeping your skis across the hill below you. Keep your head up and off the snow.

Self-Arrest With Self-Arrest Grips

Self-arrest grips make stopping easier in desperate situations. The same principles used during a ski pole self-arrest apply to the grip arrest. Always attempt to self-arrest using both arrest grips together for maximum stopping power as one grip may arrest before the other. Bring both grips together under your body to apply body weight to the arrest effort. Remember that arrest grips, regardless of design, can work only on snow that they can penetrate. It's very difficult to stop on ice, even with an ice axe! Don't expect a self-arrest grip to do any

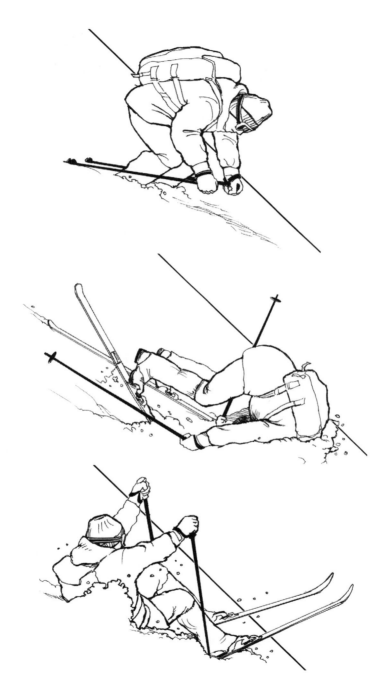

Figure 5.16 Use a rollover stop during headfirst falls on steep terrain.

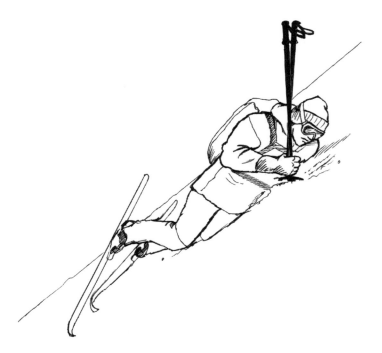

Figure 5.17   Get your weight on top of the ski pole tips or self-arrest grips for maximum snow penetration.

better. This is yet another reason to always climb the slope you intend to ski.

Falling in Deep Powder

Falling in very deep powder can be like being buried in an avalanche. You are buried, the snow chokes you, and you are drowning in a mass of white. The skiers behind you can't see you, especially if the weather is bad. Protect your head! Tuck down and cover your head with your arms. I received a ski edge cut that went from my nose to my ear once when I fell in front of another skier while skiing deep powder.

Getting Up From a Fall

Getting up from falls can increase fatigue, which in turn causes more falls. Good technique will save you a great deal of energy. There are several important things to remember to make getting up a lot easier.

- Get your skis across the fall line. Even seemingly flat surfaces have one. This eliminates slipping, falling, and more wasted energy.
- Leave your heavy pack on the snow. Get up, then put it back on.
- Always plant your poles on the uphill side to take advantage of gravity when you try to pull yourself up.
- Take some deep breaths and take your time. Plan it out and do it right the first time. *Conserve energy.*

To get up on hard-pack snow, put both ski poles together. Plant the ski pole tips as one unit on the uphill side right next to your hip as you sit on the snow. Push down on the ski pole baskets with your uphill hand, and at the same time pull down on your ski pole straps and stand up in one fluid movement (see figure 5.18).

To get up from powder or soft snow, form an X with your ski poles on the uphill side right next to your hip. Crossed poles form a platform in bottomless powder. Organize your skis so they're downhill from you, across the fall line. Grip the intersection of the poles and push down on it to push yourself up into a standing position (see figure 5.19).

Figure 5.18 On hard-pack snow, get up from the uphill side.

Figure 5.19 In powder, make an **X** with your ski poles to create a better lifting platform.

Getting up with a heavy pack can be exhausting. Leave your pack on the snow! Stand up and reorganize yourself. Place your skis across the fall line and kick out a solid stance so they don't slip out from underneath you. On steeper terrain, try putting your downhill ski on first for balance. Now put your pack on. Always pick up heavy packs with bent knees. To work on your bindings, bend at the knees (instead of bending at the waist) while keeping a straight back to keep your balance.

Conclusion

Descent entails more than skiing—when necessary, climbing down the mountain is as important as climbing up it, and telemark and parallel techniques are only the start. Ironically, though, good basic techniques take us the farthest in the backcountry. Reducing the number of falls we make increases our endurance and reduces our frustration, and learning how to fall more safely extends our borders and dares us to try new things.

Skiing the powder above Butler Gulch, near Berthoud Pass, Colorado.

6
chapter

Reading Terrain and Snow

This chapter considers specific techniques that will help you ski over, around, and through problematic terrain and snow. With good snow sense, you can ski places that you have avoided until now. Winter backcountry travel means more than skiing—it entails pathfinding through varying snow and terrain conditions. That's what makes it so interesting and fun!

Navigating Obstacles

Unknown snow conditions must be approached with some caution. There is no ski patrol to check out what lies *underneath* the snow— that's up to you. We can only tell what lies beneath the snow by what shapes or clues appear above the snow. This is the art of pathfinding in natural snow conditions.

Buried Trees

Small buried trees that cross your line of travel can appear as long, skinny mounds of snow (see figure 6.1). They should be approached with caution on downhill sections. Skis can nosedive under the buried

Courtesy of Patrick Griffin

Figure 6.1 Fallen logs may be difficult to see in foggy weather.

fallen sapling or log, trapping your ankles and causing a fall and injury. Stop and step across.

Holes and Old Mines

In the continental United States, crevasses are rare but holes left from mining activities are numerous, especially in the western mountains (see figure 6.2). Your topographical map will show mining areas with many small **X**'s. After a big storm, these holes are covered up with fresh powder, making it difficult to see them. They may appear only as a crease or slit in the snow.

Dirt and Mud

Bare dirt will stop your skis so fast you will fly over your tips before you know it, so always avoid it! Carefully step or ski around sections of dirt or mud so you won't have to stop to take off your skis. For longer

Figure 6.2   Fresh powder covers abandoned mine shafts and holes—
examine your map closely for these areas.

sections, though, it is better to carry your skis around to save time and
energy. Always warn fellow skiers by yelling "dirt" or "rock" when
you encounter obstacles.

Brush-Covered Slopes

Beware of small twigs appearing above the snow—these indicate
snow-covered brush (see figure 6.3). Brush creates air pockets under
the snow that are easy to fall through, especially during periods of
shallow snow conditions such as in the spring. Always give wide berth
to these areas when ascending or descending.

Sun Cups

In the late spring, you can see whole slopes covered with rounded-out
depressions called *sun cups*. These can reach a depth up to two feet

Figure 6.3 Twigs poking through the snow, especially during hot weather, can indicate a weak snow pack underneath.

(.6 meters) and are very bothersome to navigate through or around (see figure 6.4). Sun cups are caused by melted water running down the slopes under the snow pack and by radiation bouncing off big rocks underneath the snow. If sun cup ridges are close together you may be able to sideslip down these with tips and tails of the skis riding the ridges. It's often easier just to walk up or down these areas or to find an alternate ski route on a less sun-damaged area.

Spring Skiing

In the spring, snow melts during the day and freezes at night, turning slopes into a sheet of ice. Lightweight gloves should *always* be worn regardless of the heat to prevent the serious cuts that can occur to hands during falls. In the morning, stay out of shady areas. If a shady trail must be skied, beginners should leave their skins on to help reduce their speed. Later in the day, ascend slopes in the shade to take advantage of firmer snow and to reduce fatigue from the heat.

Rockfall

It's always a good idea to climb up your line of descent to inspect the slope, especially for rocks. You can always see pockmarked snow

Figure 6.4 Sun cup fields are best climbed on foot in the early morning or skied in the afternoon when they are softer.

where rockfall occurs daily. While climbing up, be cautious of rockfall from side walls bordering ski slopes or couloirs (see chapter 8 for a description of mountain architecture). Rock rarely falls straight down, but it curves outward—so the safest spot is really where you'd think is the worst spot, up against the wall. The center of a couloir is no good because rock comes straight down the center from above you and from the side walls. If you must ascend these slopes, do so before the sun hits the upper slopes and thaws out rocks frozen in place. Helmets should be considered for such conditions.

Corniced Areas

Cornices are places where the snow is undercut due to wind or water. On ridge lines and passes, cornice edges—when seen from above— seem strong, but you cannot determine the extent of this undercut (see figure 6.5). In poor visibility it is especially dangerous to try to downclimb around these obstacles. Find another route around. You are somewhat safer with older cornices during the morning hours in spring. These have survived the winter and have peeled off some of their layers. However, during spring or summer skiing, cornice collapse is a real danger after midday. Cornices can also occur along creek or river edges and can get quite large. Always probe them for thickness with a ski pole before attempting to get water.

Figure 6.5 It's poor technique to climb up or down slopes in the shadows of cornices.

Boulder Margins (Moats)

Rocks absorb heat, causing snow to melt out around their bases (see figure 6.6). This space is called a *moat*. On car-sized boulders, this moat can have a cornice surrounding the entire boulder. Before crossing a moat, reach over to the rock and get some handholds first, in case the snow collapses. Give some distance (especially in foggy conditions) to large boulders and bottoms of cliffs, which will have corniced edges and are prone to collapse if skied on.

Tree Skiing

It's best to learn tree skiing during excellent powder conditions. Start with trees that are spaced widely apart and then work into tighter groupings. Here are some basic precautions.

• **Goggles**—Besides preventing tearing of the eyes and improving vision, ski goggles can save your face! While I was doing research for an article on goggles, a young ski racer told me about her close call with a large aspen tree. While skiing deep powder she missed a turn, landing her face straight into the tree. Her goggles absorbed the force of the impact and probably saved her life! It is good to see that ski helmets are becoming more popular among skiers who like to push these limits.

• **Helmets**—Helmets are becoming more popular, especially among telemarkers who like to push the limits. But helmets may not make it

Fracture line of cornice

Figure 6.6   Boulder margins can become large enough for a skier to fall into.

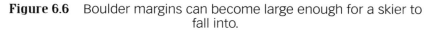

© Laurant Mclaughlin

Working the trees at Eldora, Colorado.

into the backcountry due to their weight: a 61-centimeter (extra large) helmet, for example, weighs 59 ounces. The mountaineer will probably wear a rockclimbing helmet that is meant to handle rockfall but not skiing impacts such as face-on impacts. Helmets must be strapped on during use for maximum protection. They can range in cost from $60 to $165. Some features that you might appreciate include hardshell construction to prevent penetration by skis, tree branches, or rocks and allow for shedding of snow; an insulating, impact-resistant liner; a goggle strap to keep goggles centered on shell; side openings to allow hearing during skiing; a helmet profile that allows optimum side vision; and a quick-release chin strap to keep the helmet on during impact.

- **Loose clothing**—Tuck in all loose clothing before skiing. Long, pretty ski scarves or hats can get caught in branches, causing falls. Use a neck gaiter instead. Double-check your clothing before each run.

- **Ski pole straps**—Ski pole baskets are likely to get caught in brush and tree branches, causing falls and thumb fractures, if you are using the straps. Take all straps off, including the releasable type.

- **Spaces between the trees**—Your body follows your head and your head follows your eyes. So don't look at the trees, as beautiful as they are! Look at and concentrate on the spaces between the trees. Your body will follow.

- **Tree type and terrain**—All trees can have large overhanging branches, and whole, dead trees sometimes fall across spaces between trees, blocking the way (called *deadfall*). Also watch out for old tree stumps, fallen trees, and debris, which can allow air pockets to form that will collapse under your skis. Square, angular snow shapes should be avoided as they are probably hiding a tree stump underneath (see figure 6.7). Trying to ski over small stumps is tricky and should be left to expert snowboarders and skiers. During or after a new snowfall, your skis may fall through the air spaces surrounding the tree trunk or run into it, causing injury. Look for a better line. A shallow or unconsolidated snow pack hides both air pockets and the potential of collapsing snow around smaller trees. Solar energy is absorbed by bigger trees, causing the snow to melt around the tree bottoms so that a "well" is formed (see figure 6.8). These can be small enough to grab a ski or large enough to swallow a skier! During powder storms these wells fill up with powder so that they become invisible. You won't see the trap until you fall into it. These edges can also collapse during hot weather. Skiers and snowboarders have died from falling into them and hitting trunks. The trunks of even small trees are sturdy enough to knock you out! Try to ski equidistantly between very large trees to avoid these hazards.

Bushwhacking

According to Outward Bound research, bushwhacking is the biggest cause of injury to its students. When you get stuck in a jungle, remember the following points:

Figure 6.7   Avoid angular snow shapes—they could indicate a buried tree stump.

- Be sure your glasses or goggles are on. There's nothing fun about having a tree branch snap back into your face. Always hold branches for unsuspecting others.
- Take your time. Time is energy. Go slowly and measure each step so you don't fall into a hollow or snag your skis under a fallen branch. Slow down and you'll go faster.
- Use your ski poles. Take your ski pole and use the upper shaft to punch dead tree branches out of your face. They snap off easily and make the passage much easier for those behind you.
- Use your skis. Place your skis on top of brush; don't just slide your skis blindly forward, or they'll get caught in the brush.

Creeks, Rivers, and Lakes

Water courses such as creeks or river beds are natural and fun avenues for skiing during cold weather when heavy forest is difficult to navigate. But they should be avoided during late spring or when

Figure 6.8   Snow around tree bottoms can melt, forming dangerous wells.

warming trends occur. Rocks absorb heat, weakening the ice. In addition, currents in the center of the creek or river thaw ice more quickly in the center than on the edges of the main flow. Snowplow and stem christi turns will disturb the ice the least. Examine your route carefully for holes and weak spots. A fall in 35-degree Fahrenheit (2-degree Celsius) water can cause hypothermia. Creeks have undercut snow banks (cornices), and climbing out may be impossible. Cross lake ice only during cold weather or when it consists of many feet of seasoned snow and ice that occurs in the middle of winter. Late-season lake ice should be held suspect during warm spells.

Fording a creek or river is done only when alternate routes are not available. Never cross a creek or river that is deeper than midthigh. Put your boots in your pack, roll up your pant legs, and go barefoot. Find the shallowest area to cross—the faster flow often belies a shallow spot. Deeper areas are often at the creek's edge. Carry your skis on your pack and use ski poles for support while crossing.

Also beware of log and rock crossings. Logs and rocks can be iced over with creek spray and mist. Check the log or rock carefully for ice before stepping on it. Sometimes you see photos of people with elaborate rope crossings across a stream (referred to as *Tyrolean traverses*). However, it will often save considerable time and effort to just go and cross upstream than set up such a system. Since creeks and rivers get wider the farther they get from their source, you want to go *up*stream. The crossing there will be narrower, thus shorter and easier as a result. Cross streams in early morning hours when water levels are lower because of the lack of snowmelt upstream. Snow bridges are also stronger in the morning hours before the sun gets to them. If in doubt, probe snow bridges for thickness with your ski pole, then proceed across quickly, without stopping.

Breaking Trail

Breaking trail in deep powder can be difficult for leaders and followers alike. Use your legs to break trail in powder, not your arms! Use arms only for balance and occasionally for support. Do not keep your hands in the ski pole grips—this is very tiring. Use regular ski poles, as poles with large powder baskets load with snow and are difficult to pull out of the snow. Choke up on the ski pole halfway down the pole shaft—this relieves much shoulder fatigue and tension, especially when carrying a heavy pack (see figure 6.9). Concentrate on your breathing as you lift your skis. Keep your skis close together and drag the following ski over the forward ski that has already broken the trail. Take periodic breaks and switch leaders when skiing in a group.

Skiing Backcountry Snows

It has been said that the Inuit Eskimos have over 100 words for snow. Well, we have quite a few ourselves! *Junk* and *crud* are slang terms for snow that has become hardened over time, wind damaged, or saturated with water. This heavy snow grabs skis and bindings, preventing ski edging and binding release and resulting in strains, sprains, and sometimes leg fractures. Learning to ski crud and powder correctly is important because not doing it right can cause fatigue and injury.

Matching Turns to Snow Conditions

Table 6.1 can give you some insight as to how to adapt your techniques to different snow conditions. Even the color of snow can give clues as to the type of ski technique you should use to reduce falls and increase performance in the backcountry. Sometimes snow will not support

Courtesy of Patrick Griffin

Figure 6.9 Breaking trail on the Colorado Haute Route near Vail, Colorado.

body weight—thin windslab, sun crust, crud, and powder are the worst offenders. Telemarkers often fall victim to these snows because so much of their weight is committed to the forward ski, which breaks the snow pack, causing a fall. Turns that distribute body weight over a greater surface area prevent the skier from breaking through the snow. Learn to feel what the snow can or cannot hold. Ski smoothly without making hard, percussive-type movements, which can cause a collapse of the snow. Larger, long-radius telemark turns, snowplows, or stem christis are very effective in distributing body weight over a greater surface area, preventing breakthrough. Hockey stops should be avoided. On slopes where real skiing is not possible, try kick turns and traverses to get you down. Beginners can snowplow the sun crust or do a pole drag through the slush. Skiers should remember to breathe!

Banking in Heavy Crud and Powder

Banking is a conscious use of the hands and arms to amplify whole-body angulation and rotation during a turn, and can be used by both

Table 6.1

Snow and Ski Turn Compatibility Chart

Type of snow	Snow characteristics	Ski technique
Powder	Light, sparkling	Parallel, telemark
Pack powder	Fluffy, dry, powdery	Parallel, telemark
Hard pack (neve)	Very hard, chalk-colored	Parallel
Spring ice	Shiny pearls on surface	Parallel
Black ice, verglas	Shiny or invisible	Parallel
Slush, mush, junk, hard crud	Heavy snow, high water saturation	Telemark
Soft crud	Resistant to turning, color of mashed potatoes	Telemark, parallel on steeper slopes
Avalanche debris	Snow blocks, rocks, branches, dirty snow	Parallel or snow plow
Surface hoar	Spring conditions	Parallel, telemark
Rain crust	Icy pearls	Parallel
Sun crust	Sugar colored	Snow plow, stem christi
Breakable crust	Windblown, sun damage	Stem christi, wide-stance parallel
Windslab	Chalk-colored	Wide-stance parallel
Powder and ice combination	Shiny with chalk-colored patches	Telemark, parallel
Waves, ripples, sun cups	Hard, windblown	Kick turn, snowplow, avoid if possible
Sand dunes, sand dollars	Hard spring snow	Parallel, stem christi, telemark

parallel and telemark skiers. In addition to the legs edging the skis maximally, the whole body will bank (lean) over, adding a few more degrees of edging to the snow. This surfing movement makes a big difference in heavy powder and crud. As you go into the turn, start the turn while swinging the outside arm and ski pole in an exaggerated pole planting motion, as if you were trying to punch the air. It's a fun and effective technique. You'll find it very helpful in heavy snows, especially when you link up several turns together. Parallel skiers must keep the skis together for better flotation in these conditions. Steepness may permit parallel or telemark jump turns over crud because of the added momentum to edge set down through heavy snow. Larger-radius turns can be more effective in heavier snows because you can build up some speed for the turning effort. When you are in changing snows and suddenly hit a batch of very heavy snow, absorb the sudden deceleration at the knees instead of buckling at the waist, which can throw you over your leading ski and cause a fall.

Modifying Weight on the Forward Ski

The amount of weight that is applied to the skis during telemarking changes with snow conditions. The general rule for telemark skiers is to have slightly more weight on the front ski at all times. There should be about 55 percent of the body weight on the front ski and 45 percent on the rear ski. This is fine for hardpack snow, but in powder and crud a more even distribution of body weight may prevent the front ski from nosediving in. As the snow consistency changes try different values for both skis. Parallel skiers will usually keep more weight on the rear of both skis in powder and crud so that ski tips stay on top of the snow, resulting in better control. Keeping the hands low (except when banking) also keeps your body in a downweighted position and allows for faster pole plants. During short-radius telemark turns, the trailing ski tip should not fall behind the leading ski boot binding. There's a point in telemarking when too much distance between the boots prevents you from standing up fast enough to unweigh your skis, resulting in a loss of balance and edging power.

Using Terrain to Your Advantage

Use terrain features to help you initiate turns, control speed, and maintain your line of skiing. Avoid ice patches, as you'll probably slip and fall. Look for hard snow, not ice; look for opaque, flat-looking snow that doesn't shine. Be cautious above trees, where windblown snow is often thinner than the snow below the tree, which will slow you down but still allow you to turn in control. In addition, doing a hockey stop or hard turn above a tree is not a good practice as the uphill side may be undercut, which could collapse and cause you to fall into a tree well. Why not just stop or turn below the tree?

Additionally, when telemarking on low-angle terrain with heavy snows, it is often difficult to get enough speed to make a turn. A large rolling slope formed by drifted snow can provide a sudden burst of

Skiing through the stumps at Ski Cooper, Colorado.

acceleration, which will make turning much easier. Go over the top of the slope in the telemark position but don't try to turn until you feel your skis speeding up. Use terrain and get creative—it's fun!

Conclusion

You may know many ski techniques but unless you know what snows to use them in, those techniques are useless. This chapter focused on explaining the different colors and textures of snows and what techniques they tell you to use. Learning to ski within the limitations of nature helps you to ski farther and faster. The ability to navigate through the winter wilderness is built on your understanding of what techniques to use once you determine what the snow below and all around you looks like—shapes in the snow take on special significance, and it is up to you to know what to expect. Armed with this knowledge you can get closer to nature and become a safer skier as a result.

7
chapter

Mountain Weather

Clear and quiet conditions are great for skiing, but if you are only a fair-weather skier you are missing a beautiful aspect of mountain travel. Understanding mountain weather allows you to take advantage of good conditions and avoid violent conditions. Always ask yourself, "If the weather does change, how will it affect me?" The best rule is this: Be prudent! Make camp or turn back before you are forced to. The good backcountry skier has a habit of constantly looking above and behind him for weather changes and making mental notes on the route already skied.

Mountain Weather Changes Quickly

Each mountain has its own weather pattern that is associated with its shape and surroundings, causing air currents to lift, cool, and condense into clouds—this is called *orographic lifting*. Mountain valleys are warmer during periods of warm weather, but during the winter they become cold sinks holding super-chilled air at night. With the morning sun, air heats and rises up the mountain to create wind and storms on the peak tops. After sunset, air cools and once again descends into the valleys for the night.

Changes of Season and Storm Frequency

In the United States, storms occur more regularly during the middle of winter, from January up to and including March (roughly June, July, and August in southern latitudes). During winter, the sun is lower in the sky, with sunset occurring much earlier than in summer. Skiing normally occurs between about 8:00 A.M. and 3:00 P.M. during deep winter. It gets cold quickly as the sun drops in the sky. Spring brings fewer storms and longer days more suited for ski touring. For exact sunrise and sunset times and the length of days in the United States, consult the *Farmer's Almanac.* Try national weather Web sites on the Internet for international data.

Regional Influences

Mountains close to oceans (Sierras, Alps, Cascades, and New Zealand Alps, for example) have higher humidity, and snowfalls of 3 feet (.9 meters) are common. Mountains far inland from oceans (for example, Rockies and Wasatch) have less humidity and snowfalls of 6 to 10 inches (15 to 25 centimeters) are more common, with occasional snowfalls over 2 feet (.6 meters). Humidity is a natural junkmaker as it keeps the snow saturated with water, but this wetter snow stabilizes quickly with few avalanches. Inland areas of the United States such as Colorado and Utah have dry, cold conditions perfect for dehydrated dry powder snow and powder avalanches.

How Weather Affects Skiing

You should know what weather you are heading into so you'll be aware of the kinds of conditions you and your equipment may be up against. Often the knowledge of a possible storm may cause you to cancel a ski trip and seek other plans. Or maybe you are a person who enjoys skiing the backcountry in changing weather conditions, in which case the possibility of a storm makes you want even more to keep your plans. At any rate, there are many considerations to take into account.

New Snowfall

New storms bring in new snow and powder skiing, but new snow can also impede progress by forcing you to break trail and thus increase energy expenditure and food demand. Rewaxing may be needed to accommodate new snow, taking time away from skiing. Avalanche danger may increase, forcing you to reroute. Increased cold and wind demands more clothing. During deep winter ski tours, you will need more food, stove fuel, and clothing. Snow camping should be reserved for spring tours while hut tours are more ideal for the deep of winter.

Rain

Rain is the scourge of skiers. It can follow snow when a warm, low-pressure system hits coastal mountains. Rain destroys the snow pack by cutting bonding layers between snow layers or between the whole snow pack and the ground. Skiing becomes difficult in rain because the snow is reduced to slush. You have to change your cross-country wax to Yellow Klister, which is normally reserved for very hot spring touring. Climbing skins may fall off due to moisture if they don't have a backup attachment system besides adhesive (see chapter 4, page 72). The skiing is miserable and sloppy. Goggles fog up, making navigation difficult. It might be a good time to make camp or turn back.

Planning for Bad Weather

Have alternate routes planned in case of bad weather. It's good to have several high (haute) routes and low routes to choose from. Remember that the temperature normally drops 5 degrees Fahrenheit (–15 degrees Celsius) per 1,000 feet (305 meters) in elevation. Valleys may be sunny and comfortable, but you can still find blowing and snowing higher up. High routes are exposed to more weather and so they are better suited for periods of stable weather and low avalanche danger, like in the spring. Low routes are below the tree line, sheltered from the weather and avalanche activity. These two route design options let you ski the backcountry all winter long.

Getting the Complete Weather Picture

You can get a good idea of what the weather will be doing by getting up-to-date weather forecasts and by being observant in the field.

Using an altimeter will back up your observations by detecting pressure changes in the atmosphere (see page 144). At home there are several different sources of weather information: television, radio, ski phone reports, the Internet, the local forest service, and resort ski patrol offices. Where has the storm been and where is it going? Is it coming off the ocean with wet, heavy snow and difficult skiing? Is it coming out of the Arctic, bringing light powder snow? The satellite radar image shows where the big "storm cells" are. Ask yourself: How big is the storm mass? Does it have breaks and clearing areas? A mountain travel advisory with a winter storm warning that alerts motorists of blowing wind and poor visibility will also hold true for skiers. If you know where ski resorts are located and the snow amounts they are receiving, you can deduce the direction and speed of the storm. For long-term planning, a national weather bureau will have 5-, 10-, and 30-day forecasts that are invaluable for expeditions.

Making Field Observations

The look of the sky and the feel of moisture in the air can tell you if a storm is moving in. There are many indications that bad weather is moving in—you simply must know what to look for. For example, clockwise or anticyclonic wind and cloud movement is related to high pressure and good weather. When the clouds are moving counter-clockwise, you can expect low pressure and bad weather within 24 hours. Following are some other observations you can make.

Rings Around the Sun or Moon

Rings around the sun or moon indicate moisture in the air and announce incoming bad weather. However, sometimes they just mean some harmless moisture is in the air. As the storm approaches, the halo around the orb will shrink due to increased moisture in the air. The important observation is the speed at which the halo shrinks. If there is no front, the halo will stay one size. The faster the shrinking, the higher the probability of stormy weather. While most people think a full-moon period guarantees good weather, this is not necessarily the case—it is often the opposite!

Star Visibility

The stars will twinkle brightly during periods of high pressure and good weather, especially if it's windy. If the stars seem vague or misty, then moisture is aloft. If you can't see any stars, then obviously some clouds are present. A clear night sky with a high barometer (over 30 mmHg) is a sign of good weather. A lower night barometer means bad weather is coming. Morning clouds down in the valley confirm the low barometer reading. These clouds can rise out of the valley, engulfing skiers.

Sound

"When sound travels far and wide, a stormy day likes betide" is an old saying based on the echoing effect thick clouds or a clear sky holding moisture have on sound. You'll notice that the sound of a jet plane is sharp and clear as it passes overhead during dry, clear weather. Because moisture dulls sound, the plane will sound hollow when moisture and clouds are aloft.

Compass Direction

It's easy to lose your sense of direction in the mountains when you are tired. Your compass will tell you precisely where the clouds are coming from—this way you can't miss. Remember the storm system you saw on TV? Are those clouds coming from the same direction?

Temperature

Temperature can give you clues to future weather. During winter, a period of good weather with high temperatures often precedes a few days of bad weather. This is because the low pressure cells are spaced between high pressure areas. Warm weather is pushed in front of the cold front. As the cold front arrives, temperature drops and snow and wind begin. But when it clears up, it is really cold! (As the cold front passes, it is followed by very cold air for at least 24 hours after the storm.) If you are in your sleeping bag, you can tell 80 percent of the time whether it's clear outside just by the temperature. Cloud cover acts like a blanket, keeping warmth closer to the ground. With clearing, the warmth of the earth escapes to the atmosphere.

Stages of Incoming Weather

If you watch the sky carefully you will see signs of the weather to come. Weather is not an exact science, so the following stages may not work precisely every time. But based on many years of observation, I can tell you that the odds are good that these stages will occur as presented.

Stage 1: Warm, Sunny Weather

There's nothing like good weather in the mountains! However, during changeable winter weather, a very warm, sunny day may be an indication of high pressure air being pushed by the next low pressure air mass (storm). A dropping barometer during the day and night will warn you of an incoming storm. Very warm winds called the Fohn (Europe) or Chinook (North America) often accompany these conditions, and they can hold bad weather off for days while ruining ski conditions and causing avalanches. But when the high pressure finally breaks, be prepared for storms!

Stage 2: High Cirrus Clouds

The "tails" of cirrus clouds point in the direction of an incoming disturbance. You know a low pressure system is on the way, but how big and how soon? The rule of thumb is, the bigger the tail the bigger the disturbance. The tail simply tells you that the sky is active, and the next 24 hours will reveal more specifically what's in store (see figure 7.1).

Stage 3: Lenticular Clouds and Wind

Lenticular clouds—called cap or mountain wave clouds when they rest on mountaintops—are long, lens-shaped, high cirrus clouds (see figure 7.2). They are a sign of major jet stream winds aloft, while on the ground there may be flurries even on a clear, sunny day. These

Figure 7.1   "Mare tail" cirrus clouds point to increasing clouds on the horizon.

Figure 7.2   Lenticular clouds indicate increasing winds aloft.

flurries can exceed 60 mph, obviously making it difficult to ski. You may need to hike if you are in an exposed situation, such as close to a cliff or cornice edge, because a change of weather is either coming in or passing over within the next 24 hours. If puffy, high clouds accompany the wind, there is an increased chance of an immediate storm.

Lenticular clouds accompanied by a sudden increase in wind temperature indicate that a Chinook or Fohn wind has arrived. These southerly or westerly winds ruin ski conditions and raise avalanche danger by driving warmth into the snow pack, melting the snow.

Stage 4: Altocumulus Clouds

White, puffy altocumulus clouds are a sign of good weather in most cases but can also accompany cumulonimbus clouds, which cause bad weather—especially when sighted in the morning hours (see discussion in Stage 5). The morning clouds in figure 7.3 appeared just four hours before the cumulonimbus clouds in figure 7.4.

Stage 5: Cumulonimbus Clouds

Clouds that give us the majority of our snow, rain, and hail are those marked by the term *nimbo*, which means "rain bearing." These clouds can move in while you are socked in (covered) by low clouds or mist in the valleys, and you won't even know it. They might just move over like they do on spring afternoons, threatening but just passing by. But total cloud coverage is a good indicator of bad weather to come.

Rule of Thirds. The amount of the sky that is covered by clouds is related to storm potential. A handy formula is called the Rule of Thirds: When one third of the sky is covered, there's not much to worry about. If two thirds of the sky is covered, storm clouds are moving in or passing over. If the entire sky (three thirds) is covered, the clouds have stopped moving and are solidifying into a cloud mass with precipitation (see figure 7.5)—time to make camp! Another way to think of it is to remember the phrase "clouds are thickening and lowering; or thinning and lifting."

Figure 7.3 Cumulus clouds in the morning hours can warn of incoming weather.

Figure 7.4 Cumulonimbus clouds can build up during afternoon hours, bringing with them possible thunder and lightning.

Lightning. Cumulonimbus clouds may also contain lightning, which skiers may encounter during spring ski touring on higher mountains. High-mountain rain or hail is a good indication of cumulonimbus clouds with lightning. If you feel your hair standing up, descend immediately but carefully. Many people get hurt while getting off a summit to avoid being hit by lightning. Just ski or climb down carefully—but do descend! Get down to a lower altitude until the storm clouds have blown over. Take your skis off your pack, because they can act as lightning rods. Either carry them in your hands *horizontally* or set them aside until the danger passes. Stay off ridges, summits, or high points. Avoid solitary trees or tall boulders. A party of skiers should spread 10 feet (3 meters) apart from each other, as lightning can travel horizontally. Ski on open slopes rather than down narrow chutes, because lightning follows cracks and chutes down

Figure 7.5 Twelve hours after the clouds in figure 7.4 accumulated, this fast-moving storm enveloped our tent within 10 minutes of taking the photo.

from the summit. Wet dirt and rocks conduct electricity better than dry dirt and snow (which are actually poor conductors), so stay away from them during the descent. If you need to stop, get away from all metal objects, including skis, ice axes, and other equipment. To play it safe, sprinkle snow on your pack or ensolite pad and squat down on top of it, *keeping your hands off the ground*. The rubber soles of your boots coupled with the poor conductors will protect you from ground currents.

Stage 6: Descending Ceiling and Wind

There is now a solid cloud cover above. The clouds no longer move sideways but are now descending. Cumulonimbus clouds now touch the mountaintops and descend the valley walls as fog and mist.

Compute in your head: the valley walls are 3,000 feet (914 meters) high, and the clouds descend 1,000 feet (305 meters) every 10 minutes. Therefore, 30 minutes remain before you are stuck with poor visibility and falling snow. Now is the time to make camp or return to the trailhead before the snow picks up and covers up your tracks.

Stage 7: Increasing Winds With Ground Flurries

At this point, fog and snow are in your face—it's goggle weather! Snow showers will continue to increase into a solid wall of snow (see figure 7.6). According to the National Weather Service, a blizzard is defined as a storm with heavy snow, reduced visibility, winds of 35 mph or higher, lasting at least three hours, with temperatures below 20 degrees Fahrenheit (–7 degrees Celsius).

Using an Altimeter

A weather change is always accompanied by a measurable change in barometric pressure. A barometer works by actually measuring the

Figure 7.6 Full conditions—increasing wind and cold, and reduced visibility.

weight of the air mass above it in increments of inches, millimeters, or millibars of mercury (Hg). Altimeters are both altimeters and barometers, but are usually referred to as altimeters. Altimeters are more popular in Europe than in the United States because there is more featureless Alpine landmass above tree line with fewer marked trails. However, more American adventurers are discovering them. Altimeters are scorned by many because they are thought to be too complex to use, too fragile, or just too expensive. Wristband altimeters (see figure 7.7) are more affordable (approximately $125) and easier to use.

Calibrating Your Altimeter

The key to altimeter use is repeated recalibration, which is easy to do. Just recalibrate your altimeter whenever you're at a major landmark of known altitude such as a lake, river, creek, town, pass, or summit. Unlike the United States, in Europe (and other countries) altitude is displayed on trailhead signs, huts, and ski lift terminals, making altimeter calibration even easier. In the field, keep a note of your altitude when you reach camp in case you forget. For consistency, reset your altimeter in the morning to the altitude it was the night before, even if there's a change in the barometer.

Figure 7.7   Altimeters. From left: Casio, Thommens, Avocet.

Simplifying Your Readings

The general rule of thumb for barometers is that if the pressure is falling, the weather will worsen. If the barometer is rising, the weather will get better (see table 7.1). (A falling barometer is usually accompanied by north or easterly winds, and a rising barometer is usually accompanied by south or westerly winds.) How much of a change is important? The following degrees of change should be noted:

1. *No* change is a change of .01 inches Hg or less over 3 hours (.04 inches over 12 hours).
2. *Slow* change is a change of .01 to .05 inches over 3 hours (.04 to .20 inches over 12 hours).
3. *Rapid* change is a change of more than .05 inches over 3 hours (more than .20 inches over 12 hours).

Elevation Changes Overnight

What if the elevation reading on your altimeter has changed overnight even though you haven't gotten out of your sleeping bag? If the elevation has gone up 150 feet (46 meters), it means that there is less air pressure pushing on the altimeter, so it thinks it is 150 feet higher than it actually is—this means bad weather. Conversely, if the altimeter reads 150 feet lower, it means high pressure and good conditions. The general rule is that above 7,000 feet (2,133 meters), an increase of 150 feet overnight means the chances of a storm are high. Below 7,000 feet, a change of 100 feet (30 meters) overnight is significant.

Altimeter Tips

- Keep your altimeter in the same place (on your wrist, for instance) at all times so that storage conditions are held constant. This will give you more consistent readings over time. Keep it away from hot areas such as the top of your pack, which could get warm from the sun.
- Make a foam case for handheld altimeters so that your investment is protected from falls during skiing or hiking.
- Carefully read the information booklet that came with your altimeter—make a photocopy of it for use in the field.
- Practice using your altimeter at home. What is the elevation of

Table 7.1

Barometric Readings and Weather Observations

Wind Direction	Barometer	Type of Weather
SW to NW	30.10 to 30.20 and *steady*	Fair with slight temperature changes for one to two days.
SW to NW	30.10 to 30.20 and *rising rapidly*	Fair followed by rain or snow within two days.
SW to NW	30.20 and above and *stationary*	Continued fair, no decided temperature change.
SW to NW	30.20 and above and *falling slowly*	Slowly rising temperature and fair for the next two days.
S to SE	30.10 to 30.20 and *falling slowly*	Rain or snow within 24 hours.
S to SE	30.10 to 30.20 and *falling rapidly*	Wind increasing in force, with rain or snow in 12 to 24 hours.
SE to NE	30.10 to 30.20 and *falling slowly*	Snow or rain in 12 to 18 hours.
SE to NE	30.10 to 30.20 and *falling rapidly*	Increasing wind and rain or snow in 12 hours.
E to NE	30.10 and above and *falling slowly*	In winter, rain or snow within 24 hours. In summer, with light winds, rain may not fall for several days.
E to NE	30.10 and above and *falling rapidly*	In winter, rain or snow with increasing wind often sets in. In summer, rain probable within 12 to 24 hours.
SE to NE	30.00 or below and *falling slowly*	Rain or snow will continue for one to two days.
SE to NE	30.00 or below and *falling rapidly*	Rain or snow, with high winds, followed within 36 hours by clearing, and in winter by a colder wave.
S to SW	30.00 or below and *rising slowly*	Clearing within a few hours and fair for several days.
S to E	29.80 or below and *falling rapidly*	Severe storm imminent, followed within 24 hours by clearing, and in winter by a colder wave.
E to N	29.80 or below and *falling rapidly*	Severe NE gale and heavy precipitation. In winter, heavy snow followed by a cold wave.
Going to W	29.80 or below and *rising rapidly*	Clearing and colder.

Reprinted, by permission, from Peet Brothers, Inc. 1308 Doris Avenue, Ocean, NJ, 07712

TRUST YOUR INSTRUMENTS

While climbing Mt. Blanc, a ski group I was with stayed at the Grand Mulet Hut (10,009 feet [3,051 meters]) while skiing up the standard route. The evening was clear and beautiful. That night, my barometer kept dropping with concurrent increase in my altitude readout. The next morning we awoke at 3 A.M. for the climb. It was clear, but that's not what my altimeter was telling me—according to it, there was a storm coming in. With daylight I could see that the whole Chamonix Valley was covered in clouds. My barometer was steady but low. I had seen these clouds before and knew they meant trouble. By the time we got our skis on we were covered in clouds! The moral of the story: believe your instruments!

your home and the market you go to most? Match up your barometric reading with your local television weather forecast. The more you use it, the easier it will be to use.

Skiing in Bad Weather

No one plans to get caught in a blizzard, but it happens to expedition skiers and day tourers alike. An intense blizzard causes fatigue, cold, and disorientation, making it difficult to return to your starting point. Skiing in poor-visibility conditions is difficult and potentially dangerous. Here are some ways to deal with it:

- Ski slowly downhill. Use snowplowing, sideslipping, and kick turns to make a slow, controlled descent.
- Goggles or sunglasses (with yellow lenses) should be on.
- Button up your clothing to anticipate any unexpected falls.
- The best skier should go first to be the pathfinder.
- Everyone should ski within visual contact. Always wait for stragglers.
- Use trees for visual cues. Stay in scattered trees for depth of field cues. Follow the edge of a grove of trees for terrain contour information in flat light. Some skiers have even thrown a cord out in front of them to determine slope angle in extreme conditions.
- Stay in the track of the skiers in front of you. Watch how they

Mountain cap clouds on Mt. Blanc, Chamonix, France.

handle the terrain and be ready for it. Ski cautiously and defensively.

- To minimize chilling, don't stop on the top of a windy pass during storm conditions. Ski right over the top without stopping unnecessarily.

Making Camp in Bad Weather

Always make camp *before* you have to. When making camp in a storm, it's important to remain coolheaded and calm because the wind noise, cold, and fatigue can make for a confusing situation (see chapter 11 for more information on making camp). Do things methodically and quickly. Here are some tips to remember:

1. Be sure everyone has all their cold-weather gear on.
2. Pull the tent body out and throw all gear inside, then close the door to prevent ballooning. Get cold individuals into the tent body before it's erected. This gets them out of the weather right away, reducing anxiety in a strange situation. The bodies also anchor the tent, making it easier to put up in high winds.
3. All skis should be stuck straight up in the snow for tent anchors so they aren't buried in the fresh snow.
4. Stake down the tent and double-check loose guy lines.

Conclusion

For centuries, the old mountain guide has awakened early in the morning and walked out to see the sky and feel the air. What was he looking for? What is going on in his mind? Can he know how the morning snow will be? How it will change by the afternoon? By seeing how weather works in the mountains we can learn how to work *with* it. By missing so-called bad weather we are missing the drama and intensity of the mountains. The very stuff we ski on is caused by this phenomenon called weather. With our introduction to weather we learned how our clothing, food, and ski equipment can help us make the best use of both good and bad conditions, instead of letting the conditions get the best of us.

8

chapter

Navigation Skills

The ability to navigate is probably the most important skill in the backcountry. In this chapter you will learn how to use a compass and altimeter and learn to design ski routes that make the best of terrain, weather, and avalanche safety. Navigation takes into account many factors, including ski ability, physical condition, and terrain difficulty. It is not just map and compass work. While global positioning satellites (GPS) and cellular telephones are on the increase, a solid knowledge of mountain navigation is still essential.

Getting Information About Your Route

A guidebook should always be accompanied by the 7.5-minute USGS (United States Geological Survey) topographical map of the area (skiers in other countries, like Europe, typically rely on 15-minute maps that are more difficult to use). Photocopy route information from the guidebook to save weight. Always verify guidebook information if in doubt. Ask your local ski shop personnel if they find the guidebook accurate and usable.

Types of Maps

USGS topographic (topo) maps were originally commissioned by the United States Congress as a means of promoting commerce, transportation, and the exploration of natural resources. Over 90 percent of the features must be correctly plotted to within 100 feet (30 meters) of the exact location. The maps are drawn from plane and satellite photographic data. They're useful because they show terrain relief and altitude by using contour lines, which are excellent for determining slope angle. Forest service or national park maps—whether domestic or foreign—are useful because they show backcountry roads and snowmobile routes, which make natural ski routes. These maps are updated more often than topographical maps, but they don't have contour lines. Both maps used together can give you the big picture of a given area. Map sources are listed in appendix B.

CD-ROMs that hold up to 40 maps of a given area are also available. Most are marked with latitude and longitude and UTM (Universal Transverse Mercator) markings. Some can even calculate slope angle on your route automatically! Rescue groups and ski groups like these because they can print several copies of the same map. The only problem with these smaller maps is that you may ski off the map into an unknown area. Maps of your ski route *and* the surrounding area should always be taken.

GPS Navigation Systems

Global positioning satellite (GPS) receivers use satellite signals to provide the coordinates of your location. These may be displayed as latitude-longitude or UTM coordinates, which are the most widely used coordinate systems. Both grid systems will be discussed in detail in this chapter. GPS receivers are so popular (most run about $120) that many mapmakers are including GPS readings for hut and landmark locations. Presently, your location can be known to within 100 meters (328 feet) 95 percent of the time with an altitude accuracy within 156 meters (512 feet), so an altimeter is still needed. The United States military has degraded the satellite signals for national security reasons. This policy of *selective availability (S/A)* is unpopular with many who feel that it is necessary only during wartime.

Some GPS receivers offer, for $480, optional differential (DGPS) beacons that allow users to circumvent S/A electronically, allowing for accuracy to within 10 meters (33 feet). Because GPS is becoming more popular, future satellites may include a civilian frequency. At least four satellites are needed for GPS to work. For best results, you should have as few skyward obstructions as possible. When skiing above tree line there is no problem, but below tree line, a dense forest or narrow ravine could limit reception, making a frozen lake ideal. The more channels a receiver has, the better it works below tree line where more obstructions exist. An understanding of latitude and longitude is useful when using GPS. Remember to calibrate your receiver for the data (year and scale) of the map you are using, be sure your map has longitude and latitude markings, and don't forget extra batteries!

Reading Your Map

A map is no good unless you know how to read it. Topographical maps hold a lot of information. The more you study your maps before the trip, the easier it will be to navigate once you are in the field. Besides, it's always fun to take out your maps before a trip to see where you are going!

Mileage Scale

Mechanical mileage counters that have adjustable calibration for different scales of maps make it easier to count mileage. You can use string by simply cutting a piece that is the exact length of one mile (1.6 kilometers) on the map. Be careful not to measure the whole scale! Start in the middle, at zero (see figure 8.1). String bends and can follow your route more easily than a ruler. Both methods are helpful but will give you an underestimate, because you can't take into account every move you will make that will add mileage.

Map Date

The older the map, the greater the chance that the current terrain differs from it. Look for a blue notice stating: "Photo—Revised 1984" (or other date); this means that the map area was photographed by plane and the map was updated.

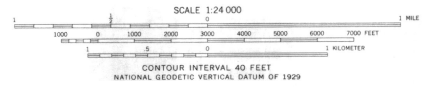

SCALE 1:24 000

CONTOUR INTERVAL 40 FEET
NATIONAL GEODETIC VERTICAL DATUM OF 1929

Figure 8.1   Typical mileage scale.

Describing Location

Describing location precisely is a valuable skill. Using common names such as Herman Lake or Pettingell Peak won't always be helpful—you may need to describe location to someone with absolutely no familiarity with the area; there may be more than one Herman Lake on the same map. Providing precise location information to a rescue party can save time and confusion (in case there are two Herman Lakes). Two major reference grids are in common use: latitude-longitude coordinates and UTM coordinates. While both are used with GPS systems, the UTM system is far easier to use in the field by skiers.

Latitude and Longitude

Like a circle, the earth can be broken into 360 degrees. Each degree has 60 minutes, and each minute has 60 seconds, just like a clock. (You just need to know that there are seconds, but you won't really use them for measurements.) There are 15-minute and 7.5-minute maps. While 15-minute maps are more common in Europe, 7.5-minute maps show more detail in a clearer manner. Try not to mix 7.5- and 15-minute maps together, as the scales are different and it will be more difficult to compute distances and travel times. Distances on a 15-minute map are double those on a 7.5-minute map, which is easily forgotten in the excitement of route planning!

A position is described as the point at which latitude and longitude coordinates cross each other. Each 7.5-minute map is bordered on its top and bottom by longitude markings and on each vertical edge by latitude markings. Zero longitude is at Greenwich, England. Zero latitude is at the equator. You can remember the difference between latitude and longitude by remembering "Latitude becomes lat, which is flat, and so is the Earth."

Latitude and longitude coordinates are printed on each corner of your map. In the simulated map in figure 8.2 you can see the markings:

106.00 to 105.52.30 (degrees, minutes, seconds) are the longitude or vertical lines on your map, and 39.37.30 and 39.45.00 are the latitude or horizontal lines. Notice the difference in these markings is 7.5 minutes—the size of your map! You can always tell latitude markings because they are the same at opposite top or bottom corners of the map. Find your position with natural landmarks around you. Now find them on the map. Using the latitude and longitude coordinates on the map, draw perpendicular lines that intersect at your location. Notice latitude and longitude figures on the map's edges. In this case, you would say, "We're at 105 degrees 53 minutes west longitude (since you are west of Greenwich, England) and 41 degrees 15 minutes north latitude (since you are north of the equator)." Seconds are not normally used in describing location.

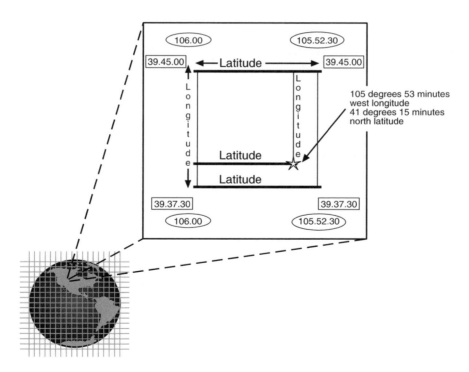

Figure 8.2 Finding your location with latitude and longitude. Longitude coordinates are circled, and latitude coordinates are boxed (map not drawn to scale).

UTM: Universal Transverse Mercator

The UTM mapping system coordinates were developed for use by troops with little or no map training (which makes it ideal for skiers, too). Instead of dividing the globe by minutes and degrees, UTM divides the globe into 60 zones, 6 degrees wide. These can be used like latitude and longitude markings to describe your location. No ruler is necessary to read them. Each UTM mark is 1,000 meters apart. Those along the top and bottom margins are called *eastings,* while those on the vertical margins are called *northings.* Northings are referenced to the equator, and eastings are referenced to the Zone Meridian in which it lies. Northing values go up the farther north you go. Eastings values go up as you go east. You can see the UTM numbers highlighted in the map on page 159, a scan of the Loveland Pass topographical map. Find your location, match up the nearest UTM number on the vertical and horizontal lines, and mentally draw perpendicular lines out to your location. In our example, Herman Lake can be described as $^{43}98^{700}$N (northing) by $^{4}23^{250}$E (easting). Don't let the little superscript numbers scare you. $^{43}98^{700}$N actually means 4,398,700 meters (2,733 miles) above the equator. Likewise $^{4}23^{250}$E means 423,250 meters (263 miles) east of the Zone Meridian. UTM markings are also handy for aligning two maps together more easily—just match up the same numbers. See the bibliography for books on GPS and UTM (books on GPS usually cover UTM in good detail).

Matching Map to Terrain

One of the hardest skills to learn is matching map features to the actual terrain you are looking at. It is an important skill because all your route finding relies on it.

Map Color

Green map shading means that it's covered with trees, brush, or meadows. Trees can protect you from high winds during the winter and protect you from the sun during the spring, providing you with better conditions. The map alone can't tell you what the vegetation is like. It could also mean fallen timber or underbrush—always look for existing hiking trail thoroughfares for alternate routes. Green usually means protection from avalanches, whereas white depicts areas without trees or vegetation, where there may be an increased potential for avalanches. For safe skiing, place your ski route "in the green" as much as possible. Old avalanche chutes are more obvious below tree lines than they are above tree lines, where steep funnel shapes depict chutes and couloirs. Reroute around these areas during high avalanche hazard.

Contour Lines and Slope Angle

Topo maps are covered with contour lines showing elevation. On a 7.5-minute map the elevation difference between lines is 40 feet (12 meters), and 15-minute maps show contours with 80-foot (24-meter) intervals. The steeper the slope, the closer the lines. Does the terrain in the map on page 159 match the photo of this area? Notice how lines are farther apart on the flatter areas and closer together on the pass in the background. It is safer to travel on low-angle slopes (lines farther apart) since most avalanches occur on slopes between 30 and 45 degrees. From a fatigue standpoint, as the saying goes, always follow the path of least resistance!

CARING FOR YOUR MAPS

Fold your maps into thirds lengthwise and then into thirds again with the map side facing out. Put them into a large freezer bag or map case so you can read the map without taking it out of the bag. The less you handle maps with wet hands the longer they will last. Waterproof maps are nice, but they are usually 15-minute maps, many of which don't show detail or latitude and longitude or UTM markings.

The less you write on a map the better. Use a fine lead pencil and be as neat as possible so details aren't covered. Erasures weaken map paper, causing tears. If you have several maps on the same route, number and name the map on its back with a pencil for fast field reference. Don't use a black marker pen as it will bleed through the map, ruining it.

Navigating With a Compass

How many of us get lost trying to find a street address? The same thing happens in the backcountry. Don't forget that fatigue and altitude can play tricks even on those who rarely get lost. Carrying maps and a compass can help you find your location and stay on course.

Mountain Features as They Relate to Skiing

Pass (1)   Passes are low points in a valley wall that allow skiers to hook up one valley to the next. Always double check the pass location on your map—it is easy to confuse low points on a ridge with passes.

Bowl (2)   A rounded headwall of a glacial valley where glacial action has molded the mountain into a concave area. They are great for skiing but prone to avalanches. Cirques (smaller bowls) may have higher walls (headwalls) that are often too steep to climb.

Point (3)   The end of a ridge or a stand-alone pinnacle. Often a navigation mistake will bring you to this impasse. Points are best avoided since they must often be downclimbed on foot.

Ridge (4)   An often skiable broad or narrow rampart usually connecting one or more points. "Knife edges" are much narrower, unskiable ridges.

Arete (5)   Bare rock technical climbing routes that may provide access to skiing routes alongside them. Similar to ridges, aretes run vertically rather than horizontally and are like ribs of the mountain itself. Aretes are typically avoided by skiers.

Chute (6)   Narrower and shorter than a couloir and often too tight for skiing, chutes might not follow the fall line, or they might split into even narrower branches. Chutes are prone to rockfall and are safest to climb during early morning hours.

Couloir (7)   Meaning "hallway" in French, couloirs are natural access routes to summits and are usually wide enough to ski and climb. Rockfall is a constant problem, so travel them in the early morning hours.

Summit (8)   This true peak top may be preceded by many false summits. Pointed summits are difficult places in which to put skis on, especially in high winds.

Col (9)   Also called a saddle, this is a low point between two peaks. Check your map before using a col as a pass—the terrain may be too steep to ski on the other side.

Face (10)   A broad, open area running vertically that often originates at a summit or ridge. Faces provide excellent skiing during stable snow conditions.

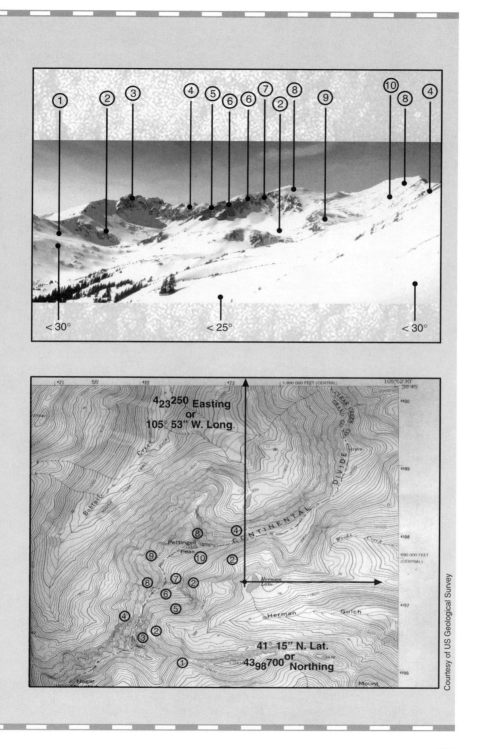

159

BUYING A GOOD COMPASS

A compass is an important piece of navigational equipment. A good compass will have the following features:

- **Lanyard (1)**—A compass must be attached to something to avoid loss. Wear the compass around your neck or tied to a pocket or pack zipper pull.
- **Straightedge (2)**—A straightedge is important for drawing triangulation vectors, bearing lines, and magnetic north lines.
- **Sight (3)**—A sight increases the accuracy of measuring. With the mirror, you can read the exact bearings of a landmark.
- **Liquid-filled (4)**—A liquid-filled (usually with oil) dial compartment dampens pointer movement and reduces the time needed for the pointer to find a bearing.

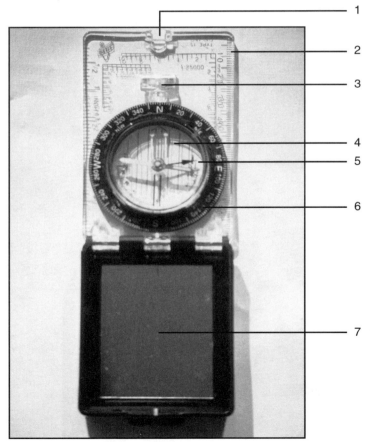

- **Enclinometer (5)**—The back pointer is used to measure slope angle and avalanche potential.
- **Adjustable magnetic declination (6)**—This built-in split movable ring lets you preadjust magnetic declination to save you from having to do the measurements in your head. This can make the difference between finding a hut and not finding it at the end of the day.
- **Aiming mirror (7)**—This mirror allows the compass reading to be read off the dial as you sight the compass at the target. It can also be used as a signaling mirror in an emergency.

Magnetic Declination

Magnetic declination refers to the magnetic pull the earth exerts on metals (including the metal of your compass needle). For precise readings, keep the compass away from radios, avalanche beacons, and wristwatches that have magnetic fields. Each area of the world is affected differently by this force. It will be slightly greater if you are on the west coast of North America than if you are on the east coast. You can navigate using magnetic bearings or "true" bearings, as long as you use one method or the other consistently.

At the bottom of your map you will see an angle drawn with a star on the vertical axis showing *true north*, and an angled line showing *magnetic north*. The declination is the difference between the magnetic pull of the magnetic North Pole and true north bearing (vertical edge of the map, i.e. grid north, see figure 8.3). Notice the date. Remember that the declination changes by 3 minutes each year. For example, it's 1999, your map is dated 1955, photo revised 1983. Look at that angle diagram at the map bottom with a magnetic north date

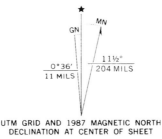

UTM GRID AND 1987 MAGNETIC NORTH
DECLINATION AT CENTER OF SHEET

Figure 8.3 The map's declination symbol should be compared to the date of the map's most recent revision.

that says 1983, and calculate: 1999 – 1983 = 16 years × 3 minutes = 48 minutes (almost 60 minutes, or 1 degree). The difference is on the minus side in the continental United States. Internet sources or map retailers can usually tell you the declination in other parts of the world. Is 1 degree a big deal? While you would rarely navigate by instruments alone, repeated errors of 1 degree over 1 mile (1.6 kilometers) could throw your course off 984 feet (300 meters). This could be a big problem in heavy forest or foggy weather. For updated specific declination information for North America correction factors, in the United States call the main USGS office at 303-202-4386 with your map name and date.

For the compass without adjustable declination, you'll need to adjust the map. Notice the magnetic declination symbol at the bottom of the map. The vertical line with the star points to true north and is parallel to the side of the map. The magnetic declination (MN) line goes off at an angle. GN pertains to UTM grid north, which is not used in our calculations. Simply draw a continuation of this line right across the map. Now draw parallel lines to this line. Point to north on your compass—this is actually magnetic north. Align the lines on your map to the north you have found. Now your map is oriented to true north, indirectly but precisely. Always tell others you are using magnetic bearings, not true bearings.

Orienting Map to Terrain

You have adjusted your declination, now be sure to line up the N with the sighting mark on the compass frame. This makes your compass frame straightedge parallel to north—a very important detail! Now place your compass frame exactly on the vertical edge of the map with the N pointing to the top of the map. Lay out your map on your backpack and move compass and map together so both point to true north. Cross-check important landmarks on the map against the same landmarks in front of you. Don't be surprised if they don't look the same; you'll need practice to develop an eye for matching map to terrain.

Using Landmarks for Navigation

Once you have your map and compass oriented to true north, you can read a bearing to your first landmark whether it's a peak or a valley. A bearing is a numerical degree description of direction. Saying "75 degrees" is more precise than saying "easterly." Keeping the red needle on the N, turn the compass frame until the gunsight is aiming at your next landmark. In figure 8.4, the first landmark is at 75 degrees. Every time you recheck your course, you must correctly orient your map and compass to true north before anything, or you *will* get lost. Recheck your bearing more often if the terrain is unusually rough or if the weather is closing off your view of the landmark. Even if the landmark disappears, you can follow your original compass bearings, keeping in mind obstacles en route.

Finding Yourself

Getting lost is not the end of the world, but it can be disconcerting. You can find yourself more easily if you have good-visibility conditions and some landmark peak tops. In heavily forested areas such as the eastern United States and Canada, a GPS receiver can be helpful. In any case, getting to higher ground or to an open area will help; you can see more landmarks and receive satellite signals.

Find Yourself With Reverse Bearings

Remember the reverse bearing of the direction you are heading in case you need to backtrack and find that your ski tracks are buried (see

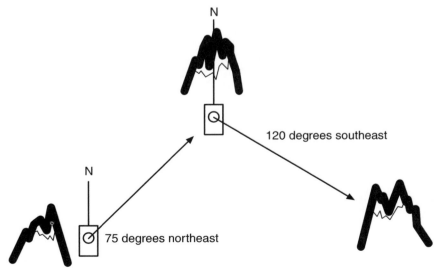

Figure 8.4 Multiple landmarks can be linked together with compass bearings.

figure 8.5). In figure 8.4, you were traveling northeast on a 75-degree bearing. Traveling up a valley would make reversing direction easy. But what about a large, featureless plain? The reverse degree (in this case 255 degrees) would help you return to your starting point.

Find Yourself With Triangulation

Triangulation can be used to locate yourself if you have good visibility and distinct landmarks. Always start by orienting your map and compass to true north. Find two landmark peaks (this can work with two lakes or passes also). The two landmarks should form close to a 90-degree angle with each other, with you as the apex of the angle. With your compass oriented to true north, read the reverse bearing *from* landmark A (see figure 8.6). On the map draw a long straight line down the middle of the compass housing from landmark A across the map. With your compass still oriented to true north, take a bearing

Figure 8.5 Old ski tracks can give clues to the proper return route, but should be followed suspiciously.

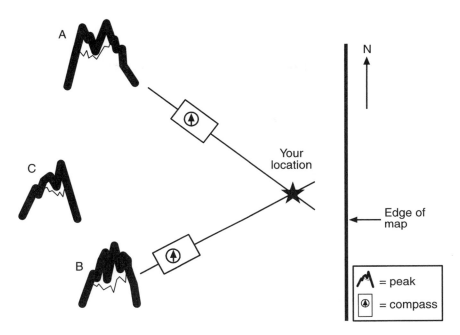

Figure 8.6   Use triangulation to determine your location.

using the compass sight off landmark B. Using the reverse bearing from landmark B, draw a line down the middle of the compass housing from landmark B across the map. You are located where the two lines cross within a 300-foot radius. Using landmarks spaced far apart (landmarks A and B) will give better precision than two that are closer together, such as B and C.

Find Yourself With Zero Horizon

There are two ways to travel in a straight line during very poor visibility. With the first method, you can leapfrog skiers. Have one skier go out 50 yards (46 meters) or as far as visibility permits. Move the skier until he lines up with your desired compass setting. Ski to that skier and repeat. With the second method, you can do the same thing sighting off trees. If you can't see at all and conditions are worsening, stop and make camp.

Find Yourself With an Altimeter

In addition to helping you evaluate weather conditions (see chapter 7), altimeters are the ultimate navigation tool during bad weather because they can measure your altitude. Since each contour line represents a different altitude, when you know your altitude you can find yourself on the corresponding contour line on the map. Viewing local terrain features will further verify your position. With that information, you can find your location on a contour line on your map, which is often enough to establish your location. It is a good exercise to circle the altitudes closest to your route to see how the route fluctuates in altitude. By studying your maps you may find ways to minimize the total number of vertical feet needed for climbing and maximize your downhill skiing. Longer and faster days can occur when there are more downhills en route.

The altimeter and a compass can be used very effectively *together*. First, find your altitude and corresponding contour line. Next, use your compass to take a bearing off a known landmark (refer back to the triangulation section for help). Where this bearing crosses your contour line marks your position. Finally, an altimeter reading can be used to verify a location previously found by triangulation.

Designing the Ski Route

Plotting out a ski route takes into account many factors that are often forgotten by novices and experts alike. Matching the skills and physical abilities of several people to a particular ski trip will increase speed and safety and make it more enjoyable.

Travel Speed

The time needed to ski untracked snow is surprising—1 mile per hour in the backcountry is typical for a group of three to four because of the interaction of many factors, including: difficulty of route, physical condition and fatigue, equipment condition, weather, snow conditions, avalanche terrain avoidance, falling, navigation problems, food and bathroom stops, climbing time, and the distance to cover.

Experience, skill, and strength will pay big dividends—even a .5 mph increase makes a big difference. That's 6 hours for 9 miles (14 kilometers) instead of 9 hours! A 10-mile (16-kilometer) day on either telemark or AT equipment on variable terrain is very good. You can add an additional hour for each 1,000 feet (304 meters) of climbing and cut 50 percent off the time for downhill sections. For instance, a 3-mile (5-kilometer) uphill may take 3 hours. But going back down will take 1.5 hours (depending on the weather), a 50 percent reduction in time. Naismith's formula allows 1 hour for each 3 miles traveled and 1 additional hour for every 2,000 feet (609 meters) climbed; the Alpine estimate allows 1 hour for every 800 feet (244 meters) climbed. Both estimates apply best to summer hiking rather than winter ski touring.

Difficulty

You're trying to get from point A to point B. One alternative is 1.5 miles (2 kilometers) shorter than your second choice. The first choice is steeper going up and down. The second is flatter but longer. Consider this—are you in shape? Is everyone in your group in shape enough to do all the climbing? How about falls? Consider the time it will take to get up from a fall for one person. Multiply that by the number of people with you. You will save a lot of time by taking the longer route that everyone can do without falling. The shorter route is not always the fastest way. Pick a ski tour where everyone's equipment is equal to the task. Be sure everyone has climbing skins before the tour if they are needed and that no one is overburdened by a heavy pack.

Natural Ski Routes

Pick a route that is easily plotted and followed. Use marked hiking, ski hut, and snowmobile trails. Summer trails may be marked with trailblazes (see figure 8.7). Always look behind you as you go because the blaze might be on the other side of the tree. Above the tree line look for cairns (rock piles) that mark summer hiking routes. You can travel faster when you don't have to stop every 10 minutes to check your map. Follow natural travel avenues such as valleys or main waterways. Avoid getting too close to dropoffs or dead-end canyons that could be encountered mistakenly during bad weather. Pick a route that affords a continuous flow of skiing unchallenged by objective dangers such as large creek crossings and avalanche hazards. The more time you spend figuring out your route, the less time you have to ski.

Escape Potential

A part of your self-rescue plan should be to look for ways of getting off your route if problems arise. It could be something serious such as an injury, or it could be something minor like a change of heart and a desire to end the ski tour. At what point will it be faster to finish the route instead of backtracking? How far is the nearest road? How far is the nearest town or ski area? You should know all aspects of the route!

Figure 8.7 Don't confuse *(a)* squared-off trail blazes with *(b)* animal markings.

Games Ski Tourers Play

Skiers play games with terrain to design ski tours. We can use natural terrain characteristics to make our tour easier to ski and navigate. Each of the following ski route designs has different features, such as different amounts of climbing and downhill skiing or the use of other transportation modes (cars or ski lifts, for example). In addition, some ski routes are more difficult to travel during bad weather than others, and some routes will be more enjoyable at different times in the ski season than others. Whatever the design, the idea is to have fun and adventure!

- **Baseline Skiing**—The most basic of ski route designs employs what is called a baseline. You can use a road or an imaginary line between two landmarks as a baseline. You can then draw a perpendicular line in the direction you want to go—for instance, you want to go east. Many summer trailheads are located on roads perpendicular to a trail. Skiing out, the compass reads 90 degrees (east), so on the return trip you will come back on the backbearing 270 degrees (west). Your ski route should also have navigational backups. In this example, a primary backup could be a stream that parallels the route. The stream runs right into the road or imaginary line, and will bring you back to the starting point with or without a compass. Stay on the same side of the stream, returning on your own ski tracks. You now have three navigational backups:

1. The perpendicular backbearing compass bearing (270 degrees)
2. The stream
3. Your ski tracks

• **Loop Skiing**—You can feel pretty safe about skiing out for the day or for a few hours as long as the weather is good. A loop tour is done in much the same way, but instead of coming back on your tracks you make a big loop that ends at your baseline.

• **Valley Hopping**—You can connect several valleys together via passes going the same direction. Valleys can provide you with relatively easy skiing and good weather, water, and camping. They are easier to ski than windy ridges. But in bad weather, valleys may hold deep snow that might not be avoidable. Trees can also provide easier navigation and shelter during poor weather.

• **High (Haute) Route**—High (haute) routes usually follow high-altitude plains, passes, and ridges. Spring is the best time for these routes. They should be avoided during deep winter and periods of bad weather unless skiers are experienced in bad-weather navigation and avalanche avoidance. High routes are exposed to wind and cold and require that you carry appropriate storm gear and extra stove fuel for melting snow for water, since you will rarely find running water up high. High routes can be skied later in the season and offer the opportunity for more interesting technical skiing such as peak skis and chute skiing. There are very few natural obstacles such as streams, forests, or brush—it is wide-open skiing!

• **Peak Ski**—For maximum vertical feet of skiable terrain, you can't beat skiing a peak. These are best done during the spring, when snow and weather conditions moderate. Always climb up your ski route to examine the snow for rocks or ice. If the snow is too hard to climb on foot, it might be too difficult to ski even if you wait for it to soften up. For the hardcore skier-climber, it may not be a problem. But for the weekend skier, another descent route may be safer and more

Skiers on the John Muir Trail near Mt. Whitney,
Sierra Nevadas, California.

fun. You can do an Alpine traverse of the peak from one side to another. This involves precise planning, a much longer day, and an Alpine start (4 A.M.) so that you get back to the trailhead before dark.

• **Base Camp**—Skiing into one spot and making camp for several days while skiing the area around you is a good way to travel. Since you don't have to carry a heavy pack every day, you can concentrate on skiing a given area in-depth. It's fun to return during the day to have lunch or take a nap at a camp that is already set up. It's great for large groups with inexperienced people, since they can go back to camp if they are cold. Base camp skiing is especially fun during the spring.

• **Circumnavigation**—One of the problems with skiing around a mountain is that you are required to ski against the grain of the peak's drainages. You must ski across gulches and ravines and will undoubtedly have to traverse some possible avalanche paths. Planning should include the possibility of some snow climbing and snow camping over several days.

• **Ski Lift**—Some ski areas will allow you to use their lift and then ski out of boundaries with the ski patrol's permission. Some resorts even have cross-country ski trails starting on the top of their mountains. You are wasting time and energy skiing up a mountain that has a lift on it. Plus, many resorts won't let you ski up against skier traffic due to safety considerations.

• **Car Shuttle**—While not wilderness skiing, per se, using a car to access terrain can be fun. Drop one car off at the end of the proposed run. Take the other car to your starting point. This is great for a day tour where you want to get as much skiing done as possible.

Conclusion

The most important navigational skill in the backcountry is the ability to match the map to the terrain around you. You need to do your homework *at home* before going on your ski tour. Maps contain the most accurate slope angle information, which is often overlooked during a planning session. Once in the field, bad weather can move in, but a thorough knowledge of the terrain and a trust in your instruments (compass and altimeter) will get you to your destination. GPS systems are more understandable when you have a good foundation in map navigation as a start.

chapter

Avoiding Avalanches

Ski tourers, unlike resort skiers, must often venture up slopes before they go down them. This automatically puts them *under* a potential hazard rather than skiing down on top of it. Even small avalanches can cause bone fractures or tendon sprains or drive you into trees or off a cliff. Small avalanches also set off bigger slides. Skiers always have a choice. They can wait for more stable conditions, or they can simply ski around a suspect slope—it's that easy. Learning about avalanches is learning about snow, the basis of all that we do. This chapter will help you to understand snow better and to predict and avoid avalanches. One should remember the old climber's maxim: follow the route of least resistance. Follow your instincts, too!

Learning About Avalanches

There is an abundance of books on avalanches and avalanche rescue (see the bibliography on page 266), and many mountaineering and ski clubs give avalanche workshops. A field class is often an invaluable learning situation where you can actually get out and learn from the experts. The American Avalanche Institute, among others, gives excellent field classes each winter.

Getting Avalanche Forecasts

Weather can be a stabilizing or destabilizing influence on the existing snow pack. Avalanche and weather forecasts are available for most mountainous areas of the world via telephone, radio, and now the Internet. These are usually updated daily. Things can change overnight! Get a new forecast *each morning*. The avalanche danger ratings in table 9.1 are only meant to serve as general observations. Low hazard doesn't mean no hazard—a low rating should ease your mind somewhat but shouldn't close your eyes. Always pay attention to the terrain you are traveling through.

What Is an Avalanche?

Every snow pack has a certain inherent strength due to the bonding of snow. When this snow pack is stressed because of new snow weight or a skier's weight, that snow pack can no longer hold together and it slides, becoming an avalanche. It takes less stress to cause a slide if there are existing weak layers within the snow pack. In addition to stress, the snow needs something to slide on that is steep enough for gravity to pull the snow down the mountain.

Avalanche Types

Avalanches come in several types, depending on prevailing climate and terrain. *Slab avalanches* are the most dangerous type. Wind compresses snow into slabs of snow that are strong enough to rest on, but not bond with, a weak snow layer (see figure 9.1). For example, early-season snows can be followed by days of dry and cool conditions that turn the snow into a weak, sugarlike snow (depth hoar). This old, weak snow pack is later covered by heavy snows accompanied by wind—a perfect avalanche situation.

These slabs can be many inches or feet thick and are very common in open areas, mostly above tree line, whenever and wherever wind deposits snow. Slabs usually occur on leeward sides of ridges (protected sides) and can be the size of a football field with tremendous weight and destructive power (see figure 9.2). Soft slabs can occur right after a windy storm, while hard slabs are older slabs that have grown larger with time, wind, and sun. Wet slab avalanches are more

Table 9.1

Five-Step Avalanche Danger Scale

Danger level/ Color	Avalanche probability/ Trigger size	Degree/ Distribution of slides	Recommended travel precautions
LOW (green)	Natural avalanches unlikely, human-triggered slides *unlikely*	Generally stable snow, isolated areas of instability	Travel is generally safe, normal caution is advised.
MODERATE (yellow)	Natural avalanches unlikely, human-triggered slides *possible*	Unstable slabs possible on steeper terrain	Use caution in steeper terrain on certain aspects.
MODERATE to HIGH (orange)	Natural avalanches possible, human-triggered slides *probable*	Unstable slabs probable on steeper terrain	Be cautious on steeper terrain.
HIGH (red)	Natural and human-triggered avalanches *likely*	Unstable slabs likely on a variety of aspects and slopes	Travel on avalanche terrain is not recommended. Safest travel is on windward ridges or lower-angle slopes without steeper slopes above.
EXTREME (black)	Widespread natural or human-triggered slides *certain*	Extremely unstable slabs certain on most aspects and slope angles. Large, destructive avalanches possible.	Travel on avalanche terrain should be avoided. Travel should be confined to low-angle slopes that are well away from avalanche path runouts.

Courtesy of Dale Atkins, CAIC (Colorado Avalanche Information Center).

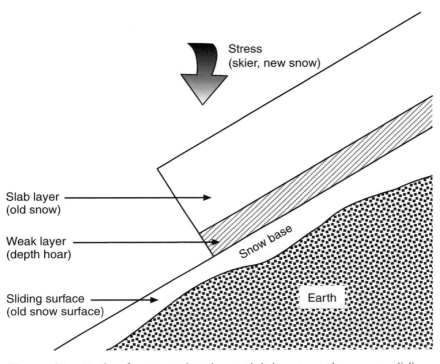

Figure 9.1   Recipe for an avalanche: a slab layer, weak snow, a sliding surface, and a stress.

common in maritime climates. These can occur when there is free water in the snow pack due to warm winds or rain.

Point release avalanches occur when a small amount of cohesiveless snow starts to slide, picking up more snow. A good example is when a snow-laden tree or cornice drops a load of snow on a slope and a slide occurs that looks like an upside-down ice cream cone. Although these naturally triggered slides can get big, they usually occur right after a storm and help stabilize a slope by triggering many small slides rather than letting a big one build up (see figure 9.3).

Hangfire avalanches occur when a small avalanche or the weight of a skier on a questionable slope pre-stresses a slope for sliding. Spontaneous sliding occurs in the process of stabilization of the slope. You just don't want to be around when it's happening! It's also incorrect to think that if the skier in front of you made it across, it's safe. Not at all. It just means that the slope is still loaded and is ready for you! Widely spaced trees do *not* provide safety. Avoid wide-open slopes immediately after a storm. They will be ready to ski soon enough!

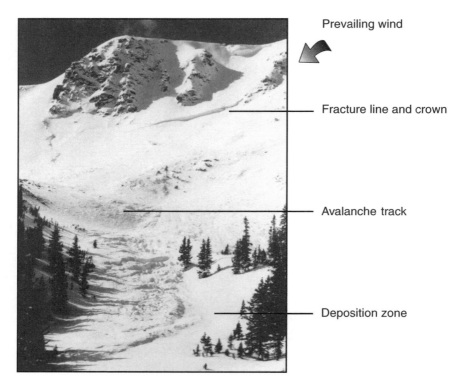

Prevailing wind

Fracture line and crown

Avalanche track

Deposition zone

Figure 9.2   Principal parts of an avalanche.

When Do Avalanches Occur?

January and February (July and August in southern latitudes) have the greatest number of snowfalls and thus the highest likelihood of unstable slopes. More than 75 percent of avalanches occur between December and March (June and September in southern latitudes). March through June are the best months to ski tour and ski steep slopes because increased snow-pack depths bring strength and stability to snow slopes (see table 9.2).

Factors Affecting Avalanche Formation

Several factors work together to create ripe conditions for avalanche formation. As you will see, avalanche hazard can even increase during clear weather!

Figure 9.3   Even sparse trees can hold enough snow
to start an avalanche.

New Snow

Snowstorms come in many varieties of moisture, wind, and duration. One inch (3 centimeters) per hour is enough snow to cause avalanches. Eighty percent of avalanches occur *during* a storm when enough snowfall is present. What is sufficient? A storm total of 4 inches (10 centimeters) of fresh snow with enough wind can increase the danger dramatically. Twelve inches (30 centimeters) of new snow over 12 hours is not the same as 12 inches over four hours. The longer time gives the snow time to bond to the snow-pack surface, whereas shorter time doesn't allow for bonding.

Wind

The avalanche hazard can even increase during clear weather. How? Wind can transport snow from the windward side of the mountain to the leeward side, forming snow deposits called snow pillows or deposition zones (see figure 9.4). The deposition zone can be either concave or convex. An avalanche report may say that there is a northwesterly flow and a high hazard above tree line on southeasterly aspects. Moderate winds of 20 to 25 mph will pick up just enough

Table 9.2
Snow and Avalanche Conditions by Month

Month	Weather	Snow conditions	Avalanche conditions
October *April***	Hi T°: ↑ Freeze 0°C* Low T°: ↓Freeze 0°C	Snow-covered north aspects, bare south aspects	Small slabs on steep slopes at high elevations with north aspects. Increasing danger with new snow on old, hard summer snow
November *May*	Hi T°: ↑ Freeze 0°C Low T°: ↓Freeze 0°C	Shallow, weak snow cover; little snow below 10,000 feet	Depth hoar formation, small slabs and releases to ground
December *June*	Hi T°: ↓ Freeze 0°C Low T°: -18°C (0°F)	Shallow, weak snow cover; slabs near or above tree line	Depth hoar formation, hard slabs above tree line, slab releases to ground
January *July*	Same as December *Same as June*	Weak but increasing snow cover	Deep instability, slabs at all elevations
February *August*	Same as January *Same as July*	Increasing depth and strength, good coverage at all elevations	Large, deep releasing slabs early in the morning; sliding surface layers at month's end
March *September*	Hi T°: ↑ Freeze 0°C Low T°: ↓ Freeze 0°C	Increasing depth and strength, good coverage at all elevations, sun crust on south aspects	Avalanches confined to new snow; wet slabs below 9,000 feet on steep, rocky areas except north faces
April *October*	Hi T°: ↑ Freeze 0°C Low T°: 0°C	Maximum snow depth; corn snow on east, south, and west aspects	Dry, new snow avalanches; danger of wet snow avalanches increases in afternoon
May *November*	Hi T°: ↑ Freeze 0°C Low T°: ↑ Freeze 0°C	South aspects melt out; poor skiing below tree line, good skiing above tree line and on north-facing slopes	Cornice fall and wet snow slides
June *December*	Hi T°: ↑ 18°C Low T°: ↑ Freeze 0°C	No skiing below tree line, good skiing above tree line	Cornice fall; conditions stable except for fresh snow

*T = Temperature   **Southern latitudes shown in italics. Coastal areas may have more snow and lower temperatures.
In the second column, ↑ means "above" and ↓ means "below."
Reprinted, by permission, from Dale Atkins, CAIC (Colorado Avalanche Information Center).

Figure 9.4 Wind transporting snow from the windward to the leeward side of the mountain, where it "loads" the slope shown in figure 9.2.

snow to drop off on, or load, leeward slopes, which now become starting zones for an avalanche. Wind can actually transport more snow into leeward starting zones at rates higher than a storm! Higher winds can keep the snow suspended in the air long enough to push the starting zone farther down the leeward side of the mountain, increasing the hazard. Pay attention to wind forecasts even in clear but windy weather. Direction, speed, and duration are the most important components of wind and should be noted on a continual basis.

Temperature During the Storm

It is preferable that a storm start off with warmer temperatures than with colder temperatures. Warmer temperatures mean heavier snow that bonds better to old snow, improving the chances of bonding of new storm snow, resulting in lower avalanche hazard. A storm coming in cold and leaving warm will prevent snow from bonding to the snow pack and may not support the weight of new, denser storm snow. If there is wind during the storm, the sliding potential skyrockets!

Poststorm Conditions

The colder it stays after a storm, the longer it takes for the snow pack to stabilize. Cold weather keeps the snowflakes the way they were when they fell. That's dangerous. You want a nice, slow warm-up over 48 hours in which bonding can take place. At times it can actually get much colder *after* a storm (see chapter 7). This cold recrystallizes snow, causing a debonding action that increases avalanche potential on snow that was safer when it fell! Watch for very cold weather (below 20 degrees Fahrenheit or –7 degrees Celsius).

Conditions Between Storms

Look for the amount of sunshine and wind occurring with storms and between storms. The more wind, the more windslab development. Deep snow layers undergo evaporation and dehydration during periods of bright, sunny weather and become depth hoar crystals (weak and unstable snow crystals). If there has been a lack of snow for a few weeks (or months of summer) the snow pack will have a smooth, icy surface. Four to six inches (10 to 15 centimeters) of new snow will have nothing to anchor to, making for prime avalanche conditions.

Setting for an Avalanche

Besides weather influences, the natural characteristics of the environment can set the stage for avalanches. Rocky slopes affect avalanche formation differently than smooth, grassy slopes. During the summer hike into the areas you like to ski; you might start to see things differently.

Slope Ecology

The slope's appearance in the summer affects its ability to generate avalanches in the winter. While grassy slopes are obviously slick, rocky and bushy slopes generate air pockets that allow for deep, weak snow layers—these cause avalanches. A topographical map may show major avalanche chutes below tree line, but bushy areas may not be identified. Ask local forest rangers about the slopes on your route.

Above and Below Tree Line

Avalanches start more often above tree line than below it, but once started they can run into forested area. Dense trees mean safety, but widely spaced trees do not. Trees can hold clues to signs of past avalanche activity and future events. Look at the forested slopes around you for signs like vertical chutes and clearings that run down a hillside (see figure 9.5), or tree damage on the uphill sides of bigger trees. Clumps of snow in the tree branches and avalanche debris on the snow are signs of *very* recent avalanche activity.

Aspect of Slope

Aspect is the direction the slope faces. Northern slopes face north, for instance. During the winter, every aspect of a mountain is a possible avalanche slope. Three conditions influence avalanche potential on a given aspect: sun, wind, and temperature. Wind will amplify sun and temperature effects as slopes become loaded with snow, causing any slope to become dangerous. Always immediately recognize the aspect of each slope you encounter.

Figure 9.5   Look for distinctive avalanche chutes at and above tree line.

Prevailing Temperature and Time of Day

The use of the terms "cold" and "heat" in most avalanche texts can be confusing. Remember, snow does not exist above 32 degrees Fahrenheit (0 degrees Celsius). Any descriptions of temperature refer to temperatures *below* 32 degrees Fahrenheit. Both heat and cold are needed for the bonding of snow. Ironically, the same sun that melts snowflakes apart melts snowflakes together when coupled with cold temperatures. This is the thaw-freeze cycle. The snow pack is weaker when it's thawing (daytime) than when it's freezing (nighttime). With sunrise, the air temperature penetrates the snow pack, melting frozen bonds within the snow pack. Climbing slopes early in the day is preferable to late-day climbing due to increasing hazard with increasing daytime temperatures. With sunset and falling air temperatures, the snow pack starts to solidify again. This occurs after the afternoon avalanche cycle, which is amplified during the spring with the warmer season.

South and west faces are not necessarily more stable during the dead of winter in the cold Alpine environment. They may not stabilize due to the low temperatures prevalent at high altitude. South and west faces can be solid in the early morning but hazardous in the afternoon, especially after 2:00, *all winter.* There's a delayed reaction before the radiation can reach deeper levels of the snow pack, where delicately balanced weak snow can be waiting to be cut off, causing the snow above to slide.

The sun hits the east faces first, so ski eastern aspects before sunrise. Don't wait for the sun to get to them, when they will be more likely to slide. Avalanches are less likely to occur on slopes during the spring, when the snow pack is older and more stable. Plan your route to go from east to west if at all possible. The morning sun heats the eastern snow pack some, so you can climb on skis or on foot faster. For the descent, go down a west-facing slope that has warmed up and softened enough for skiing but not enough to cause slides. Start down before 10:00 A.M. so you are off the west exposures by noon. This ensures safety during the whole winter and spring. During spring conditions, snow may *pinwheel,* or cartwheel down south-facing slopes—an indication of snow-pack warming and increasing instability. Try to ski on less sun-exposed slopes (north-facing or other slopes in shade).

During winter there are more storms and more new powder snow, regardless of aspect. With prolonged cold temperatures, the powder is slow to bond and stabilize. This means that all aspects are prime for avalanche. It might be better to wait for more stable weather and less hazardous avalanche conditions. In the field, sudden storms mandate that you assume high hazard and avoid avalanche-prone slopes.

Field Testing for Avalanche Potential

The goal of snow testing is to determine the strength of the snow pack, which in turn indicates avalanche potential. Four information-rich tests should be carried out in order: slope-angle measurement, then three tests involving a snowpit—the snow hardness test, the shovel shear test, and finally the Rutschblock test. To make a forecast stronger, take a holistic view of your environment: the amount of new snow, prevailing daytime temperatures, and wind speed and direction.

Slope-Angle Measurement

Planning a ski route is a key element in avalanche avoidance. Avalanches commonly occur on slopes measuring between 30 and 45 degrees, but each snow is different. Wet, slushy snow with low strength and cohesion can slide at a relatively low angle of 15 degrees. On the upper end of the scale, powder snow usually can't stick to slopes greater than 45 degrees. There is less slab formation at higher angles, but a rare slide can occur at angles up to 60 degrees. Old, age-hardened summer "neve" snow that is similar in consistency to styrofoam is very stable at all angles.

There are five different ways to measure a slope: by using an inclinometer, a topographical map, your ski poles, your fingers, or a tree. Short of using engineering tools, these will be approximate measurements that will be useful and will help you build a slope-angle consciousness. These methods will appear in order of accuracy.

- **Topographical maps**—Using topographical maps with a map-angle conversion scale (Life-Link, Inc.) is the most accurate method available to the layman since these maps are made to such exacting standards. This method is more accurate than just looking at a map with the unaided eye, and it can tell you in advance about the angle of the slope that is on your route. The map-angle conversion scale measures the distance between contour lines, converting that distance into slope angle. Generally, the closer the lines are together, the steeper the slope.

• **Inclinometer**—Angles can be measured with a professionally-made inclinometer (Life-Link, Inc.). Find a nearby slope that resembles the slope you are studying. Inclinometers are usually laid down on the snow on top of a ski pole. Be careful to compensate for the poles' taper during measuring by aligning the pole with the rest of the slope. Some compasses have built-in inclinometers as well.

• **Ski poles**—Measuring slope angle with your ski poles can determine a 45-degree and 35-degree slope fairly well (see figure 9.6). Both poles must be the exact same length. Hold one pole as perfectly straight up as possible. Hold the second pole at a 90-degree angle to the first pole at the top of the ski pole grip. Where the slope meets the ski pole tip is 45 degrees. If you can move the horizontal ski pole one third of the way down the shaft until the tip meets the slope, the slope angle will measure about 35 degrees. These are the slope angles you want to avoid during periods of high avalanche hazard.

• **Fingers**—Another method is to frame the slope from a distance between your thumb and forefinger held at a 90-degree angle, as if to

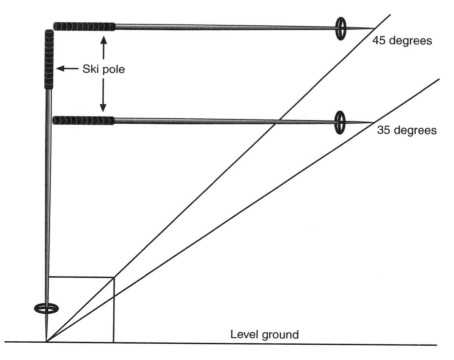

Figure 9.6   Determining slope angle using ski poles.

frame the slope in a photo. This gives only a very gross estimate measurement.

• **Trees**—Trees always grow exactly vertically unless disturbed. Deduce slope angle from determining the angle between a small tree and the slope.

Snowpit Testing

You'll need to dig a snowpit to perform the remaining three tests. The accuracy of a snowpit depends on how closely it resembles the slope to be skied. It should be on at least a 30-degree angle in an undisturbed area away from trees, rock outcrops, and other obstacles. Dig a square hole in the snow, about four feet (1.2 meters) deep. Square off the walls of the pit and make them as smooth and clean as possible. Probe the pit floor with your ski pole to determine whether weak layers exist under your feet. If so, dig another foot (.3 meters) deeper. The following tests should be done at three different sites for an average of readings. With practice, you'll be able to dig and test a pit within 15 minutes.

Snow Hardness Test

Resistance to penetration measures the density and strength of the snow-pack layer. The sharper the object needed for penetration, the stronger (and safer) the snow pack. Brush smooth the uphill side of the pit wall. Use your hands and fingers to penetrate the snow pack to test the hardness and strength of the layers in front of you (see table 9.3). Look for hollow gaps between layers or sugar snow falling out from between layers as you dig your pit. The more hard layers, the better. More weak layers means a weaker snow pack.

Snowflake shapes in new snow should always be observed. Depth and type of new snow indicate the extent of new snow sliding. The classic dendrite flake with six branches is seen during cold snow conditions. Light powder snow blows away in your hand and generally stresses the snow pack less than warm, heavy snow. Rimed snow crystals are snowflakes coated in ice—they are often formed in big storms where snow crystals collide with water droplets. This is also good slab snow.

Shovel Shear Test

Cut a block-shaped piece of snow at the top of your pit about a shovel-width square. Stick the blade of the shovel in the snow on the uphill side and pull the shovel straight toward you (see figure 9.7). The shear

Table 9.3

Snow Hardness Table

Snow texture	Penetration test	Possible snow type	Snow strength
Very soft	Fist	Powder, depth hoar	Less cohesive, weaker
Soft	Four fingers	Pack powder	↑
Medium	One finger	Soft slab	↕
Hard	Pencil	Hard slab	↓
Very hard	Knife	Hard slab, age-hardened snow	More cohesive, stronger

Snow strength increases by degrees.
©1993. Adapted with permission of the publisher from *The Avalanche Handbook* by David McClung and Peter Schaerer. The Mountaineers, Seattle, WA.

test should be done three times for an average of readings. Did the snowblock fall out as you stuck your shovel in? That's weak snow. The more effort you need to pull the snow out, the stronger the snow pack (see table 9.4).

Rutschblock Test

The shovel shear test is a good way to find weak snow layers, but it also is a poor way to judge the strength of those layers. A proven method of stability testing is the jump or Rutschblock test. Popular in Europe, it is gaining more acceptance in the United States. According to Dale Atkins of the Colorado Avalanche Information Center, the Rutschblock test is the best test of snow stability because the snow strength is directly stress tested with the weight of the skier.

You did your shear test, now dig out your pit so it's as wide as your skis along the uphill wall. Make parallel trenches parallel to the fall line going up from your pit (see figure 9.8). To isolate a block that is also as long and wide as your skis, take the rear of your ski and slice down as far as possible behind your block. Now for the fun part—put your skis on and carefully climb up until you are standing on the slope right above your block. Now gently step onto it. The block can fail immediately, sliding on a weak layer, or fail according to any of the levels presented in table 9.5. Dale says if he can jump hard on his block twice, it's "bombproof," meaning it's solid. The skier should perform

Figure 9.7 Performing the shovel shear test is a good way to get a preliminary feel for snow strength.

Table 9.4

Shovel Shear Test Results

Very easy	Snow column fails during cutting or insertion of shovel
Easy	Snow column fails with very low shovel pressure
Moderate	Snow column fails under moderate pressure
Hard	Snow column fails under firm, sustained pressure

Courtesy of Denny Hogan, Silverton Avalanche Center

Figure 9.8　The Rutschblock test uses body weight to test snow-pack strength (this snow pack failed).

Table 9.5

Rutschblock Test Results

Results of test	Hazard*
Block fails as you dig it or walk above it	Extreme
Block fails as you step onto it	Extreme
Block fails with sudden deep knee motion	Extreme
Block fails with one jump	Moderate
Block fails with two jumps	Moderate
Block fails with repeated jumping	Low
Block does not fail	Low

*See table 9.1 for description of hazards.
Courtesy of Dale Atkins, CAIC (Colorado Avalanche Information Center).

more than one Rutschblock test to get a representative testing of the snow pack, as one test site may not represent the ski slope exactly.

Ski Testing for Avalanche Potential

Some of us have felt snow settling with a noisy "whomp" as we skied across a meadow. Our weight has triggered the snow layers under us into collapsing. This is so-called "noisy snow." When this happens on a steeper and larger slope, an avalanche is a real possibility. When no other route is available, continuous ski testing during descent can provide some margin of safety. A ski-testing descent allows you to descend a slope and continuously check the slope for avalanche potential. If it does slide, you'll be above it instead of being trapped in it (although you can still get buried in an avalanche). Be sure your ski traverses are no more than 15 feet (4.6 meters) apart so that you test all the snow (see figure 9.9). Be particularly wary where the slope suddenly steepens, called the *transition point*, where gravity is most active on the snow.

Extremists may want to use a roped ski test to determine avalanche potential on steeper and narrower chutes. Testing should occur within a zone of suspected weak snow, just as the slope angles off. A strong

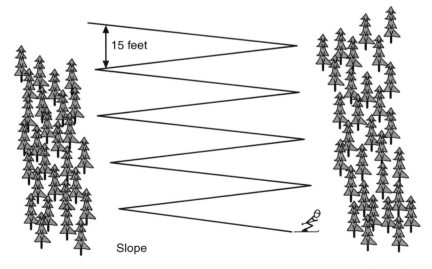

15 feet

Slope

Figure 9.9   When no other route is available, continuous ski testing during descent can provide some margin of safety.

belay stance is mandatory. If the slope fails, you will be holding not only the skier but all the snow falling on top of him! Stomp and jump on the snow, test and retest until you are convinced of its safety. If your skis don't penetrate the hard snow on a leeward slope, don't assume it's safe! It could be a hard slab waiting to release. Shooting cracks that form near your skis are a sure sign of instability.

Finding Safer Routes to Travel

It's much easier to ski around a suspected avalanche path than to try to second-guess nature. Why not just ski around it and get on with the tour? The following tips will cover several terrain conditions and how to navigate around them. Backcountry skiing is, above all, the adaptation to the precincts of nature.

Skiing as a Group

The killing radius of an avalanche includes not only the slope, but the runout pattern or zone of the slide. In dubious conditions, skiers should never ski above, below, or to the side of other skiers. Only one person should cross a suspected avalanche path at any one time. Never take rest breaks in runout zones.

Sometimes crossing huge areas one at a time is not practical due to the time it takes. In this case, ski at least half a football field apart. Always be aware of escape routes and islands of safety such as large trees or rock outcrops that may protect you from a slide. When you cross a chute or slope with evidence of sliding, move quickly while using these islands for protection. Angle your path downward to use gravity to speed your passage through heavy snow. Watch out for large avalanche debris that might cause a fall.

Look for Windrippled Snow

A good sign of slope stability is the presence of snow ripples, or *sastrugi* as they are called in Europe (see figure 9.10). This is a sign of ongoing snow compaction by the wind over a long period of time, and a strong snow pack is less likely to slide. However, rarer snow ripples sometimes do hide a hard windslab underneath them, which is dangerous. Usually, windripples over four inches high indicate safe (but possibly more difficult) skiing. If there is doubt, probe or ski test

Figure 9.10 Wind ripples may be a good sign of slope stability, but they can also hide a hard slab avalanche.

the slope—if it sounds hollow when you jump on it, there is probably a hard windslab underneath.

Beware of Old Ski Tracks and Established Avalanche Paths

Old ski tracks don't mean safety. There have been many cases where skiers have skied a slope one day without avalanche activity just to get caught in a slide on the same slope the following day! Wind may have loaded the slope overnight. Recent avalanche activity is telling you that there is a slide cycle taking place. Re-evaluate the snow pack each day for avalanche potential. Areas with past sliding histories should also be avoided during questionable conditions.

Use Short, Linked Turns

Smooth, short, linked turns will allow you to ski down the side of a suspected avalanche slope rather than all over it. This will disturb it less than wide turns (parallel or telemark). Wide turns will keep you traversing the danger zone too often. The less time you spend on the slope, the better; the less snow you disturb, the better.

Ski Straight Up or Climb Up on Foot

If you have to climb up a slope during low visibility and can't see the top, you can disturb less snow in hazardous conditions if you ski climb (see chapter 4, page 75) straight up along the edge of the potential slide area. This will limit snow-pack disturbance and doesn't affect the rest of the slope. You can often find a bare rocky shoulder to climb on foot that is parallel to the slope that you want to get up.

Bracket Your Run in Deep Powder

A large face should be suspected of being unstable during deep-powder conditions. Even hard-snow conditions (hard slabs) are inviting, but very dangerous. Bracket skiing allows for ski testing the slope while protecting other skiers from slides (see figure 9.11). The strongest skier (S1) should ski the outer edge of the run, while other skiers (S2

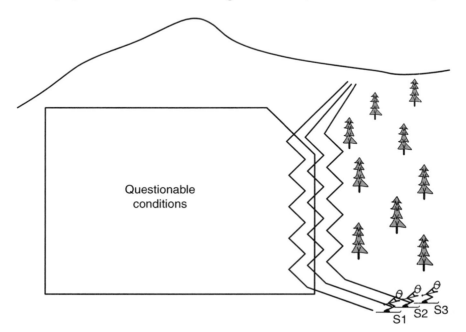

Questionable conditions

S1 S2 S3

Figure 9.11 Bracketing your run on wide open slopes provides some safety during questionable conditions.

and S3) stay within the area tested. If a slide does occur, all skiers should get as far in the trees as possible, find a tree, and hang on.

Take Ridge Routes

Snowy ridges and shoulders are excellent travel routes. Being alternately sun-drenched and wind-packed throughout the winter, they provide solid snow (though some may be bare dirt) that makes walking easy. You can often hike faster than you can ski, especially in shallow-snow conditions. Keep clear of any cornices, as fractures can occur far back from the edge of the cornice itself.

Avoid Cliffs and Crevassed Areas

Traversing above cliff areas should be done with great care at all times. Small avalanches can push you off a cliff into a creek or river gorge. If at all possible, reroute around such obstacles when mapping a ski route. Always go one person at a time. If need be, set up a fixed rope so that skiers can clip into the rope during the traverse or belay skiers one at a time. Crevasses form natural fracture zones for slides, which are then triggered by glacial movement. A slide could carry you into a crevasse if you are above it.

Skiing U- and V-Shaped Valleys

When skiing inside a U-shaped valley, stay to the far side of the valley away from the corniced ridge that is overhanging the valley. The leeward side (side facing away from the wind) of the valley holds the snowy deposition that could avalanche. The windward side (side facing the wind) can be quite wind-packed and relatively safe. Look for sastrugi (wind ripples) on windward faces signifying wind-packed snow.

Stay out of V-shaped valleys, canyons, and couloirs during questionable conditions on big mountains. They are natural skier eaters. If unavoidable, stay as high up as possible on the windward wall of the valley, using natural protection as you go.

Avalanche Safety Plan

The biggest problem in avalanche rescue is the speed of efforts relative to the short survival time of avalanche burial. Fast extrication and the maintenance of an air pocket around the face have both been shown to increase survival, as most deaths occur mainly due to suffocation. Skiers must be able to self-rescue quickly! Practice in finding buried beacons must be mandatory for backcountry skiers.

Avalanche Safety Equipment

Ask yourself three questions before heading out:

1. What are you going to do if you or the group gets caught in an avalanche?
2. How are you going to rescue yourself or the group if you do get caught?
3. Do you have the tools to get the job done effectively?

The following safety equipment is mandatory for ski touring parties headed for high-mountain tours during every season when extensive snow pack is present.

Avalanche Shovels

Avalanche debris is made up of very compacted snow, ice, dirt, and rock. You need a strong, large-blade shovel made of Lexan plastic or heavy aluminum. Lexan shovels (Life-Link) have been shown to be as strong as aluminum but lighter in weight. When stressed, Lexan flexes while metal cracks, resulting in a shovel that is not usable. Any shovel can break if used for prying rocks. Get a lightweight shovel as you will carry it always with little use (hopefully). Most shovels range from one to two pounds and can cost between $35 and $45.

Avalanche Cords

An avalanche cord is a 100-foot (30-meter) cord that trails behind the skier. It's colored bright red for visibility and marked with arrows pointing to the wearer. Tests have shown they work only 40 to 60 percent of the time. In fact, some have been found wrapped around the necks of buried victims. Don't rely on the cords—buy a transceiver!

Avalanche-Probe Ski Poles

Avalanche-probe ski poles are becoming very popular among off-trail skiers. The handles and baskets can be pulled off and the poles joined into one long probe pole.

Avalanche Transceivers (Beacons)

An avalanche transceiver or beacon beeps loudly when you are within range of a victim's device and more quietly when you going away from the victim. Swiss research has shown that one avalanche transceiver can search as fast as 490 people with probe poles! There are several brands available (figure 9.12 shows two). All use AA batteries and can last up to 300 hours. Most have three-year warranties and cost between $200 and $300. Modern beacons come with internal speakers and/or LED readouts that show signal strength. External speakers allow hands to be free from keeping an earplug in. But in noisy, high winds, an earpiece with an LED is very useful. Some have a visual battery level indicator. Wearing an avalanche transceiver doesn't mean you can ski avalanche slopes without getting hurt.

Transceiver Frequency

Everyone in a large ski party should be equipped with a personal beacon of the *same* frequency. Most of the beacons made today have essentially the same features. Practice has been shown to be the critical factor in search success. You need to develop an "ear" for the faint signals coming from your transceiver—this can save a life! In 1994, the International Commission for Alpine Research (ICAR) endorsed the 457 kHz frequency as an international standard. This extended the search range from a 50- to 70-meter (164- to 230-foot) area, versus the previous 20 meters (66 feet) possible with the old

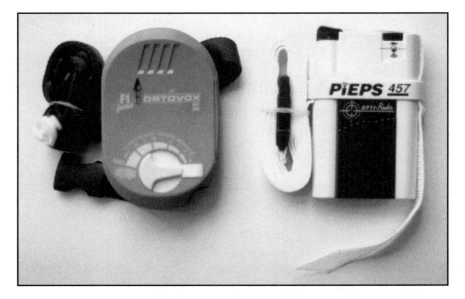

Figure 9.12 Avalanche beacons. From left: Ortovox and Pieps.

2.275 kHz transceivers. However, manufacturers recommend not exceeding 40 percent of those values (20 to 28 meters or 66 to 92 feet). Should people still use the old transceivers? Until you buy a new one, yes. An old transceiver is better than no transceiver. Remember that one transceiver won't work by itself—you need two to work. Dual-frequency transceivers are no longer made.

Optimum Working Conditions

For optimum working conditions, follow these rules:

1. The transmitter must be attached to the victim's body and not the pack, which might be thrown off during a slide.
2. The beacon should always be worn *under* clothing for maximum battery life. It should not be worn over the sternum, where it may cause injury during a crash.
3. The victim's transmitter must be turned on.
4. The batteries of all transceivers must be working. Always use fresh batteries.
5. The search must be done with volume controls turned up and not down for maximum reception.
6. All searchers must have their beacons turned on and switched to "receive."

AVALANCHE SAFETY

Before Crossing a Suspected Avalanche Path

These steps should be followed *before* skiing onto a slope of doubtful stability:

1. Plan your route for minimum exposure to danger by using natural protection.
2. Plan an escape route—spot a tree or a large rock you can grab onto if an avalanche starts. Keep your eye on these islands of safety.
3. Use the buddy system. Make sure your friend is watching your crossing so he can watch you if the slope slides.
4. Remove ski pole runaway straps so you can easily discard the poles if you are caught in a slide. Leave packs on.
5. Button up clothing. Put your hat on.

6. Be sure every beacon is on "transmit!"
7. Proceed without hesitation, one skier at a time, allowing only one skier to be in the danger zone at any given time. Ski more slowly if it means not falling. Falls *do* set off slides!
8. If everyone doesn't have a shovel, be sure people with shovels go last.

If You Are Caught in an Avalanche

1. Yell loudly and then close your mouth to keep snow out.
2. Follow your escape route if possible.
3. If you are knocked down, dump your equipment. Get rid of poles, pack, and skis!
4. Fight for your life! Use swimming motions to stay on top of the slide or go to the closest side of the slide.
5. Cover your face with your hands if burial is imminent so you can push the snow away from your face quickly before things stop moving to make an air pocket to breathe in. Your arms are no good to you if pinned to your sides.
6. Keep snow pocket walls scraped and free of ice. Your hot breath will cause the pocket to glaze over and the ice will seal it airtight.
7. Save your breath! Snow is a good transmitter of sound but outside noise may mask your yells.
8. Calm down and breathe slowly to use less oxygen.

If Other Skiers Are Caught in an Avalanche

1. Wait! Look up and listen! Are *you* safe from a secondary slide?
2. Mentally mark the point where you last saw the skier.
3. Turn transceiver to "receive." Do a quick search.
4. Search *below* the place you last saw the skier. Look for discarded equipment.
5. If you are the sole survivor, don't give up. Keep looking! Use a grid search pattern.
6. Let less-buried victims dig themselves out. Spend precious moments digging out completely buried victims.
7. Dig victims out carefully so you don't hit their faces with the sharp blade of your shovel. Keep digging until you find the victim, until you determine that the victim is completely unreachable due to obstruction by large ice blocks, or until avalanche danger is too great for you to stay with the victim.

Finding Victims

Avalanche rescue must take place efficiently and methodically. The first 15 minutes of burial are the most critical. After that time, survival potential goes down drastically. All efforts must be made to coordinate surviving skiers into a search team, regardless of weather conditions.

An avalanche will most likely carry a skier into the deposition zone where the slide comes to rest. Occasionally, it can deposit the skier in catchalls such as road cuts (see figure 9.13), bends, or trees. The victim could also be thrown free of the avalanche flow by gravity. In rare cases victims can escape and walk off in shock, not knowing what they are doing.

Search the area along a vertical line from the point where you last saw the victim to the final resting point of avalanche debris. Frame the search area into a box that can be methodically scanned for reception. Electromagnetic waves are best received when they are parallel to each other. This is why the rescue beacon should occasionally be slowly rotated in all directions at the initiation of searching to find the strongest signal. The strongest orientation should be maintained for

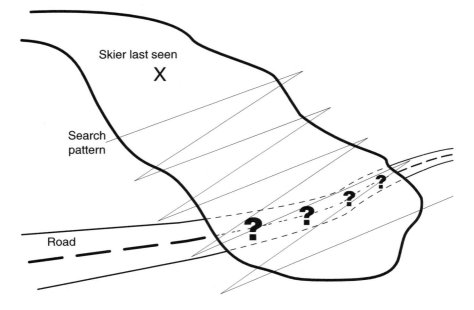

Figure 9.13 Avalanche snow flows like a river and may deposit a skier on any obstacle it encounters, such as a road.

the rest of the search. This becomes more critical the farther you are from the victim. Zero in on a weak signal by reducing the size of the search area while reducing beacon volume to make it more sensitive. Slow your movements immediately upon picking up a signal. The transmitting beacon should be within a six-foot (1.8-meter) square area. Once you have a stronger signal, "bracket" your scanning while further reducing beacon volume (see figure 9.14). Wind can make listening to beacon signals very difficult. Putting the earpiece inside your ski cap can minimize this problem to some extent.

You've probably seen pictures of a line of rescuers with long probe poles searching in avalanche debris. This is the probe search, which may be your only choice when searching for victims without beacons. Searches should form a tight line and make probes every 30 inches (76 centimeters). Probing should proceed in a methodical and disciplined manner. The victim could be in any body position, from standing straight up to a fetal position. Large accident scenes will have elaborate search-and-rescue management. In the typical small ski group, everyone searches and digs.

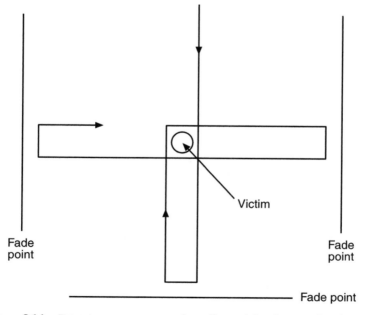

Figure 9.14   Decrease your search radius while decreasing beacon volume to increase your chances of success.

Avalanche First Aid

Turn the victim's beacon off in case other victims need to be found. Use first aid ABCs—Airway, Breathing, Circulation, Shock:

- **Airway**—Clear the mouth and nose of snow and dirt.
- **Breathing**—Check for a pulse. Begin CPR even while others are digging. If the victim starts to choke on debris, you may have to do the Heimlich maneuver by getting into the snow with her.
- **Circulation**—Bleeding should be stopped using direct pressure.
- **Shock**—Calling the victim's name immediately may save him from going into continued deep shock.

Keep the victim's head and neck from moving until the extent of injury is determined. Once stabilized, insulate the victim with extra clothing to protect against deepening shock and impending hypothermia and frostbite.

Going for Help

When you go for help, you are responsible for contacting the right people and for relaying sufficient information for a rescue. Telephone 9-1-1 to initiate an avalanche rescue. Mountain rescue or ski patrols will direct the rescue. As a survivor, you will accompany the rescue team to the site if you are physically able. This first rescue team is a "stage one" team that will assess the situation and administer immediate first aid. If more manpower is needed, a "stage two" team that is made up of more people and equipment will be sent. An avalanche dog may accompany either team.

Mark your route on retreat by breaking tree branches along your trail so you can find the site again. Mark the avalanche location on a topographic map with the words "avalanche accident" before leaving the scene, in case you pass out upon reaching civilization. Otherwise, you may accompany the rescue team by snowmobile or snowcat if helicopters can't be used due to bad weather or if there are delicate avalanche conditions where the wind force of the helicopter blades may cause additional slides. A rescue may be called off if avalanche danger is too high for rescuers or if a reasonable amount of time has passed with no success.

An avalanche warning sign on top of Berthoud Pass, Colorado.

Conclusion

In chapter 8 you saw how planning the route beforehand can help you avoid avalanche hazards. In this chapter we looked at understanding how weather and snow interact in building avalanche scenarios even on clear days! Skiers need to look at the total environmental picture. The topography of the surrounding mountains coupled with a knowledge of what is going on in the snow pack can give us clues as to the danger that may or may not lurk under our feet.

10

chapter

Backcountry Nutrition

Mealtime is a time to recharge physically and psychologically. Proper nutrition increases stamina and alertness, and therefore safety. Many athletes are confused about their nutritional needs, and skiers might not realize that nutrition for nonathletes is far different than that needed for the ultraendurance demands of backcountry skiing. While protein is finally getting some attention, carbohydrates still remain king of the nutritional ammunition available to skiers. Today's skiers should resist fads and build a solid and disciplined approach to nutrition.

Nutritional Demands of Skiers

The energy demands of AT or telemark skiers while climbing are identical. A 170-pound male skier with a 40-pound pack burns approximately 972 kilocalories per hour when climbing full-time. (Multiply, in kilograms, body weight plus pack weight by .17 kilocalories per kilogram to get a kilocalorie-per-minute rate). Including resting, and climbing only 60 percent of the time, the figure totals 3,498 kilocalories in a six-hour day. Factors such as skill level, slope angle, weather, and pack weight will further affect this figure. For comparison, a Tour de France cyclist may consume 6,000 kilocalories a day, while an Arctic skier may use 5,200 kilocalories a day.

Nutrition and Altitude

At altitude, nutrient absorption is not impaired, but the hunger sensation is dulled. Accompanying weight loss is often referred to as high-altitude anorexia. Even well-trained individuals may lose weight at altitude even though caloric intake remains the same as at sea level. This phenomenon may be caused by a combination of both neurological and biochemical imbalances due to reduced oxygen pressure at altitude. Physiologists consider any altitude changes exceeding 6,000 feet (1,829 meters) a physiological change in altitude. Any such gain can decrease the appetite for food and water between 40 to 60 percent of normal. Whatever the reasons, the bottom line is that you *need* to eat while at altitude even though you don't feel hungry.

Taking in fluids at the Fowler-Hilliard hut south of Vail, Colorado, in the southern Gore Range.

Planning Your Diet

A huge breakfast will make you feel heavy and sluggish and not ready for exercise. You can't eat all you need in three meals anyway. You have to eat like a bird, eating several minimeals spaced over the whole day (see table 10.1). The body can also absorb more nutrients from smaller meals than larger ones, because the body's blood flow is concentrated on the muscles during skiing rather than on the stomach. It's important to actually schedule food and water breaks ahead of time because altitude and exercise blunts your hunger and thirst.

Water

Water is essential. Hard exercise at altitude combined with dry mountain air increases moisture loss via breathing, speeding dehydration. This can result in decreased blood volume, reducing the delivery of glucose and oxygen to muscle and nerve tissue. Always prehydrate or hyperhydrate yourself with an extra 10 ounces of water before leaving camp. For a six-hour day, prepare two quarts of water (preferably mixed with a carbohydrate powder) and force feed water at a rate of 10 ounces per hour. Marking off your plastic quart bottle can help you keep track of water intake. Always use a wide-mouth water bottle. These allow you to pour melted snowwater into them much easier than a narrow-neck bottle. To keep liquids hot, bury your bottle in an insulated vest or jacket in your pack. You can make your

---

Table 10.1

Timing of Water and Food During a Six-Hour Ski Day

Time	Hour	Nutrient and Amount
8:00AM		Breakfast plus 16 oz. water (includes hot drinks)
9:00AM		Start of skiing
10:00AM	1	10 oz. water, 1 oz. GORP
11:00AM	2	10 oz. water, 1/2 athletic bar
12:00PM	3	10 oz. water, 1 oz. GORP
1:00PM	4	10 oz. water, 1 athletic bar (midday "lunch")
2:00PM	5	10 oz. water, 1/2 athletic bar
3:00PM	6	End of skiing, arrive in camp/hut—14 oz. water, 1 oz. GORP

---

own thermos by surrounding the bottle with pieces of half-inch ensolite foam surrounded by duct tape. New water bladders that fit on the pack work well, but can be difficult to fill unless you have a funnel—and the mouth hose can freeze in cold conditions. Do not carry water bottles on the outside of the pack. In the cold weather, they'll freeze solid.

Carrying more water has an additional cost: more water means more stove fuel to melt snow and thus more weight to carry. Each quart weighs 2.2 pounds (1 kilogram)—but you need it! Cold water has been shown to be absorbed faster by the body than hot liquids and doesn't cause side cramps as some think (fatigue does). On the trail, before you finish all the water, add clean snow to your water bottle to extend your supply. Although you can catch up on water intake in camp, drinking water on the trail reduces thirst; increases comfort; and maximizes muscular power, speed, and endurance. Once in camp, finish off the rest of the day's sports drink and drink 16 ounces of water if possible (hot chocolate and soups are included). This is when your body is in a state of glycogen depletion and at maximum readiness to accept carbohydrates for the next day. At night, keep water handy to quench thirst.

Sports Drinks

Water is fine for meeting your body's needs for exercise lasting less than 90 minutes, but not six to eight hours. It is a challenge to eat and drink as much as we should while skiing. Sports drinks may offer the answer by letting you drink your calories. For example, two quarts of Twin Labs Ultrafuel can give you 800 calories! Most athletic drinks of 6 to 7 percent carbohydrate are absorbed as quickly as water. Higher concentrations cause the body to actually draw water back into the stomach to dilute the fluid so it can be absorbed, making dehydration worse. To maximize absorption, some athletic drinks use glucose polymers so that higher carbohydrate concentrations (over 6 percent) can be consumed.

Sweat is 99 percent water, and electrolyte lost is insignificant in cold weather sports except in extreme expeditionary situations. Your sports drink should emphasize replacement of carbohydrates and water. Because electrolytes are so important they are conserved automatically by the body's defense systems. The main electrolytes of the body, sodium and potassium, actually increase in relative concentration because of dehydration during exercise. Because of this natural increase, salt tablets and potassium supplements should never be used—the normal diet provides adequate amounts of both (USRDA, Sodium = 500 mg/day, Potassium = 3,500 mg/day). Water is needed to reduce the electrolyte concentration so that the body can absorb them because electrolytes without water are unusable. Potassium deficiency is more likely to occur when a person has a disease involving vomiting and diarrhea (giardia, dysentery) where electrolytes and fluids are both lost in high amounts. Research by Costill (1982) has shown that a potassium deficiency is rare even with people who have large sweat losses and have a diet low in potassium. Supplemental potassium can also cause lethal heart rhythms. If you need a hot drink to warm up, hot chocolate is better than a salty soup since your body needs the carbos more than the salt. For the record, potassium can be found in dried fruits such as bananas and apricots.

Sugar and Exercise

People love to eat sweets in the backcountry, but it has a price. Sweet, sugary fruit juices have a high sugar (sucrose) content that slows stomach emptying and worsens dehydration. Dilute your fruit juices with plain water for better absorption. Sugary foods give you a quick boost of energy followed by a big crash and loss of energy. This is due to the large amount of insulin that is secreted into the bloodstream upon consumption of sugar, which supermetabolizes all the sugar in the bloodstream. Pancakes drenched in maple syrup and toaster pastries are not athletic foods. Honey is only part fructose (fruit sugar) and is mostly sucrose, like refined sugar. Better sources of fructose are athletic bars and drinks. Fructose has been shown to decrease insulin secretion and maintain stable blood glucose over a greater time. Eat complex carbohydrates and protein before exercise and save the candy bars for later.

Caffeine

Caffeine is a true ergogenic (work-enhancing) substance that has greater effect with moderate users than with heavy users. It increases athletic performance by increasing the metabolism of stored body fat for endurance. This in turn saves body glycogen (stored body sugar) for later use. It is a stimulant and mood elevator. Unfortunately, coffee and tea both cause dehydration while causing the same insulin reaction as refined sugar. Caffeinated soda also has a high concentration of sugar and should be avoided. A good practice is to drink one cup of water for every cup of coffee or tea consumed. Instant coffee or coffee bags are good, but for stronger coffee, bring a small filter. Don't overdo it. Drink one good cup instead of three bad cups. Add hot chocolate and sugar in moderation before exercise.

Alcohol

Alcoholic beverages should be consumed only in small amounts and only in camp or in the huts. Skiing drunk is as dangerous as driving drunk. European research has shown that alcohol consumption can increase susceptibility to mountain sickness by decreasing the breathing rate during sleep, thus reducing oxygen uptake at altitude. Alcohol also keeps us colder and dehydrated by dilating blood vessels, which increases evaporation of water out of the body. Alcohol is not a substitute for water in any circumstance!

Athletic Bars

The original athletic bar was probably Pemmican, which was developed in the early 1900s by Coman and Gutenko for the Byrd-Ellesworth Antarctic expeditions. People lived solely on this food for 154 days! Today, "Power Bars" have become so popular that we use the brand name to describe all athletic bars used for exercise. Athletic bars are fast, portable, and efficient. There are so many brands that you can take along several types just for variety. Try to taste-test them *before* a trip—some taste better than others. And remember, only a very few are soft to eat when cold. Extruded bars (Power Bars, Steel Bars) stay too solid to eat, while grain-based bars such as Cliff Bars are more palatable at lower temperatures. Keep the day's supply inside clothing to keep them soft. If you can't eat them, you can't use them. Although some are designed to deliver carbohydrates during exercise, others can also be used as a source of extra protein at main meals, especially at breakfast if you don't like oatmeal.

Proper Ratio of Carbohydrates, Fats, and Proteins

Carbohydrates do not operate in a vacuum—you need protein and fat as well! An old saying in exercise physiology is that carbs are the fuel

that keeps the fires of protein and fat going. While the 40-30-30 ratio has been getting a lot of press, it has yet to receive documented research support. A ratio of 60 percent carbs, 25 percent fat, and 15 percent protein has been proven on the Steger polar expeditions and on two 28-day traverses of the Colorado Haute Route (in which I participated). A 4,400-calorie diet can fit into a 1.5-pound package (figure 1.5 pounds per person per day). Table 10.2 was designed for a strenuous six-hour ski day but can be cut down to fit a smaller time period. To get the ratio, count the grams of each food type consumed. Convert them into calories respective of type and divide each by the total calorie count (carbos = 4 calories/gram; fat = 9 calories/gram; protein = 4 calories/gram). For instance, in table 10.2 there are 653 grams of carbohydrates. Multiply 653 by 4 and you get 2,612 calories. Divide the total calories by the diet total of 4,339 calories and you get 0.6019, which equals 60 percent. Carbohydrates provide 60 percent of the calories in this diet.

Table 10.2

Nutrition for a Six-Hour Ski Day for One Person

BREAKFAST

Item	Amount	CHO (g)	Fat(g)	Protein(g)
Granola Bar	1 bar (2.4 oz.)	32	8	4
Malt-O-Meal	1/3 cup	51	0	4
Dry Milk	1/4 cup	9	0	6
Butter	1 tbsp.	0	4	0
Sugar (brown)	2 tsp.	8	0	0
Walnut Pieces	1 oz.	3	16	7
Coffee/Tea	1 cup	0	0	0
Honey	1 tbsp.	14	0	0

TRAIL

Item	Amount	CHO (g)	Fat(g)	Protein(g)
Athletic Drink (Ultrafuel powder)	7 oz.	200	0	0
Peanut Gorp	3 oz.	52	27	15
Athletic Bars (Cliff Bars)	3 bars (7.2 oz.)	156	9	30

DINNER

Item	Amount	CHO (g)	Fat(g)	Protein(g)
Dehydrated Dinner	2 1/2 cups	80	25	50
Cheddar Cheese	3 oz.	0	27	21
Hot Chocolate	1 cup	23	2	1
Dry Milk	1/4 cup	9	0	6
Hard Chocolate	2 oz.	16	9	2
Amount (grams)		653g	127g	146g
Calories (kcal)		2,612kcal	1,143kcal	584kcal= 4,339kcal total
Percentages (this diet)		60% CHO	26% Fat	14% Protein
Steger Arctic Expeditions[1]		60%	25%	15%
U.S. Army Winter Rations[2]		58%	31%	11%
Everest Climbers[3]		57%	29%	14%

[1] Shaklee Corporation Research/International Arctic Project.

[2] Edwards, J.S.A., D.E. Roberts, and S.H. Mutter. 1992. Rations for use in a cold environment; *Journal of Wilderness Medicine* **3**: 27-47.

[3] Reynolds, R.D., J.A. Lickteig, M.P. Howard, and P.A. Deuster. 1998. Intakes of high fat and high carbohydrate foods by humans increased with exposure to increasing altitude during an expedition to Mt. Everest; *Journal of Nutrition* **128**: 50-55.

Carbohydrates

Despite fad diets to the contrary, research clearly supports carbohydrates as the best exercise nutrition. There are several reasons. Carbohydrates provide 4 calories per gram of carbohydrate consumed. Unlike protein and fat, our body's carbohydrate reserves can last only up to 13 hours, so we must take in new supplies. Carbohydrates provide quick energy and are the easiest to digest. Fat requires twice as much oxygen for metabolism as carbohydrates. This is important during both exercise and sleep. During exercise, blood and oxygen are shifted from the digestive system to the muscles, decreasing the body's ability to break down nutrients; during sleep at high altitude, the amount of oxygen saturation is already decreased, making carbohydrate digestion much easier for the body. Carbohydrate intake during exercise has been shown to maintain blood insulin levels necessary for the absorption of glucose by muscle. Research shows that the body relies more on blood glucose during altitude exposure and acclimatization. Carbohydrates have also been shown to reduce the symptoms of altitude sickness. In addition, on his polar expeditions Steger found that a high-carbohydrate diet increased multiday endurance both psychologically and physiologically. Using carbs also helps to "spare" fat so it can be used later during longer periods of exercise.

Carbohydrates (for example, whole-grain pasta and rice) should be eaten during main meals. How much carbohydrate is enough for best performance? Dr. Michael Colgan, in his book *Optimum Sports Nutrition,* states that a 165-pound individual should consume 70 to 90 grams of carbohydrates per hour over several hours of heavy exercise. Sports drinks and athletic bars need to be teamed together to meet the demand. Some athletic drinks like Ultrafuel can provide more than 25 grams per 8 ounces of water per hour (see table 10.3). New sports gels (usually made of maltodextrin) are like athletic bars in a tube and may be more digestible during exercise. Both athletic bars and gels should be accompanied by adequate hydration.

The best sources of carbohydrates are those that do not stimulate a big insulin response with blood sugar changes, specifically those that have low glycemic index. Examples of low-index foods are apples, oranges, lentils, sweet potatoes, whole-wheat pasta, brown oats, and rice. High-index foods such as glucose, honey, white pasta, raisins, and white flour should be used in moderation.

CARBO LOADING

Carbo loading can be done just before a ski tour for extra energy and endurance. As most marathoners know, the biggest cause of fatigue— "hitting the wall"—is the depletion of glycogen. Glycogen is the stored form of glucose, or blood sugar. Carbo loading provides extra glycogen storage that allows the athlete to work longer and harder.

Carbo loading involves eating a moderate level of carbohydrates (50 percent) for three days followed by a high-carbohydrate diet (70 percent) for three days before the ski tour while reducing workouts at the same time. This method normally increases glycogen stores by 85 percent.

Proteins

It is good to see protein getting more attention. Protein is second only to carbohydrates in importance as a fuel source. Protein provides 4 calories per gram consumed and is vital for endurance and tissue building and repair. Protein intake for moderate to hard skiing can average 1.2 to 1.6 grams per kilogram of body weight—about two times the RDA. Tour de France cyclists use 1.8 grams per kilogram! Proteins should be combined with carbohydrates for best utilization. Breakfast foods like oatmeal are very low in protein and should be replaced with Irish oats, muesli, or even an athletic bar (see table 10.3). Proteins ingested at breakfast will be metabolized with the carbohydrates taken in during the day's skiing. They should also be part of dinner as muscle and tissue repair takes place best during rest and sleep. Good protein sources are dried milk, cheese, dehydrated meat or fish, and nuts.

Fats

You don't need to consciously eat fat in the wilderness. There is plenty stored in our bodies and in the food we consume. The average person normally carries 30 to 40 days of fat stores already (nice to know if you get caught in a survival situation). Body fat keeps you warm as it is the primary fuel for sitting and sleeping, but don't overdo fat consumption. The Steger polar expeditions found that too much fat actually reduced endurance and caused stomach upset over time. Fat provides 9 calories per gram. It is best metabolized during exercise

Table 10.3

Food Sources for the Backcountry Skier

BREAKFAST ITEMS

Item	Quantity	Carbos(g)	Fat(g)	Protein(g)	Cals[1]
Malt-O-Meal	1/3 cup	51	0	4	260
Oatmeal—Instant	1 pouch	27	2	3	100
Irish Oats	1/3 cup	41	4.5	8	690
Health Valley Granola	2/3 cup	43	1	5	201
Wheaties	1 cup	24	1	3	150
Granola Bars	1 bar	32	8	4	210
Instant Breakfast	1 pouch	25	5	6	250
Breakfast Bars	1 bar	24	6	3	140
Butter	1 pat	0	4	0	35
Honey	1 tbsp.	17	0	0	65

(1) = "Cal" and "kcal" can be used interchangeably and mean the same thing

LUNCH ITEMS

Item	Carbos(g)	Fat(g)	Protein(g)	Cals	Weight(g)	Taste
Hard Chocolate	8	4.5	1	76.5	28.4	VG
Cliff Bar	52	2	4	250	68	VG
Power Bar	42	2.0	10	225	65	A
Steel Bar	68	4	16	368	85	VG
Mountain Lift	33	4.5	12	210	60	EXC
PR Iron Man (40-30-30)	24	7	17	230	56.8	G
Bear Valley	56	12	16	400	106	G
Peanut GORP	52	27	15	511	85	VG

(A = Acceptable, G = Good, VG = Very Good, EXC = Excellent)

DINNER ITEMS

Item	Quantity	Carbos(g)	Fat(g)	Protein(g)	Cals
Tortillas (whole wheat)	1	0	4	4	160
Pasta (whole wheat)	2 oz.	38	.5	10	190
Beans (black)	1 cup	41	1	15	225
Rice (brown)	1 cup	50	1	5	230
Bread (french)	2 oz.	26	0	4	120
Cheese (Cheddar)	1 oz.	0	9	7	109
Salami	1 oz.	0	10	6	120
Chili Mac [2]	20 oz.	77.5	17.5	30	600

Chicken a la King [2]	20 oz.	80	25	50	750
Chick Vegy [2]	20 oz.	87.5	11.2	32.5	575
Triscuits	6 wafers	20	4.5	3	130

(2) = Mountain House Dehydrated Dinners

LIQUIDS

Item	Quantity	Carbos(g)	Fat(g)	Protein(g)	Cals	Sodium(g)
Dry Milk	1/3 cup	12	0	8	80	12
Hot Chocolate	1 cup	23	2	1	110	140
Gatorade	8 oz.	15	0	0	60	NA
Ultrafuel (liquid)	8 oz.	25	0	0	100	0

when combined with carbohydrates. Fat can actually *increase* dehydration as it requires more water to digest.

As previously mentioned, fat requires too much oxygen for utilization and reduces oxygen availability to the body. However, fat is not all bad; in fact, fat metabolism provides the enzyme 2, 3-diphosphoglycerate (2, 3-DPG), which is necessary for maintaining oxygen delivery to muscle at altitude. Many skiers don't realize that while tasty, the traditional trail food GORP (Good Old Reliable Peanuts) is not a good athletic food because nuts and seeds are high in fat and are difficult to digest during exercise. Keep your GORP but try mixing in more carbs. Avoid saturated fats and try a mix of sesame sticks, dried apples, cranberries or blueberries, rice cakes, and chopped-up athletic bar. Or leave the fatty GORP at home and try an athletic bar instead!

Vitamins and Minerals

Most people don't eat a balanced diet of wholesome fresh fruits and vegetables, our best sources of vitamins and minerals. Dried fruits and dehyrated fruits and vegetables are readily available at most outdoor food retailers. When you're out skiing, the most convenient way to consume these important vitamins and minerals is to take vitamin supplements. Vitamins are the spark plugs that keep our metabolic engine working efficiently. Consider using a full-spectrum multivitamin with a high B-complex in addition to antioxidants such as Vitamins C and E. Some studies suggest that Vitamin E may reduce oxygen requirements of tissues, improve coronary circulation, and help prevent delayed-onset muscle soreness. It has been shown to increase $\dot{V}O_2$max at high altitude, up to 14 percent at 15,000 feet (4,572 meters). Women in particular should keep up their iron intake to maintain blood hemoglobin, which is responsible for carrying oxygen to muscles. See if your athletic bar includes vitamins and minerals in addition to proteins.

Considerations for Winter Camping

The food taken for a short day tour is much easier to prepare than the food needed for several days of snow camping or hut skiing. You can do a day tour with just a few athletic bars and a quart or two of water. Even fresh food can be taken if it's not freezing. Multiday tours demand more care in your selection of foods.

Fuel-Efficient Dehydrated Foods

Three things have to be balanced out in camping nutrition: fuel weight, food weight, and calories delivered. The more fuel used for cooking and making water, the more fuel that has to be carried—and carrying this weight will require expending more calories. Calories should be used for more important things—like skiing. Pick foods that need little fuel to cook. Pancakes and real (not instant) rice take lots of fuel to cook and should be reserved for hut skiing, along with the wine and steaks. Dehydrated soups and stews are excellent examples of fuel-efficient food. "Expanders" like potato flakes, couscous, and instant rice can be added to soups or dehydrated meals, making for a very filling and satisfying meal.

Fresh food is the best source of nutrition and is a good choice for hut trips, but it is rarely possible to use it during winter camping. Freezing temperatures destroy fresh fruits by bursting cellular walls. Many dehydrated foods are already available in your supermarket. Macaroni and cheese is an old favorite. Rice now comes in cooking pouches that can be cooked simultaneously when preparing water for another dehydrated dish. Dehydrated camping foods (even vegetarian ones) have come a long way since their introduction in the 1950s. Dehydrated foods retain all their natural nutrition while lacking only water. There are no long cooking times and no dishes—you can eat right out of the package the food came in. Both features save precious stove fuel, which means you have to carry less fuel (weight). Winter camping demands foods that allow for *in-tent* cooking—in other words, foods that can be prepared in a small space. Dehydrated foods also reduce food handling, with marginally clean hands reducing the chances of self-contamination and sickness. Typically, due to increased calorie demand, a summer meal for two turns into a winter meal for one.

Melting Snow for Water

Water in its liquid state is a precious commodity when found in a creek or river since it saves the substantial amount of fuel that you would ordinarily use just for turning snow into water—you can use your ski poles, some cord, and a wide-mouth quart bottle to fish for water without getting wet (see chapter 6 for creek precautions). Always use your largest pot to melt snow. The larger pot bottom exposes a greater surface area to flame and heat (see the equipment list for cooking kit supplies). Hand-pack the snow into the pan tightly. The more snow, the more water. Extra snow can be held in a backup pot to be added as snow melts. Always use a lid, even though it's snow! More heat is retained, less fuel is wasted, and more snow is melted. After melting the snow, place a paper coffee filter over your wide mouth quart bottle and pour the melt water in. This works great for removing debris from snow melt water.

Packing Food and Cutting Weight

Remember, if you can't fall on it don't bring it (even if you are going to a hut). Generally, tortillas or french bread rolls last longer than crackers! Glass is taboo. Wine should always be carried in plastic liquor flasks and, like everything else, packed into plastic storage bags. To save weight, try restaurant-size sugar packs for sweetener in place of honey. Get rid of excess packaging (see figure 10.1). Buy honey containers that have screw-on lids, not squeeze bottles, and bag them anyway! A pinhole in the dehydrated food bag will make the bag more compressible for packing. Cut back on the heavy stuff (peanut butter, tuna) that you can do without for a few days.

Trip Food Planning

When planning a trip, bring friends over for a map-reading and menu-making party. You can all get psyched for the trip and also find out what foods people want. Refer back to table 10.2, which gives a sample menu for a strenuous one-day tour. With that as a base, it's

Figure 10.1 Pack foods efficiently to keep them protected and reduce pack weight.

easy to make up a menu for a weekend and it's good practice for making menus for longer trips. Once you make up a five-day menu, you can just repeat it for longer ski tours. Use a day planner computer program to schedule meals if you're planning a long ski tour.

One idea is to let each person or couple be responsible for making one dinner for everyone. Utilizing dehydrated foods allows you to carry a variety of foods. Stick to simple, nutritious foods such as rice and noodles, and don't take foods you haven't tried. What tastes good at sea level may not taste so good at altitude because your hunger and thirst are dulled. Patience, imagination, and spices will allow you to find compromises for the varying tastes of the group. Spices (salt, pepper, chili powder, and so on) are important to help keep your meals more interesting. Store spices in plastic film canisters inside a plastic storage bag.

All foods should be bought before a ski tour. They are much cheaper at a large discount food or outdoor store than in a small town at the trailhead. Completing last-minute chores can be nerve-wracking, so try to get things done as far in advance as possible. You can buy dehydrated meals a week or more before the trip, as they stay usable almost indefinitely. Try different dehydrated foods purchased from a local shop. If you like them, look for them in a mail-order catalog, where you might get a better price.

Caches

On very long multiday tours, food caches may have to be preplaced. Ideally, your cache placement can be accessed within one round-trip ski day from a trailhead. The cache should be in a water- and animal-proof metal canister. Five-gallon plastic buckets with lids are also strong enough for this purpose. It should be double–duct-taped, sealed, and placed high in a tree to protect it from animals. Place the cache next to a prominent landmark so it can be found in bad weather. Mark the cache position on your map using UTM or latitude-longitude coordinates. A GPS reading would be helpful as well (see chapter 8). Take placement notes along with you on the tour to avoid any confusion due to fatigue.

Survival Food

Always be prepared for weather changes or navigational errors. Take an extra dehydrated dinner per person while on an extended ski tour (even a hut tour). Dehydrated dinners have minimal weight and don't occupy much space. At the very least, carry a few extra athletic bars in your daypack in case of an emergency.

Conclusion

We often overlook our nutrition during ski touring, thinking more about the status of our equipment and how it will make us ski faster or farther. However, without a good nutritional base that is designed for athletic stresses, our bodies may not cooperate. Olympic and professional athletes spend much time and money on designing the most up-to-date nutritional support for their activities. Like most athletes, backcountry skiers have their favorite foods that haven't changed in decades. It's time to reevaluate the foods we eat along with the amounts of water we should be drinking.

11
chapter

Hut Skiing and Winter Camping

The essence of backcountry skiing is the ability to be totally self-sufficient in the winter wilderness. This is where all of your skills come into play. If you can camp in the winter, you can camp anywhere. The quiet, the solitude, and the beauty are unequaled in all but a few sports. Winter camping can be some of the most fun you can have if you know what you are doing. Every year there are warmer sleeping bags, stronger tents, and more efficient stoves. But you still have to know how to use them!

Camping Equipment

Good winter camping and backpacking gear will provide years of warmth and comfort during your winter excursions. In this section we'll look at what equipment is needed and how to select it.

Backpacks

If the pack fits and carries enough, buy it! Backpacks can range in price from $200 to $300, and there are many quality brands to choose from (North Face, R.E.I., and Mountain Smith are a few). *Do* buy your

Skiing through Desolation Valley, Sierra Nevadas, California.

pack and other gear close to home in case you need advice or you need to return it. *Don't* buy gear on the road—you could get stuck! Always look for a good name and a lifetime warranty as a start. A pack of 3,000 cubic inches is good for overnight hut or camping trips, while one of 6,000 cubic inches is better for multiday expeditions. A smaller daypack of about 2,000 cubic inches should be big enough to carry a pair of ski boots, making it usable for spring ski tours where approaches on foot may be needed. A pack that is too small requires you to hang items from it, which can grab trees and throw you off-balance. A bigger pack gives you carrying options for the future. Fit your pack so that adjustment straps are only half tight. This allows for extra adjusting room later for additional clothing or if you gain weight!

Frameless packs are best used for skiing because they hug the body, minimize load shifting, and are less likely to snag on trees. Elaborate suspension systems allow the skier to custom-fit the backpack to the body. Side compression straps that prevent load movement are great for carrying skis. Women should investigate newer packs that offer narrower shoulder straps with hard-soft sandwich foams that cushion while maintaining strap shape, and that disperse weight more evenly over the collarbones with greater comfort.

Packs never seem to have enough pockets for sunblock, maps, cameras, headlamps, and other assorted gear. A water bottle (weight: 2.2 pounds per quart) doesn't have to be carried in the top flap. For skiing, carry it within the pack to maintain a lower center of gravity. Heavy bottles packed on top increase the tendency for the pack to push the skier over. At the sides, bottles get in the way of poling movements, and they can freeze in cold weather. Newer packs with water bladders carried within are a better idea. A top flap that can be detached for use as a waist bag is great for short trips out of base camp. An exterior avalanche shovel slot keeps your shovel handy and increases interior space. Otherwise, shovel handles can be carried behind side compression straps while the blade can be carried within the pack up against the back. Some sleeping bag compartments with a zipper at the bottom of the pack also act like a compression sack—a big plus for handling larger winter bags. Additionally, a thick-padded hip belt and a sternum strap—both with fast-release buckles—keep the pack firmly attached to the body during skiing. A lumbar pad on the lower back protects the back from sharp items in the pack and minimizes pack shifting.

Fitting the Pack

Many shops provide sandbags for weight so that adjustments can be made professionally. There are usually two aluminum stays, or frame pieces, in the pack, which can be molded to the back's contours.

Several straps are used to adjust for the ride of the pack on the back. Upper straps pull the pack higher on the back, while the lower straps shorten the arm loops, lifting the pack up off the hips. Weight on the hip joints can get uncomfortable. Alternate the weight between your hips and shoulders during the day to reduce pressure pain at these points. Large pull loops on all adjusting straps make tightening and loosening with heavy gloves or mittens easier. Before skiing down, tighten exterior compression straps to eliminate load shift. The pack should be almost too tight on your back so it feels like it's part of it. With practice, the pack can actually help your skiing by amplifying turning efforts.

Pack Weight

We would all like lighter packs. But how much weight is too much? A general rule is that a pack's weight shouldn't exceed 25 percent of body weight. For my 170 pounds, that's a comfortable 42.5 pounds. A woman weighing 110 pounds shouldn't have a pack weighing over

27.5 pounds. This is just a general rule based on years of observation, but there will be exceptions. In a group, heavier weight should be given to the fittest and strongest people because they can probably handle the weight more easily. With comfortable pack weights, people ski longer and stronger and have more fun.

People used to think that they could save weight by sawing their toothbrushes in half. This is cute, but a toothbrush is not the problem. In the winter you need more clothing, food, and fuel. Table 11.1 shows several weighty items of interest with some possible substitutes. When packing, match the center of gravity of the pack with that of the body. Heavy items (water, fuel bottles) can be placed in the main body, not the top flap. The sleeping bag can go on the bottom, while middle-weight items can be packed in the middle of the pack (see figure 11.1). Use several compression bags to minimize volume! By compressing bulky clothes and sleeping bags into a tighter load, you reduce outward centrifugal load shifting during skiing (which can throw you off-balance), and your pack will feel lighter.

Separate gear by category into separate *waterproof* nylon stuff sacks of different colors, which are easier to find in the darkness of your pack and safer from water and stove fuel leakage. Use heavyweight freezer storage bags to hold smaller items like a compass, maps, toiletries, and such. These bags are nice because you can see what's inside them, and they're reusable and recyclable. For packing out trash, use several smaller bags instead of larger garbage bags since they can be packed tighter and damage from any breaks will be isolated.

Sleds

Sleds can be good for hauling food and equipment as long you don't have to do much traversing, where you'll need someone in the rear to tether the sled so it doesn't slide downhill. It can be excellent for carrying kids and gear to a hut for the family who wants to ski together. Store-bought sleds can range in price from $150 to $400—because of their cost, many stores rent them. Homemade sleds can be constructed using a child's toy sled, but usually the plastic is not durable enough for backcountry use.

Tents

Most modern tents are double-walled, modified dome tents with independent free-standing frames. The modern dome tent design shown in figure 11.2 was originally modeled after the aerodynamic

Table 11.1

Cutting Weight During Winter Camping

Water	One quart of water weighs 2.5 lb. Take one bottle but add snow consistently to supplement your reserve.
Camera	Use a small travel camera or a throwaway camera—they take better pictures than you'd think.
Food	Use dehydrated foods made for camping. Stay away from canned foods and foods packed in glass; always transfer these and any boxed goods (with cooking in-formation) into plastic baggies, and poke pinholes into dehydrated food bags to reduce air volume and bulk. Remember that cheese and peanut butter are luxuries.
Reading	Xerox all route descriptions instead of taking the whole book. If you need to read, get a used paperback and cut it in half to reduce bulk.
Water pump	Use purification tablets.
Tools	A small pair of pliers is lighter than a composite tool (Leatherman, etc.), and you already have a knife.
Clothing	Polypropylene underwear is lighter than wool.
Sleeping pad	Use Ensolite instead of a Thermorest.
Bulky clothing	Use compression bags.

Mongolian yurt. The shape is spacious and extremely stable in high winds. The tent fly protects the tent body from snow, wind, and flying debris. A fly should fit taut around the tent body and extend to the ground, holding in heat and keeping out wind. A flapping tent fly makes sleep impossible, which can make for a very tiring next day. The fly should have multiple tie-ins for guy line installation. Single-wall Gore-Tex tents are warmer and lighter, but they're also less spacious. Both inner and outer tent fabrics should be kept uniformly taut so as not to stress any one seam. Add nylon loops to tent edge stake-down points if you want to use wider skis for anchors.

A ceiling vent is a good feature, allowing for the evaporation of moisture from snow and sweat. Additional ventilation is possible by leaving door zippers open a few inches. Get a tent with a large vestibule where you can cook and stow gear (outer boots and packs). Using an interior floor cover such as a space blanket can protect the floor from boots and fuel. Exterior ground "footprint" tarps are needed only in rocky or muddy conditions. Tents come in sizes that can hold two to eight people and can range in price from $200 to $1,000.

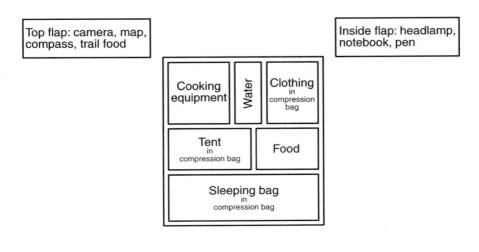

Top flap: camera, map, compass, trail food

Inside flap: headlamp, notebook, pen

Cooking equipment	Water	Clothing in compression bag
Tent in compression bag		Food
Sleeping bag in compression bag		

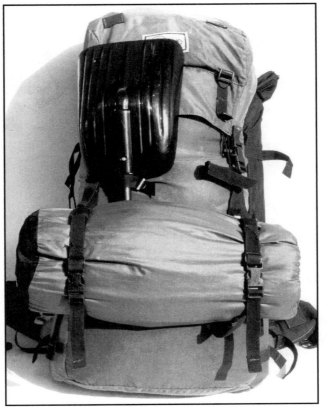

Figure 11.1 A properly loaded ski pack means less load shifting and easier skiing.

Figure 11.2 North Face VE-25 dome tent. Notice how the ski bottoms face inward so the tent guy lines won't be cut by ski edges.

It's better to get a bigger tent to accommodate winter equipment—two people will fit more comfortably in a three-person tent. Clean your tent using the same washing methods as your sleeping bags (see page 227).

Tent Color

Some tents are so dark you can't see inside them! In the 1970s, Murray Pletz of JanSport was the first to recognize the positive psychological properties of the bright colors now used in most expedition tents. Bright colors lift the spirits and have been shown to aid recuperation and rest. Bright tents provide internal illumination, saving precious battery and candle reserves. Finally, bright yellow tents stand out from the ground or air, which is important for finding your tent in whiteout conditions. Unfortunately, many tentmakers ignore these concepts. Some tentmakers even make white tents!

Tent Poles

Lightweight aircraft aluminum poles are the strongest and lightest available. Pole sets are usually shock corded so they snap together. Replace damaged shock cord yourself using 4 mm shock cord. If metal or fiberglass poles don't slide easily together, lubricate them with a little silicon spray. Be sure that all the tent poles are there before each trip! Tent poles either fit into tent pole sleeves or are clipped onto the tent. Both designs are equally rigid in high winds, but clip-ons allow faster setup and takedown in windy conditions. With sleeve designs, poles can actually freeze to the pole sleeve in harsh conditions. Always *push* poles through tent pole sleeves to prevent poles from disconnecting. Attach the tent pole bag to your pack so it can't get lost.

Pyramids

Pyramid tents are another tent option—they have no floors, which makes them lighter to carry. This also makes them safer for using liquid-fueled stoves because there's no floor to catch fire and you have a higher roof. Because heat rises to the tent's peak, they are best used for warmer spring touring. They also take additional time to set up because their structure relies on one center pole and multiple snow anchors along each edge. Snow blocks used to anchor the edges should be sloped to help snow slide right off (see figure 11.3).

Tent Rigging

No tent is strong if it is not placed and secured properly. External guy lines using 8 feet (2.5 meters) of 4 mm Perlon accessory cord should be installed at all recommended locations. Always use black or brightly colored cord, as white cord will blend into the snow and trip you up. In high winds, internal guy lines can be installed to increase tent strength by 30 percent. Kits for these are sold commercially. Tying punge cord around tent pole intersections can also increase tent rigidity. Remember that round cordage resists knot freezing and that flat-type lacing is much harder to handle with mittens. Use guy line tighteners that can be adjusted easily. Always install large 16-inch (41-centimeter) by 4 mm Perlon zipper pulls. This makes entering and exiting the tent much easier, especially late at night when you are half asleep!

There are several types of anchors you can use while snow camping. If you are making base camp and using your skis daily, which eliminates using them an anchors, lightweight snow stakes or deadman anchors work well. At night use skis, shovels, ski poles, or

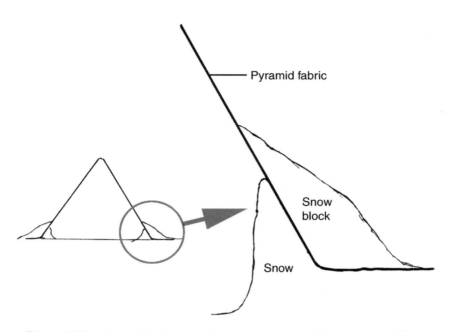

Figure 11.3   Snow blocks used to anchor pyramid tents should be sloped to allow snow to slide off.

ice axes, for example. Never take avalanche ski poles apart in an effort to use each piece as an anchor, because they will freeze in place, making removal difficult. Bury ski poles whole horizontally with the guyline looped around the center of the pole. Deadman anchors rely on their shape and the depth you bury them for strength. Several one-gallon nylon stuff sacks can be filled with snow and buried (like a "deadman") to make great tent anchors. Add a small, metal S hook to the drawstring so you are able to attach guylines easier. Bury a log or a big piece of ice as a deadman instead of a ski pole. Get creative!

When breaking camp, zip tent doors closed in windy conditions to prevent ballooning. Release tent poles at corners to flatten the tent before doing anything else, making it easier to handle in windy conditions. Throw out the factory storage sacks that came with your tent and stuff your tent into two compression sacks instead (one for the tent body and one for the tent fly). One person can carry the tent poles and tent fly while another carries the tent body. Use same-colored compression sacks and pole bags so they are not confused with other tents if you have more than one tent.

Sleeping Bags

Put your money into your sleeping system. Your sleeping bag is where your mental and physical energies recuperate for the next day. If you don't sleep well, you don't ski well.

Warmth

While you can get away with a 20-degree Fahrenheit (–7 degrees Celsius) bag for hut touring, a –20-degree Fahrenheit (–29 degrees Celsius) bag is recommended for snow camping. There is no industry-wide standard for rating sleeping bag temperature ranges. One company's –20 bag can be different from another –20 bag. To complicate matters, some people sleep colder than others. If you're the type of person who uses an electric blanket at home, buy a –20 bag! It might be heavier, but you'll be warmer and happier in the long run. Get a long bag so that you can warm and dry your inner ski boots at the bottom of the sleeping bag while you sleep (put them in a stuff sack first to keep your bag dry). Winter bags must have a good hood and draft tube running the length of the bag to keep out drafts. Get a bag with double zippers so you can vent your feet if you get too warm. Winter bags have a narrower cut to minimize internal convection currents, resulting in increased warmth. At the store, try the bag and see if zippers are free pulling and not snagging on excess material, and get a product with a lifetime warranty and a good return policy.

A clean bag is a warm bag. Always store your down or synthetic bag in a cotton storage sack so that the bag can dry thoroughly. Follow manufacturer's cleaning instructions. Tumble-drying a sleeping bag with a tennis shoe is an old idea that can ruin the loft of the down.

Sleeping Bag Materials

Nylon, often in combination with a Gore-Tex–type membrane, is used as an outer shell in all winter-rated sleeping bags. Softer inner liners have been developed that mimic silk and make sleeping more comfortable. Different insulating materials should be chosen accord-ing to the temperature range and compressibility characteristics desired.

• **Goose down**—Down weighs less than Polarguard, is more compressible and warmer by weight, and some say it lasts longer. Down feathers come in different quality levels and fill densities (see chapter 1). Down is a better investment if it comes built in a Gore-Tex

DryLoft shell that protects the down from snow, water, and spilled drinks.

- **Polarguard**—Goose down loses all its insulating properties when wet. This is not a problem in drier continental climates, but it can be in humid maritime climates. Polarguard is a better choice and is often used by Arctic explorers. Polarguard is a continuous filament from the bottom to the top of the bag. It is cheaper, easier to clean, insulates when wet, and lasts forever. New variations on Polarguard such as HV (High Void) and 3D are lighter and more compressible.

Sleeping Pad

The sleeping pad increases comfort and is an important part of the sleeping bag equation. Insulated pads that self-inflate are great, but heavier than a plain Ensolite foam pad. Blowing air into the mattress introduces moisture, so it's important to air out the pad by leaving it laid out at home with the valve open. Carry your pad in a stuff sack to protect it from sharp objects. Use ice axe tip covers to protect your pad from damage if carried on the outside. Noninflatables like Ensolite and Ridge Rest are lightweight and insulate against the cold quite well.

Inner and Outer Bags

Sleeping in layers extends the temperature range of your sleeping bag. Since –20 bags are expensive, try to add a pile fleece liner with a full-length zipper inside a summer down or Polarguard bag. Don't forget to use a compression bag to reduce volume. An outer shell like a Gore-Tex bivouac sack adds several degrees to your bag and functions as a high-performance emergency shelter. Vapor barrier inner bags prevent the loss of body heat and moisture, keeping the sleeping bag dry to minimize further body dehydration while retaining body heat. Though good in theory, the popular market has not endorsed this idea.

Change Your Clothing

Avoid wearing your ski clothes to bed. Your body is covered with a thin layer of sweat, no matter how dry you feel. For maximum warmth, always put on *dry* underwear. One strategy when snow camping or hut skiing is to rotate two sets of underwear and socks at bedtime (expedition- or medium-weight, depending on the season). The next morning, don't change. The underwear just changes roles. Sleep with a polar fleece balaclava for increased warmth matched up with a polar fleece pillow cover stuffed with clothes.

© Brian Litz

Skiers approach the Peter Estin hut in the Tenth Mountain Division Hut System near the Elk Mountains, south of Aspen, Colorado.

Stoves

Stove manufacturers recommend that you don't cook in your tent. Having said that, let me also say that I have cooked inside my tent for 30 years without incident. Alpine climbers cook inside their tents all the time. Tent fires are extremely rare and are a result of total negligence. During winter camping, indoor cooking—either in the tent or tent vestibule—is a necessity. High winds and blizzard conditions make it mandatory that you know how to cook inside.

Stoves allow you to conserve natural resources and stay warmer in an efficient manner.

Cooking inside the tent requires patience and coordination. Use a piece of Ensolite pad to insulate the stove against the snow and maximize fuel efficiency. To reduce the chance of stove flare-ups, open up the valve once to let off excess pressure before lighting. Then light your match or lighter *before* you open the stove valve to light it. Always light the stove at the lowest setting with a pot on the stove. In case of flare-up, the flame will go outward instead of upward and won't burn the roof. Flare-ups last only a second so don't panic—just turn the stove off and try again.

There are two basic types of stoves: those using pressurized cartridges and those using liquid fuel. Each has good and bad features. Each should be maintained according to manufacturer's specifications for safe, efficient performance. Practice using them at home before taking them on a trip.

• **Liquid fuel stoves**—Liquid fuel stoves are usually hotter than cartridge stoves but require a lot more care, as you need to pump and prime them. This sometimes results in getting fuel on your hands and tent, so they are best used in the tent's vestibule. Fuel bottles have been known to leak fuel while inside packs, soaking clothes and sleeping bags. Regardless of the drawbacks, many prefer these stoves, which can often use different fuels such as white gas or kerosene. These stoves are great for groups for whom larger meals must be prepared. In this situation, a cooking tent may be invaluable to isolate cooking in one area.

• **Cartridge stoves**—Many mistakenly think that these stoves are not cold-weather or high-altitude stoves; however, they've been the stove of choice for Himalayan climbers for decades. The higher they go, the more powerful they get. Cartridge stoves (Bleuet and Primus are two brands) don't require pumping or priming—you just turn them on (see figure 11.4). Newer fuel mixtures of butane and propane don't need prewarming in a sleeping bag, but it doesn't hurt to prewarm them, and it actually increases their efficiency. Start new cartridges in the vestibule to be sure that all connections are tight. If something does happen, you can throw the whole thing out the door. Some models hang from the roof of the tent, providing more living room but requiring additional finesse in handling. Newer fuel cartridges are self-sealing, preventing leakage. The only drawbacks are that cartridges are more expensive than liquid fuel, and the tanks do take up pack room and must be packed out after use. Cartridges are becoming more environmentally friendly now that more recycling programs are accepting them.

Utensils

For snow camping, two people can use a one-quart pot kit for cooking *and* eating, while a two-quart pot can come in handy for melting snow. Plain aluminum pots are lighter than stainless steel, but Teflon coatings do make clean-up easier. Stove, utensils, kitchen cloth, and lighter can all nest together into one cooking pot, which can fit into one stuff sack. Don't use metal cups, which burn fingers and spill easily. Insulated commuter-style drinking mugs reduce the need to reheat liquids, saving stove fuel, and a no-spill lid prevents messes. Inside a tent every move is amplified, another reason to have a water resistant sleeping bag. Lexan spoons, knives, and forks are lightweight and keep your Swiss army knife cleaner. To conserve fuel, measure what water you need before boiling a whole pot.

Figure 11.4   With care, a cartridge stove can easily be used in a tent.

Headlamps

A good headlamp with both a narrow and wide beam is a must for night travel, rescue signaling, or just plain cooking. It must be able to operate in low temperatures. A lamp using standard AA batteries (especially rechargeable batteries) should have a battery pack that is worn inside the clothing for use in very cold conditions. If the battery pack is worn on the head, use lithium batteries to prevent cold degradation in extreme conditions. Rechargeable batteries don't last long in the cold. Always test your batteries before leaving the house and bring backup batteries and bulbs (both high- and low-intensity) for emergency use. Lithium batteries are very reliable in extreme cold and have unlimited shelf life. A standard AA bulb works fine for daily chores, lasts longer, and saves money over halogen or krypton bulbs. For minimalists, a small flashlight (Techna) can be worn on the side of the head. A small hanging tent light can be valuable while preparing meals. Use the same size batteries for all electrical appliances for maximum interchangeability. Place a piece of duct tape over on-off switches to prevent accidental activation while in a pack. Headlamps can range from $10 to $70, and lithium batteries can cost $2 to $20 each.

Placing Your Camp

Always establish camp before you have to. Don't wait for darkness to make camp! The ideal campsite would be right at the tree line. This way you could have a great spot to make camp while taking advantage of the treeless bowls above for skiing. This ultimate campsite would of course be on a level spot, next to a creek in a sheltered wooded area, with no overhanging branches laden with snow that might come down in the night. This ideal campsite would also be at the eastern edge of the forest so that when the sun came up your tent would get the first rays of the sun. But often we cannot find such an ideal location.

Camping Below Tree Line

Of course, in a storm, camping below tree line is always preferred. Get into a thick grove of trees to protect the tent from violent winds. A small opening within a thick grove of trees is ideal. Don't camp

DIGGING A SNOWPIT

If you are caught above tree line, you can dig a shallow pit to place your tent in and with the displaced snow build a circular mound of snow around the pit to block driving wind. The harder the wind, the deeper the pit. Most open snowfields are cleaned of loose snow by the constant winds, so your snowpit won't get buried with too much blowing "spindrift" snow unless it is snowing very heavily. But I'd rather dig out the snow occasionally during the night than deal with the wind. Burying tent edges with snow prevents the tent from being lifted off the ground in high wind as well.

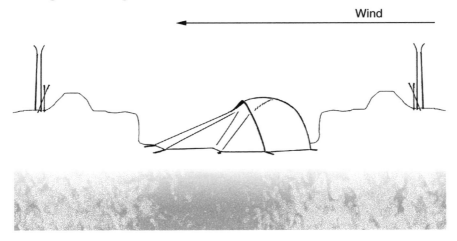

Wind

underneath trees that hold large snow deposits. These can get big enough to destroy a tent. Look out for dead trees hanging within live ones ("deadfall") that can fall suddenly in a windstorm. Don't camp below rock walls as there's always danger from falling snow or rock.

Camping Above Tree Line

Although the views are great above tree line, camping can be more complicated. In leeward areas snow is carried over from the windward side, increasing avalanche hazard. Wind is your enemy. On the windward side your camp may be buffeted by high winds. Wind is worse than snow because it works on a tent by loosening guy lines, weakening your tent, and keeping you awake. Snow is the better choice since it can partially bury a winter tent, acting to insulate it.

Look for evidence of past or present avalanche activity on the slopes above you. Always ask, "What will happen if it does slide?"

Setting Up Camp

You're stopped for the night and the temperature is dropping fast. You've exercised hard, so put on extra clothing to stay warm. Practice putting up your tent at home before you go camping. Try to put it up quickly with your gloves on. It's not easy, but it can be done. Handling tent wands with tight glove liners is easier.

There are several steps in setting up your camp at the end of a long ski day. Once you have found a level spot, repeatedly ski pack and boot pack the area into a sleeping platform. The entrance should be facing opposite the prevailing wind. Pack out a four-foot (1.2-meter) square area in front of the door so that when you go outside to relieve yourself you won't fall waist deep in snow. Dust as much snow off your clothing as possible before entering the tent. This keeps the floor and your sleeping bags drier. A space blanket on the tent floor protects the floor from wear and tear. Sleeping pads and bags go down next. Put your extra gear against the walls of the tent to keep cold tent walls from touching your sleeping bag, thus keeping it dryer. Have your feet pointing toward the entrance so you can get out more easily.

Before coming in, pack your cooking pots with snow for water. Take your boots off outside the tent and put on camp booties to prevent snow from entering the tent. Get into your sleeping bag and change into a dry set of underwear. Drink some cold water, followed by a warm drink (hot chocolate or soup)—this begins carbo loading for the next day. Your body is most receptive to carbs at this time. With practice you can be warm inside your tent within 30 minutes after stopping!

After dinner, you may want to study your maps or do some reading. Use a headlamp, since candles and oil lanterns use large amounts of oxygen, drip wax or fuel, get in the way, and generally make a mess. Carry extra batteries and forgo the romantic ambience. If you need a candle, keep your tent ventilated and use plumber's candles, which burn cleaner and longer. As you read, melt more snow to fill up your water bottles for the next morning and for drinking during the night. Hot water bottles placed inside your sleeping bag can increase your warmth immediately and will prevent their freezing overnight—plus, the extra warmth feels great! Place your boot liners inside your bag as well so they are warm for the morning ski. Place cooking pots and stoves where you won't bang into them if you roll over while sleeping. Remember—a neat tent is a happy tent!

Before turning in, walk outside one more time. Check guy lines to see that they are tight so you won't have to get up later to do it. If it's snowing, check to see that snow is not overloading the tent roof unevenly. Give your inflatable mattress a few more breaths since the cold has probably condensed the air inside. Keep your headlamp and toilet paper right at your head so as not to disturb campmates if you need to get up.

Hygiene While Camping

A small hand towel works well for drying dishes after being used as a hot pad during meals. It fits into your pot and pan, keeping the contents from banging around. If you use dehydrated foods that can be prepared and eaten in their packages, there is not much dishwashing. Scrape excess food remnants with a knife or fork and bury the biodegradable scraps in the snow, away from your tent so as not to attract animals. Add a bit more water and swish out the remaining food. Alcohol wipes work great to cut grease. Wipe clean with your towel.

A clean body is a warmer body. Minute body hairs keep the body warmer if the hair has loft (dead air space) itself—but if you are dirty, the dirt will occupy the dead air space, thus keeping you colder. You can do the whole job with a full-size face towel, a small plastic bottle of biodegradable peppermint soap, and about two cups of hot water (alcohol wipes also work here). A travel-size bottle of deodorant is nice to have as well.

Another question is of course: How do you go to the bathroom out there? During the day it's not a problem. But at night you'll be happy to have installed large zipper pulls on your tent doors and clothing. That way you can do things while half asleep! Once outside, get at least 25 feet (8 meters) away from the tent and away from all water sources. Dig a deep hole, even if it is only snow, for human waste so that it will decompose more quickly, and *always* carry toilet paper out with you. Paper kitchen towels can be used as toilet paper, also—cut them into quarters for easier use, store them in an airtight bag, and always bring them home with you for disposal. Always wash your hands or use alcohol wipes or gel afterward. In horrible weather conditions when it is dangerous to go outside, men can use a plastic quart-size wide-mouth bottle as an emergency bathroom backup. In the morning, the bottle can be sterilized with boiling water. Some companies sell urination reservoirs for women that are made specifically for this purpose.

Expedition Planning

Day tours and half-day ski tours are fun in themselves and can provide excellent training for longer multiday ski tours. With groups it's important to have organizational meetings to discuss food, equipment, and route. Each person has their own level of comfort and their own ideas of goals for a trip. For example, talk about whether you want to set daily mileage goals and move camp day to day, or if you would prefer just to make a base camp from which you can ski the surrounding area. A planning calendar is helpful for scheduling daily mileage and menus. The chapters in this book can help you identify areas that need work. Whether you are going snow camping or hut skiing in Colorado, Europe, or Alaska, you need to plan out what you *want* to do in light of what you *can* do based on your own and your fellow skiers' abilities. It's always better to start conservatively with an easy multiday hut tour before trying winter camping, for instance. Do a shorter distance, do an easier climb. Take more food than needed, take more clothes than needed. Build on a series of progressive experiences.

Sometimes it's helpful to make a trip-planning outline:

1. Where do we want to go?
2. How much time do we have?
3. Who wants to go?
4. Are they experienced in this type of skiing?
5. Do they have all the equipment needed? (See the equipment list at the end of the book.)
6. Are they strong enough?
7. What will the weather be like?
8. What will the avalanche conditions be like?

9. How far is it?

10. How steep is it?

11. How hard is it?

More Alpine expeditions are using democratic leadership in which everyone has a say in decisions. Those with more experience should lead discussions on routing and timing of skiing. Expeditions usually mean more people, more waiting, and more time. Everyone should start out with the same quality of equipment, regardless of experience level, so that breakdowns are minimized. Having everyone eat and drink is particularly important to keep body and mind together. With more people there are always more disagreements, but most conflicts can be resolved with patience and listening. To build team efficiency and to reduce confusion during multiday ski tours, have the same people do the same jobs. This builds specialization and saves time and tempers when making camp at the end of the day.

Hut and Yurt Skiing

Hut skiing can be a great way to enjoy backcountry skiing (see figure 11.5). Almost every mountain state and Canadian province has ski huts. Yurts, originally developed by Mongolian nomadic tribes, are also becoming popular in North America as backcountry dwellings. In Canada and Europe, huts are owned by Alpine clubs. By joining these clubs you can get maps and reservation information. Most huts in the United States are not staffed, while the ones in Europe usually are, offering room and board. Always call local guide services to get exact dates when services are available. In North America, bed and breakfast inns can be found in most mountain towns and usually offer inexpensive lodging.

Being in a hut with a lot of strangers is similar to communal living. You need to respect each other's rights. Cell phone users should be courteous and get out of earshot if they must make a call. Being helpful in getting firewood, washing dishes, and keeping the place neat is always a plus, too. Huts are a great place to make friends with others who share your passion for skiing, but with a large group of people it can get unavoidably noisy. Earplugs are a real lifesaver! Upon departure, be sure everything is swept neat and clean and that all power sources are turned off. Leave some firewood in the wood box and fill up the melting pot with snow for the next visitors.

© Brian Litz

Figure 11.5 Typical skiing conditions and hut accomodations on the Tenth Mountain Hut System, Colorado (Fowler-Hilliard hut shown).

Spring/Summer Skiing

Backcountry skiing doesn't stop when the lifts close—it just goes into high gear! Skiing through June is not uncommon in the American Rocky Mountains, and year-round skiing is always available in northwest North America (see figure 11.6). Of course, for those with the means, skiing in South America, Australia, and New Zealand is possible. Hard neve snow with ice in the morning is generally the norm, so freshly tuned skis are a must. If the snow doesn't freeze the night before, avoid skiing because it won't support body weight.

TRAIL SKIING ETIQUETTE

Backcountry skiers are not immune from manners when they are around other skiers and would do well to observe the following courtesies:

- Ski under control at all times.
- Keep a lookout for skiers coming down the trail. *They* have the right of way.
- When overtaking a skier below, you must avoid the skier. Yell to the skier, warning them of your approach.
- Do not stop on a trail where you are not visible from above. If stopping, get off the trail so people don't have to ski around you.
- When entering a downhill resort trail, yield to other skiers.
- Observe and obey all posted signs.
- Keep your dog at home—dogs aren't allowed on many trails. If you bring your dog, make sure you can keep it under voice control.
- Do not ski under the influence of alcohol or drugs.
- Do not leave an accident site unless you have given your name to rescue personnel.

Conservation

Backcountry travelers often damage the very nature that they love. Exposed tundra is easily damaged with heavy ski boots. Snow protects delicate nature from damage, but it also covers a multitude of sins. Biodegradability is relative. Burying toilet paper, eggshells, or orange peels in the snow won't make them disappear. Pack everything out, *especially* toilet paper. Toilet paper should be placed in plastic bags to pack out or it can be burned as an alternative, as ashes are biodegradable. Human waste will biodegrade but it should be deposited at least 200 feet (61 meters) from water sources. Use a stove in high-use areas to conserve tree cover.

Skiing With Children

Always underestimate the abilities of children to cope with cold and fatigue. Take the shorter trip, use the easier route. Rent warmer telemark boots, even if they are heavier. Chemical heat packs and a

Figure 11.6 A mountain bike can take you up unopened roads for early summer ski tours.

thermos of hot chocolate can provide instant warmth and comfort. Let kids try out used short and light Alpine-width skis you can find at a secondhand store for $5 a pair. Old Alpine skins can be split in half to form two skins for easy touring. Or you can use some cross-country wax (see chapter 4). A basic cable binding is worth a purchase since it will last through several foot growth spurts, but boots should be rented. Teach kids the beginner techniques listed in the ski technique chapter (see chapter 5). Although sleds can provide tired children a free ride, the children can get colder because they aren't exercising. Be sure children have plenty of carbs and hot liquids to keep them going. Kids should always learn basic winter survival skills and how to use a whistle. Make sure they are using sunblock and have good sunglasses—a sunglass retainer strap will help keep them in place.

Hiring a Guide or Instructor

You actually save time and money by learning about backcountry skiing from a guide instead of going hit-or-miss on your own. Giving

PHOTOGRAPHY TIPS

Photos of your skiing adventures preserve great memories. Here are some ideas to make photography easier.

- Oversized buttons and controls are bonuses for a winter camera. Wear glove liners when you go shopping for one.
- Always use a polarizing lens for 35mm cameras. Get the right kind of film—100 to 200 speed film allows for good color saturation and forgives some overexposure.
- For all cameras, get the sun behind the photographer. Take photos in the early morning and later afternoon when the light is softer.

- Always take more than one shot if it's important. It's cheaper and faster to take more photos than to have copies made.
- Always carry extra film and batteries. Cold eats up both.
- In subfreezing conditions, keep camera and film inside clothing.
- Get people to wear colorful clothing to show up against the snow.

a gift certificate for instruction is a good way for couples to provide instruction for each other. Most guides in Europe and Canada are generally certified through the Union Internationale des Association d' Alpinisme (UIAA). In the United States, the American Mountain Guide Association (AMGA) has its own parallel certification process. American mountains are in many ways more demanding since they lack elaborate hut systems and helicopter rescue services. The American guide may therefore be more experienced in snow camping and unsupported wilderness multiday tours than European guides who ski hut to hut. You don't have to be certified to have a good, helpful nature, be safe, and be knowledgeable about backcountry skiing. Many excellent guides are *not* certified. Reputation is key. Find out about guides by contacting local climbing and ski shops. Phone the guide, and ask whether you may speak to some past clients. Get a price list and try it!

Conclusion

When you learn to camp in the winter, you are learning a very basic mountain skill: self-sufficiency. Learning to camp in the winter provides the hut skier with an understanding of snow living that is put to good use if the skier is forced to bivouac en route to a hut. This knowledge makes the hut skier more comfortable in the winter environment. Snow camping is an art. Choosing the proper stove and learning to use stoves correctly is an important part of snow camping that should be practiced.

12
chapter

Emergency Survival

While beginners suffer from naiveté, "experts" can fall victim to their own complacency, whether in the face of bad weather, an avalanche, injuries, cold, or fatigue. Mountain emergencies usually occur in bad weather, often hours or days from help. What happens before and after such occurrences is the skier's responsibility. It's up to you to be as prepared as possible for any kind of mountain situation.

Preventing the Survival Situation

Dangers in mountain travel are usually divided into subjective dangers and objective dangers. Subjective dangers, which include physiological or psychological problems such as frostbite, hypothermia, and fatigue, were covered in chapter 3. Objective dangers involve environmental factors such as weather and avalanche hazards. Poor judgment is the number-one cause of backcountry accidents. It starts in the ski shop when poor-quality equipment is purchased or rented. Everyone should have enough equipment to survive on their own. For some reason, some people go out underequipped to save weight—but this doesn't save lives. Poor judgment can continue with choosing a ski route that is far too difficult or underestimating the length or difficulty of tours and the amount of physical energy needed to complete them. Another bad idea is making a habit of skiing alone. Turning back is unfortunately seen as defeat instead of a sign of intelligence. While generally there is safety in numbers, there is no safety when the people you travel with are unsafe. Much like pilots file a flight plan, why not file a ski plan? Tell a friend where you are going— if no one is home, leave the information on a telephone answering machine. Include date of departure and location of the tour, with a second location you might go to in case you change your mind. State whether you have food, pack, or avalanche equipment. Leave a note on your dashboard. Car keys should be hidden on the car and everyone in the group should know where they are. No matter how much you prepare, you can't remember everything every time. Many people think they are too experienced to use a list. Their attitude changes after some time in the backcountry. Survival potential depends upon each piece of equipment that we carry. In the equipment list at the end of the book, equipment is organized for hut skiing, snow camping, and day tours. Day tours are where many people get into trouble. A few hours can turn into a few days when we least expect it.

Preparing to Survive

Learn how to survive in an emergency. Once you've purchased good equipment, learn how to use it effectively. Learn how to survive alone if you get separated from your group, and always carry emergency supplies in your pack and jacket.

Learn to Survive Alone

Skiers make a mistake when they depend on others for help. The *team* has the tent. The *team* has the food. But what happens if the *team* disappears? Now you have nothing. Decide what equipment on *your* body and what information in *your* head will increase your survival. The ski team is stronger when each person is self-sufficient. Redundancy in equipment increases your ability to handle an emergency. Everyone in the group should have an avalanche shovel for building snowcaves; everyone should carry their own sleeping bags—you do them no favor by carrying their bags for them; each skier should carry a supply of emergency food, like athletic bars, and divide community food amongst all. Two people can benefit from one tent if one takes the body and another takes the rain fly.

Bring Prepositioned Equipment

If you are stranded alone without a sleeping bag or tent, your odds of survival are better if the clothing you have on contains prepositioned equipment. Military pilots wear a survival vest that contains prepositioned survival equipment. Your jacket can become a survival

Alpine terrain near Rogers Pass, British Columbia, Canada.

vest with contents that should never be removed unless you are in a survival situation. A small knife is handy but not critical. A zipper pull compass can give you direction. Two butane lighters can give you fire. Add a small whistle and a mirror for signaling. These items will not be in your way during regular skiing—but you'll appreciate that they're there if you find yourself in a situation where you need them.

Carry a Daypack

Everyone should have a good daypack in which to carry a set of equipment that can help one survive during heavy winter conditions. A fanny pack might be okay for day skiing out from a hut or basecamp, but it can't replace a daypack for the amount of protection (clothing, survival gear) the daypack can carry. Therefore, a daypack should be carried for every ski tour, no matter how short. Two-hour tours have a bad habit of turning into longer tours. See the items marked as day tour backpack contents in the equipment list.

Weapons and Tools

Antarctic ski expeditions such as Steger and Messner have carried firearms to ward off polar bears. Outside the Poles or true wilderness areas such as northern Canada, animal attacks are very rare. Bears injure 20 to 100 people annually in the United States, but this occurs mostly during the summer at highly visited national parks. Experts advise that if you are attacked you should resist maximally, as playing dead is totally ineffective. Pepper spray is now the weapon of choice according to most animal experts. You should contact forest ranger stations for animal advisories, especially during the spring. Research has shown that women are *not* more prone to bear attacks during menstrual periods.

You don't need a huge knife to survive if you know how to use the knife you have. A Swiss army or other utility knife with a sawblade is excellent. This sawblade cuts through a 3-inch (8-centimeter) pine branch very easily—very important for building shelter or gathering fire fuel. It weighs only 3.5 ounces. All of the other blades and accessories make this type of knife attractive for routine chores. Lacking a knife, you can climb up a tree and use your heavy ski boots to break off dry, dead wood at the base for use as firewood.

A snow shovel is standard equipment for building survival shelters even during low avalanche hazard. If you don't have a snow shovel, use a cooking pot or the end of the ski. I've even used a big flat rock.

You can even stomp a hole in the snow with your boots and get into it if you have to. Gloved hands are the last resort since they will get wet and invite frostbite. Snow saws are optional.

Setting Survival Priorities

You are in a survival situation. You are lost and/or separated from your group en route to a hut. The future is unknown. Night is falling rapidly and things must be done quickly before the real cold hits you. The following steps should occur in this order:

1. Dig in—find shelter
2. Find water
3. Regroup psychologically
4. Make a fire
5. Signal: alert and locate
6. Prepare for rescue

Step 1: Find Shelter

To get out of the snow, get into it! As a building material, snow is soundproof, blocks wind, and holds in heat. A story from the Will Steger Antarctic expedition illustrates this. Skier Keizo Funatsu got lost in a blizzard while caring for his dogs. Disoriented in the whiteout, he had no choice but to lie down and let the snow cover him. Like his dogs, he was soon covered with snow, and he lived to see the next morning. Though an extreme example, it gives testimony to the sheltering properties of snow.

Considerations for Emergency Shelters

Snow depth determines the type of shelter that should be built. Use your ski poles to probe the snow to determine the type of shelter to build. During shallow snow conditions, where some bare ground may be showing, a lean-to shelter can be made. With a thick snow pack, snow caves and tree wells are preferred over trenches and igloos. Igloos take too much time and energy to build, and trenches are a last resort because they become cold sinks that collect frigid air. If above ground, build your shelter on the edge of dense forest to avoid trees bombing your shelter with windblown snow. Build it facing south to take advantage of any available sunlight and warmth. Avoid deep canyons and valleys, as cold always flows to the lowest part of the terrain. Place your shelter up the side of a valley whenever possible. Always collect pine boughs to use for insulating your body from the snow, and get into the HELP position (talked about in the next paragraph) once inside your shelter. Don't use your skis for the roof of a shelter if you expect to stay in the shelter for an extended period of time. You'll need the skis for foraging for water and firewood. With all snow shelters, stick your skis outside the entrance—somebody might see them!

When inside your shelter, stay in the HELP position (Heat Escape Lessening Position). HELP was originally used by boaters forced to await rescue while floating in very cold water. It is the same fetal position used by mountaineers during forced bivouacs. With a sleeping bag, a person can use a prone HELP. Always use an insulating layer between you and the snow made with available materials such as Ensolite or Thermorest pads, backpacks, or even a thick layer of pine boughs. If you have two snow hats, put both of them on for added warmth. Bring your knees up to your chest and fold your arms across your chest to protect the core area of your body. Stay in your shelter to conserve body heat and lessen exposure. Urinate in your pants if you have to, but stay in your shelter. Eat snow for water instead of leaving shelter and warmth to go look for it.

Making Shelters

- **Deep snow pack: Snow cave**—Prepare to get wet when you dig a snow cave. Plus, it will take over an hour to make a good one. It's important to have a good solid snow pack when you dig a snow cave. There are many stories of snow caves collapsing, so always *sleep with your shovel.* Snowdrifted hillsides can be good places to build a snow cave. Dig your snow cave during the light of day while you have energy. Pace yourself so you don't get all your clothing wet from snow without and sweat within. Take turns digging with other people in the group. The entrance to any snow cave or shelter should be kept as small as possible and below floor level within the cave to prevent heat loss (see figure 12.1). Always vent the snow cave when using a stove.

- **Deep snow pack: Trench shelter**—A trench shelter is like a horizontal subterranean snow cave. It's best used when you are stranded on a large, flat plain. The problem is with cold settling into the trench. Dig down far enough to stand in it, then dig a snow cave sideways (see figure 12.2). The original hole can act as an artificial cold sink. Probe snow-pack depth before digging.

- **Deep snow pack: Tree well shelter**—Tree wells are great for shelter since the wind has done most of the digging for you (see figure

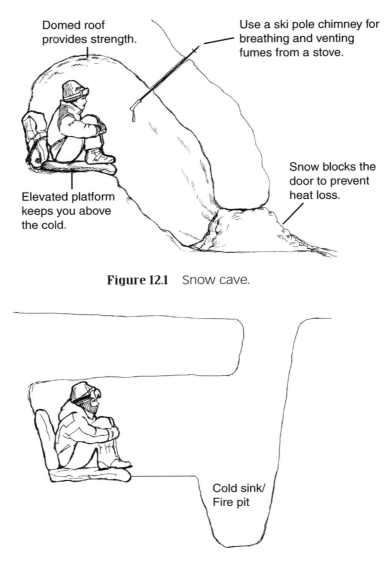

Figure 12.1 Snow cave.

Figure 12.2 Trench shelter.

12.3). Enlarge the well with a shovel so you can stretch out and cover the top with branches and pine boughs. The Hug-a-Tree program designed for lost children uses trees as a place of shelter. In California there once was a search for two children who were benighted in a snowstorm. The next day they were found in a tree well shelter alive and well, even though night temperatures had been in the teens.

Figure 12.3   Tree well shelter.

• **Shallow snow pack: Lean-to shelter**—Lean-to shelters can be made with tree branches and pine boughs against a frame supported between two trees or as a half-teepee with branches radiating out from a central tree support (see figure 12.4). A fire reflector can be situated in front of the openings for heat. Lean-tos can be drafty, so the ends should be closed off. Lean-to shelters can also be made against huge fallen trees or just a snow wall. If you have a tarp for a door, you can make a fast shelter.

• **Shallow snow pack: Tarp-igloo shelter**—Make a ring of snow blocks and cover it with a tarp (see figure 12.5). A pole can be added to the center, which is helpful in keeping snow from gathering at the center. Without a pole, it still works well in light snow. It can be very comfortable.

Bivouac Strategies for Hut Skiers

All the strategies in this chapter can be used if you are benighted en route to a hut. It wouldn't hurt hut skiers to be more knowledgeable about snow camping techniques. Individual Gore-Tex bivy bags are more the norm in the United States, while multiperson bivouac sacks are still used in Europe. Bivouac sacks are best used inside an emergency structure whenever possible. A small two-person tent without fly or poles can act as a three-person bivy sack if it's

Half teepee with fire reflector.

Lean-to with fire reflector.

Figure 12.4   Lean-to shelters.

Snow blocks hold down tarp.

Figure 12.5   Tarp-igloo shelter.

windproof—this is basically what a European bivy bag resembles. A 10-foot (3-meter) square nylon tarp is also handy for making emergency shelters. One ski manufacturer shows how you can clip four skis together into a teepee—this is helpful *if* you have a tarp that will fit over them. Keep the teepee low to prevent heat from rising to the top of the teepee, where it won't heat anyone. Small lightweight Ensolite pads are invaluable for bivouacking and lunch stops. A small lightweight gas stove can also be carried for emergencies.

Step 2: Find Water

Dehydration greatly amplifies fatigue, impatience, and poor decision-making. It is well documented that you can survive by eating snow for water. You can last days without food, but remember that you *will* die from dehydration, so the choice is clear. James Scott, lost in the Himalayas, ate snow for 42 days while awaiting rescue (James Scott, *Lost in the Himalayas*). A man survived for 13 days in the Sierras after a plane crash by eating snow. Always avoid red snow, which is made of decomposing microorganisms. When eaten, even the "clean" snow underneath has been shown to cause severe stomach cramps and vomiting. Only use clean snow and clear off the top two inches (5 centimeters) to be safe. Melting the snow in your mouth makes it go down more easily.

Step 3: Regroup Psychologically

Group shock is a real phenomenon in which everyone knows something must be done but no one knows what should be done *precisely*. One might encounter in this group silence, blank faces, apathy, or high emotion. Do not take words spoken at these times seriously. You've made a mistake, someone got hurt, you have to spend the night out. *Your first survival act is to make the conscious decision to survive.* Fear, worry, self-rebuke, and guilt all must be ignored. You have only one job now—that is to survive.

A Psychology Lesson

The average person has reserves of energy and endurance that are rarely used. *You can endure it.* There are several mental attributes that can make surviving a little less painful and frightening.

- Humor—It's important not to panic. Just relax and go with it. If indeed you must stay out overnight, you'll be miserable but you'll live.

- Objectivity—Really, how bad is it? Size up the situation and prioritize the solving of problems. Do you have enough water? Is there shelter? Do you really think the bears are hunting you down now as you wait to be rescued? No, they are sleeping. Stop imagining things.

- Ingenuity—Use your brain, be creative, remember what you learned in this book!

- Patience—We have fast food, fast news, and fast travel. Survival takes time, so try to relax.
- Hope—Rescue groups are relentless. Once they lock on to a rescue, they will continue to search until they find you. Your job is to stay alive.

USE YOUR MIND TO STAY WARM

Meditation can really help you stay warm and relaxed. If you are tense and scared, tight muscles squeeze blood vessels, decreasing the amount of warm blood going to the extremities. Survival literature contains many instances where meditation has been vital to survival. Here is a meditation that can help you sleep and rest in difficult situations: Calm your mind. Take several deep breaths. Picture the sun within your stomach. Feel the heat going from the center of your body into your fingertips. Repeat the following in a soft, inner voice: "My hands are warm, I feel the warmth flowing into my hands. My hands are warm. I am relaxed and my hands are warm." If you believe that this can work, it will!

Surviving as a Team

Every skier is different and all have varying levels of temperament, technical ability, and judgment. Whatever the mix, certain principles can be followed that will result in the best effort and outcome of a difficult situation.

- **Principle 1: Do not move.** Do *not* move unless there is a very good reason to make the switch: a better site for an emergency shelter, a better tent site that is more protected from the weather, more available firewood, or a larger open meadow that can be used for ground-to-air signaling. Once you are there, stay put.

- **Principle 2: Stay together.** Ski groups usually range in size from 3 to 10 or more people. Staying together means there is no major movement without everyone going. I'm not saying that one or two people may not go on exploratory patrols within a half mile in good weather, but if it is snowing no one should move. Ski tracks are easily buried and can vanish in the fog. Having all the brainpower and muscle in one place makes survival easier.

- **Principle 3: Cultivate teamwork.** Making decisions can result in leadership conflicts. Experienced skiers have a responsibility to make correct decisions to the best of their ability. Those decisions must be objective and always point toward one goal: the survival of the most members of the group. However, the group as a whole should endorse the final decisions together.

Step 4: Make a Fire

Fires are not a condition for survival. People survive all the time in the winter without fires. But the warmth and psychological lift of a fire cannot be ignored. They also add daytime smoke signaling possibilities.

Use a small earthen pit if barren earth exists. Or boot-pack a firepit in the snow about two feet (.6 meters) in diameter in a sheltered area. Make it one foot (.3 meters) below the snow level to provide for a windbreak. Make a platform out of green tree bark to keep the fuel off the snow. Once the fire is going, it will create ash thick enough to insulate itself from getting extinguished from melting snow.

Around the bottom of trees you'll find dry pine needles and very small twigs and leaf debris that can be used for fire fuel. Save the wet twigs for later when they can be dried once a fire is going. Look for fire fuel in your pack: toilet paper, dollar bills, cotton socks, and pages from a book all will make good fuel. The biggest error in building any fire is using twigs and branches that are too big. The second error is using too many branches so that the fire is suffocated. Fire is a mix of fuel and oxygen. *You need both.* Try toothpick-size twigs first, then small drinking-straw–sized twigs. Have pen-sized twigs and larger wood standing by to take advantage of any flame that is created. Keep the fire small—it will keep you warm and won't keep you running for more firewood.

Butane lighters are an overlooked winter survival tool. Hurricane matches, flint and steel, and such don't even come close. Carry several butane lighters for starting stove and wood fires in the wild (remember the ones in your jacket?). They have long life, and can survive machine washing if accidentally thrown in there before your trip. I've even used them to dry a wet twig to the point of combustion! A headlamp can also be used as a fire starter. Inside the lamp's battery holder, carry a small amount of steel wool. Connect both ends of the battery with the steel wool. This completes the electrical circuit, causing the steel wool to burst into flame. Don't forget to wear your gloves!

Step 5: Signal for Help

Boaters have long used the alert/locate signaling system in emergencies. First you have to *alert* people that there is a problem. Use signaling that can be noticed far away: a cellular phone, headlamp, mirror, smoke, satellite beacon, or flares. Once a rescue is evident, you can bring rescuers right to you through *locate* signaling by using a headlamp, whistle, or strobe light. Those marked alert/locate can be used for both functions.

- **Alert/Locate: Pattern Signaling/SOS**—Search pilots report that the land becomes a hypnotic blur beneath their wings. You must make your position obvious! The letters SOS or even a simple X that is big enough will tell someone you need help. These markings are known as pattern distress markings to pilots. It must be big enough to be seen by a pilot. Think about the size of a swimming pool, about 25 yards (23 meters) in length. Deep snow is the best for making this signal. Walk (don't ski) through the snow to make the letters. Neatness counts, so it shouldn't look like animal tracks. Make the letters at least two feet (.6 meters) wide and two feet deep. Fill the letters in with pine boughs for better visibility. You can use an arrow to indicate travel direction as well.

- **Alert/Locate: Mirror Signaling**—According to military survival experts, a signal mirror can knock a pilot out of the cockpit! Skiers are surrounded by mirrors—a compass mirror, sunglasses, camera lenses, tin foil, metal pots, plastic bags, and so on. One man was rescued after using a piece of ice as a mirror! Mirroring should be done slowly over the edge of the horizon (see figure 12.6), moving the mirror side to side using the fingers of one hand as an aiming sight. This should be done even if no aircraft can be seen or heard, because mirror signals have been seen over 100 miles (161 kilometers) away even with mountains.

- **Alert/Locate: Daylight Smoke Signaling**—A smoky campfire can be seen from many miles by air. Setting a tree on fire would be the last resort. However, smoke doesn't work in all conditions. High mountain winds can flatten out smoke instead of allowing it to rise so it can be seen.

- **Alert: Satellite Rescue Strobes**—Some satellite EPIRBs (Electronic Position Indicator Rescue Beacons) weighing 2.2 pounds (1 kilogram) not only transmit data concerning where you are, but who you are, because you must fill out a user questionnaire upon

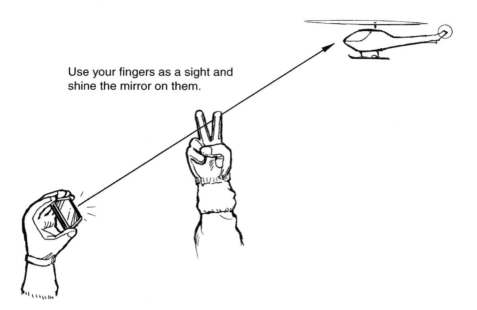

Use your fingers as a sight and shine the mirror on them.

Figure 12.6 Use a mirror to signal for help.

activation. They are so popular in Canada that the normal certification process was dispensed with. For larger groups and for people with chronic health problems, such a beacon could provide fast rescue. The 406 MHz satellite radio frequency eliminates false alarms because the user can be identified immediately. Pinpointing location using GPS technology speeds rescue, reducing the chances of injury or mishap to rescuers as well.

• **Alert: Cellular Phones**—Over the last few years, many climbers and skiers have initiated rescues using cellular phones. Worldwide cellular coverage via satellite is just a few years away. Plus, new technology will allow cellular phone calls to be traced using GPS technology. It is up to the outdoor community to use these devices responsibly. Range varies widely in the mountains, and hilltop transmission is always better than in a valley. Get a phone that can use a AA battery pack and take lithium batteries. A rescue will be in the palm of your hand—but you still have to survive.

• **Alert/Locate: Rescue Strobes**—Rescue strobe lights are better than rescue flares because flares only provide a three-shot opportunity for signaling. Once you've used your three flares, that's it! A rescue strobe light such as the ACR Firefly can penetrate heavy snow and fog and is visible at night up to 5 miles (8 kilometers) in the line of sight, and lasts up to eight hours. They are used by military and civilian pilots, weigh 4 ounces, and use alkaline or lithium batteries. They give off a flash of 250,000 peak lumens per flash per second for eight hours. A camera flash can be used as well.

- **Alert/Locate: Headlamps**—Headlamps are not as bright as rescue strobes, but they're bright enough to be seen from a search plane or by viewers in the valley below in good weather. Multiple flashes will get anyone's attention. Continuous flashing will get them moving toward you. Repeating three short flashes then three long flashes is the international SOS signal. Always carry extra batteries and bulbs!

- **Locate: Tent and Clothing Color**—Safety must come first when choosing colors for the backcountry. Bright clothing can help a skier be spotted while an avalanche is still in progress or after a long fall. Waving a bright jacket at a pilot will make you stand out. A yellow tent can be seen from a half-mile (.8 kilometers) away.

- **Locate: Whistle Signaling**—A whistle is always better than the human voice for distress signaling. A whistle takes much less energy than yelling. Whistles can cut through wind and forest noise and cannot be mistaken for another rescuer's voice. A plastic coach's whistle is loud and won't freeze to your lips like a metal one. Eight sharp blasts should be used every 15 minutes in case a rescuer is close by without the victim knowing it.

Step 6: Prepare for Rescue

Once you've been rescued, don't give up. Rescue death occurs when the victim gives up after being reached by rescuers. The will to live is sometimes the only thing keeping us from going into extreme shock and death. Remember—it's not over until it's over. Don't let go of your defenses. Even if you are in good hands, you still have to make it back—then you can pass out!

Rescue by Air

The request for a helicopter rescue cannot be taken lightly. Helicopters are powerful yet sensitive beasts that can do amazing things. However, several fatal helicopter crashes during rescues have raised questions about determining need. Learn the correct surface-to-air arm signals so pilots will understand whether or not you need help (see figure 12.7).

Helicopters do not fly well in high winds or low visibility. Most helicopters, except high-altitude choppers, are strained to their limits during mountain rescues (see figure 12.8). A twisted ankle or broken arm is not a reason to call a helicopter. Those emergencies should be dealt with by the ski team. A head or back injury where any movement of the victim may result in death is appropriate for helicopter rescue. This may also include massive trauma to the leg, where excessive movement may result in nerve damage or uncontrolled bleeding.

Preparing a Landing Zone

1. The landing zone must be an open field, ideally sloping off at one end for takeoff. If you aren't in a place like this, an injured skier may have to be moved to a place where the helicopter can land. If the skier cannot be moved, wait for professional help to arrive.

Yes, rescue is required   No, rescue is not needed

Figure 12.7 International surface-to-air arm signals for a helicopter rescue.

Courtesy of MSgt. Jack Loudermilk, retired, U.S. Army

Figure 12.8   Flight crew searches for signs of life in the forest below—could *you* be seen?

2. Lake ice is good if late in winter with minimum thickness of 16 inches (41 centimeters).

3. A wind indicator such as a windsock (ski pole and scarf) is absolutely necessary for the pilot to see wind direction.

4. Scatter pine needles on the snow to help the pilot with depth perception.

Moving Around a Helicopter

1. Do not approach the aircraft unless you are given permission by the flight crew.

2. Never approach the aircraft from the uphill side.

3. Always carry skis to the aircraft horizontally in your hands, not over your shoulders.

4. Always wear goggles or eyeglasses when near the aircraft.

Rescue by Ground

Make yourself obvious to people on snowmobiles or snowcats by making tracks radiating out from your shelter like a spiderweb. You

Courtesy of Flight for Life, Denver, Colorado

Flight for Life helicopter transports an injured skier above Breckenridge ski area, Colorado.

can make arrows in the snow pointing back to your shelter. Break branches and brush to get attention. Keep a smoky fire going at all times so people can see smoke and smell it.

Conclusion

Every skier should have the means and knowledge to be self-sufficient in the winter wilderness. All skiers should carry their own sleeping bags, shovels, and extra food. The lost skier is somewhat like a "man overboard" in a white frozen sea who must save himself while letting others know of his plight. By carrying just a few small tools in your clothing at all times you dramatically increase your ability to survive. Brightly colored clothing and camping equipment can help rescuers find us. As helicopter rescues increase in the backcountry, we need to learn to use them only when we absolutely need them.

Appendix A

Tourist Offices for Alpine Countries

Austria

Austrian National Tourist Office
11601 Wilshire Boulevard,
    Suite 2480
Los Angeles, CA 90025-1760
310-477-3332

Canada

Alberta Department of Tourism
10025 Jasper Avenue, 15th Floor
Edmonton, AB T5J 323
403-427-4321 / 800-988-5455

France

French Government Tourist Office
9454 Wilshire Boulevard, Suite 715
Beverly Hills, CA 90212
310-271-6665

Chamonix Tourism Office

Office de Tourisme Chamonix
    Mont-Blanc
74400 Chamonix Mont-Blanc
Telephone: 33-4-5053-0024
Fax: 33-4-5053-5890

Germany

German National Tourist Office
122 East 42nd Street
New York, NY 10168
212-661-7200

Italy

Italian Government Travel
500 North Michigan Avenue,
    Suite 1046
Chicago, IL 60611
312-644-0990

Switzerland

Swiss National Tourist Office
608 5th Avenue
New York, NY 10020
212-757-5944

Norway

Scandinavian Tourist Board
655 3rd Avenue
New York, NY 10017
212-949-2333

Appendix B

Map Resources

CD-ROM Maps

TOPO!
Wildflower Productions
375 Alabama Street, Suite 230
San Francisco, CA 94110
415-558-8700
Web site: http//www.topo.com

U.S. Topographical Maps

Maps East of the Mississippi
U.S. Geological Survey
Maps and Publications
12201 Sunrise Valley Drive
Reston, VA 20192
800-872-6277/703-648-6045

Maps West of the Mississippi
U.S. Geological Survey
Denver Federal Center
P.O. Box 25086, Mail stop 911
Denver, CO 80225
303-202-4700

U.S.G.S. Western Mapping Center
345 Middlefield Road
Menlo Park, CA 94025
650-853-8300

Federal Information Center
(For additional information)
800-688-9889

U.S. and Foreign Topographical Maps

Trails Illustrated
P.O. Box 4357
Evergreen, CO 80437
800-962-1643

Map Link
30 South La Patera Lane, Unit #5
Santa Barbara, CA 93117
805-692-6777
Web site: http//www.maplink.com

OMNI Resources
1004 South Mebane Street
Burlington, NC 27216
800-742-2677/336-227-8300
Web site: http//www.omnimap.com

Chessler Books
P.O. Box 4359
Evergreen, CO 80437
800-654-8502/303-670-0093
Web site: http//www.chesslerbooks.com

Appendix C

Weights and Measures

1 quart water	=	2.2 pounds
1 quart water (32 fluid ounces)	=	2 pints
1 pint	=	480 grams
1 pint	=	16 ounces
1 cup	=	240 grams
1 inch	=	2.54 centimeters
1 centimeter	=	.3937 inches
1 foot	=	30 centimeters
1 meter	=	39.37 inches
1 kilogram	=	2.2045 pounds
1 pound	=	.4536 kilograms
Convert F to C	=	(F - 32) x 5 ÷ 9
Convert C to F	=	(C x 9 ÷ 5) + 32

Celsius (C)	Fahrenheit (F)
-40	-40
-20	-4.0
0	32.0
1	33.8
5	41.0
10	50.0
15	59.0
20	68.0
25	77.0
30	86.0
35	95.0
40	104.0

SHOE SIZE CONVERTER	
Metric Size	U.S. Size
35	3.5
36	4
37	4.5
38	5.5
39	6
40	7
40.5	7.5
41	8
42	8.5
43	9
44	10.5
45	29
46	11.5
47	11.8

Equipment List

Two asterisks mark day tour backpack contents. Unless otherwise noted, "quantity" depends on the size of the group, amount used, and days spent out.

Ski Gear

1	expedition backpack
1**	backpack (waistpack optional)
1**	pair skis
1**	pair ski boots
1**	pair climbing skins
1	tube climbing skin adhesive (optional)
1**	pair ski poles (metal/avalanche probe)
1	pair crampons (optional)
1	ice axe (optional)
1**	avalanche transceiver (with fresh batteries)
1**	avalanche shovel

Repair Kit**

1	Swiss army knife
2	binding screws
2	drywall expansion sleeves
1	pair of adjustable ski pole inner bushings
1	quantity duct tape (25 feet— stored on ski pole or in pack)
1	pair of pliers or composite tool (optional)
1	binding adjustment tool
1	sewing kit (leather needle with dental floss ok)

Clothing

1**	pair gaiters
1**	top synthetic underwear (expedition-weight)
1**	bottom synthetic underwear (expedition-weight)
1	top synthetic underwear (medium-weight)
1	bottom synthetic underwear (medium-weight)
1**	Dry-Lite T-shirt
1**	ski hat (pile fleece or wool/nylon)
1**	balaclava (or extra hat)
1**	neck gaiter
1**	pair heavy gloves/mittens
1	pair glove liners
1	pair lightweight cross-country gloves
1	cotton handkerchief
1**	pair heavy ski socks
2**	pair ski sock liners
1	pair cotton socks
1**	Gore-Tex storm suit top
1**	Gore-Tex storm suit bottom
2	pair briefs
1**	pile fleece vest
1	pile fleece jacket (optional)
1	pair camp booties (or use ski boot liner)
1**	pair orthotics
1	quantity chemical heat packs

Snow Camping Gear

1   water pump/tablets
1   sleeping bag (-20 degree F. minimum rating)
1   sleeping bag cover (optional)
1   compression bag for sleeping bag
1   tent (with vestibule)
6   stuff sacks
1   Thermorest/Ensolite pad
1**   15-inch square Ensolite pad (to insulate stove)
1   camping stove
1   quantity stove fuel
1   Lexan spoon, knife, fork
1   cooking pot and lid
1   thermos drinking mug

Cooking

1   camp towel
1   quantity coffee filters
1   quantity alcohol wipes
2**   water bottles (32-oz., wide-mouth)
1   thermos drinking mug
1**   1/2 roll of toilet paper or 5 kitchen towels, in plastic storage bag
2   extra plastic storage bags
2**   small butane lighters
1**   headlamp
4**   extra batteries (lithium batteries optional)
2**   extra light bulbs (1 high intensity, 1 regular intensity)

Sun Protection

1**   crushproof sunglasses case
1**   bottle sunblock (SPF 45)
1**   stick lip balm (SPF 45)
1**   sunvisor or baseball cap
1**   pair sunglasses
1   set sunglass retainer straps
1   pair prescription glasses (if necessary)

1   extra pair prescription glasses (optional)
1**   pair goggles (with fog lenses)
1   antifog cloth or antifog paste product

Survival Equipment**

1   compass (with mirror)
1   map of travel area
1   altimeter
2   butane lighters (kept in jacket at all times)
1   plastic whistle (kept in jacket at all times)
1   quantity duct tape (25 feet—this is already in your ski repair kit)
2   athletic bars
1   space blanket
1   Ensolite pad

First Aid Supplies**

Blister Kit
1   quantity moleskin
1   quantity second skin
1   quantity bandaids

Stomach Kit
5   antacid tablets
5   antidiarrhea tablets
5   throat drops
5   aspirin tablets
5   ibuprofen tablets
1   bottle eyedrops

Personal Camping Gear

1   book (optional—for leisure)
1   notebook
1   pencil
1   tube toothpaste
1   toothbrush
1   washcloth
1   comb (optional)
1   set earplugs
1   antiperspirant spray
2   alcohol wipes/day/person

Bibliography

Avalanches and Hazards

Daffern, T. 1992. *Avalanche safety for skiers and climbers,* 2ed. Seattle, WA: Cloudcap.

McClung, D., and P. Schaerer. 1993. *The avalanche handbook.* Seattle, WA: The Mountaineers.

Backcountry Skiing

Chouinard, Yvon. 1992. *Climbing ice.* California: Sierra Club Books.

Dawson, L. 1997. *Wild Snow.* Golden, CO: AAC Press.

Graham, J. 1997. *Outdoor leadership: Technique, common sense and self-confidence.* Seattle, WA: The Mountaineers.

The Mountaineers. 1997. *Mountaineering: The freedom of the hills.* Seattle, WA: Author.

Tejada-Flores, L. 1981. *Backcountry skiing: The Sierra Club guide to skiing off the beaten track.* San Francisco: Sierra Club Press.

Conditioning

Bigard, A.X. 1988. "Ski de randonnée, cout et rendement energetiques d'une active de haute montagne," *Medicine du Sport* **62**(3): 126-132.

Colorado Altitude Research Institute. 1992. *Recommendations for visitors coming to high altitude.* Keystone, CO: Author.

Federiuk, C.S., A.D. Zechnich, and G.A. Vargyas. 1997. "Telemark skiing injuries: a three year study," *Wilderness and Environmental Medicine* **8**: 204-210.

Ilg, S. 1989. *The outdoor athlete: Total training for outdoor performance.* Evergreen, CO: Cordillera Press.

Vives, J.R. 1996. "The physiological responses of moderately active individuals to four modes of snow locomotion." Published Doctor of Education dissertation, University of Colorado, Greeley, CO.

Glacier Skiing

Selters, A. 1990. *Glacier travel and crevasse rescue.* Seattle, WA: The Mountaineers.

Libkind, M. 1992. "Going lite: Seven days and thirty five pounds," *Couloir,* April, 3, 12-13.

Hut Skiing

Dawson, L.W. 1991. *Colorado 10th mountain trails.* Aspen, CO: Who Press.

Gibb, H., and L. Gibb. 1982. *Ski touring with kids.* Boulder, CO: Pruett.

Litz, B. 1995. *Colorado hut to hut: a guide to skiing, hiking and biking Colorado's backcountry.* Golden, CO: Fulcrum Press.

Summit Hut Association. 1996. *The hut handbook.* Denver, CO: Westcliffe.

Steger, W., and J. Bowermaster. 1992. *Crossing Antarctica.* New York: A.A. Knopf Publishers.

Vadasz, Bela and Mimi. 1994. "Ski lite," *Couloir* **7** (2): 38-41.

Mountain Medicine

Casey, M.J., E. Hixson, and C. Foster. 1990. *Winter sports medicine*. Philadelphia, PA: F.A. Davis.

Hackett, P. 1997. *Mountain sickness*, 2ed. Golden, CO: American Alpine Club.

Houston, C. 1993. *High altitude illness and wellness*. Merrillville, IN: ICS Books, Inc.

Wilkerson, J.A., C. Bangs, and J. Hayward. 1986. *Hypothermia, frostbite, and other cold injuries*. Seattle, WA: The Mountaineers.

Wilkerson, J.A. 1992. *Medicine for mountaineering*. Seattle, WA: The Mountaineers.

Navigation

Letham, L. 1997. *GPS made easy*. Seattle, WA: The Mountaineers.

Mooers, R.L. 1972. *Finding your way in the outdoors*. New York: E.P. Dutton & Co.

Peet, William J., II. 1976. *The sportsman's altimeter/barometer: a where, when and weather guide*. Ocean, NJ: Peet Brothers, Inc.

Search and Rescue

MacInnes, H. 1972. *International mountain rescue handbook*. New York: Charles Scribner's Sons.

Ski Equipment

Carbone, C. 1994. *Womenski*. Boston: World Leisure Corporation.

Masia, S. 1987. *Ski maintenance and repair*. Chicago: Contemporary.

Neptune Mountaineering, Inc. 1998. *Backcountry ski equipment*. Boulder, CO: Author.

Soles, C. 1995. "Ski mountaineering necessities," *Rock and Ice* **65**: 113-120.

Soles, C. 1997. "Winter bags," *Rock and Ice* **77**: 114-126.

Ski Technique

Parker, P. 1988. *Free heel skiing*. Chelsea, VT: Chelsea Green.

Sanders, R.J. 1979. *The anatomy of skiing*. New York: Random House.

Sports Nutrition

Clark, N. 1997. *Nancy Clark's Sports Nutrition Guidebook*. 2nd ed. Champaign, IL: Human Kinetics.

Coleman, E., and S. Steen. 1997. *The ultimate sports nutrition handbook*. Palo Alto, CA: Bull.

Colgan, M. 1993. *Optimum sports nutrition*. New York: Advanced Research Press.

Edwards, J.S.A., D.E. Roberts, and S.H. Mutter. 1992. "Rations for use in a cold environment," *Journal of Wilderness Medicine* **3**: 27-47.

Reynolds, R.D., J.A. Lickteig, M.P. Howard, and P.A. Deuster. 1998. "Intakes of high fat and high carbohydrate foods by humans increased with exposure to increasing altitude during an expedition to Mt. Everest," *Journal of Nutrition* **128**: 50-55.

Survival

Scott, J. 1993. *Lost in the Himalayas*. Australia: Lothian.

Weather

Barry, R. 1992. *Mountain weather and climate*. New York: Routledge, Chapman, and Hall.

Ludlum, D.M. 1991. *National Audubon Society field guide to North American weather*. New York: A.A. Knopf Publishers.

Index

Index

Index

About the Author

Jean Vives is uniquely qualified to write this book. He has more than 30 years of backcountry skiing and mountaineering experience. Plus, his doctoral research on backcountry skiing won him the Charles S. Houston Award from the Wilderness Medical Society. In addition to skiing the Haute Route in the Swiss Alps between Chamonix and Zermatt, he has *twice* skied the Colorado Haute Route from Winter Park to Crested Butte. The latter took 28 days to complete and covered 170 miles, making it the longest ski tour in the United States using Alpine touring equipment.

Vives has published numerous articles on backcountry skiing that have appeared in *Outside, Powder,* and *Ski* magazines. A former codirector of Aspen Alpine Guides and member of Aspen Mountain Rescue, he has climbed and trekked all over the world. As a professor at Kathmandu University in Nepal, he taught high-altitude exercise physiology. Vives lives in Boulder, Colorado.

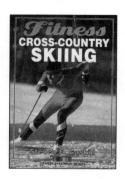

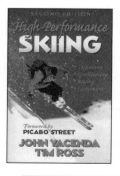